MW00615928

THE RISE OF
BLUEANON

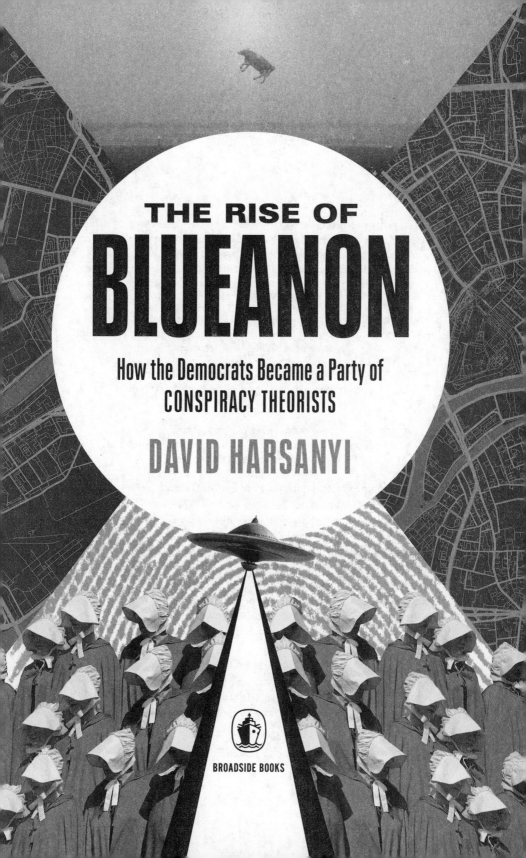

THE RISE OF
BLUEANON

How the Democrats Became a Party of CONSPIRACY THEORISTS

DAVID HARSANYI

BROADSIDE BOOKS

HarperCollins books may be purchased for educational, business, or sales promotional use. For information, please email the Special Markets Department at SPsales@harpercollins.com.

Broadside Books™ and the Broadside logo are trademarks of HarperCollins Publishers.

FIRST EDITION

Book design by Leah Carlson-Stanisic
Collages created by Leah Carlson-Stanisic from Adobe Stock and Shutterstock, Inc. images

Library of Congress Cataloging-in-Publication Data
Names: Harsanyi, David, author.
Title: The rise of BlueAnon: how the Democrats became a party of conspiracy theorists / David Harsanyi.
Description: First edition. | New York: HarperCollins Publishers, [2024] | "Broadside."
Identifiers: LCCN 2024020820 (print) | LCCN 2024020821 (ebook) | ISBN 9780063360631 (hardcover) | ISBN 9780063360624 (ebook)
Subjects: LCSH: Right and left (Political science)—United States. | Conspiracy theories—Political aspects—United States. | Political Culture—United States.
Classification: LCC JC574.2.U6 H37 2024 (print) | LCC JC574.2.U6 (ebook) | DDC 320.50973—dc23/eng/20240618
LC record available at https://lccn.loc.gov/2024020820
LC ebook record available at https://lccn.loc.gov/2024020821

ISBN 978-0-06-336063-1

24 25 26 27 28 LBC 5 4 3 2 1

For Szerena and Laszlo

Don't call everything a conspiracy, as they do, and don't live in dread of what frightens them.

—ISAIAH 8:12

CONTENTS

INTRODUCTION:
PANIC, DENIAL, AND THE PARANOID STYLE OF DEMOCRATIC PARTY POLITICS

*The central belief of every moron is that he is
the victim of a mysterious conspiracy.*

—H. L. MENCKEN

For several years now, I've been accused of being a dupe for Russia, even though I've never once written or said a single favorable word about Vladimir Putin.

When I'm not fronting for Slavic autocrats, I'm being paid off by the National Rifle Association, American Israel Public Affairs Committee, Federalist Society, Big Oil, Big Pharma, Big Grocery, and a host of other groups that have, quite rudely, never given me a penny to spread their message.

In the contemporary political world, a conservative might be dumb or maybe evil, owned by insidious billionaires or foreign governments plotting to overthrow our democracy, but they can never be good-faith political adversaries. Democrats no longer argue about policy. They accuse you of sedition.

Indeed, with the Democratic Party's "progressive" turn in the past few years has come a religious superiority complex that imbues them with an uncompromising certitude. For those who see themselves as only legitimate champions of justice, tolerance, and decency, it is inconceivable that anyone could honestly prefer the selfish, violent intolerance of the conservative agenda. There must be some unseen force pulling the strings. A conspiracy is almost surely afoot.

Loosely defined, a "conspiracy theory" is a belief that some influential but furtive groups are plotting or responsible for events or phenomena beyond our control. The notion is propelled by a never-ending string of disparate events and half-truths, threaded together to create a narrative that's often impossible to disprove. These conspiracy theories, conveniently, grow with every question and every denial.

Now, this book doesn't argue that Republicans, or any political faction, are immune from conspiratorial thinking. Whether people believe Beyoncé is running the Illuminati or Rothschild space lasers are wreaking havoc on the environment, every faction has its unhinged conspiracists. This is the norm since Pericles of Athens.

To some extent, every demographic group is susceptible to this paranoia. It all depends on your upbringing, your political disposition, and your generation. Middle-aged Americans, for instance, are more likely to believe that John F. Kennedy was assassinated by the CIA, whereas Millennials are more likely to believe "jet fuel can't melt steel beams." Today's college students? They are more likely to believe . . . well, lots of insane things.

Politics has always had the unfortunate ability to transform seemingly rational, decent individuals into hysterical, unthinking mobs of partisans. Anyone who follows today's political discourse knows this all too well.

This book makes the case that over the past decades, the American left and its institutions have mainstreamed a unique brand of political paranoia. The modern Democratic Party's policy prescriptions—even what it views as our most pressing societal problems—are increasingly tethered to groundless or sensationalized anxieties, myths, revisionist histories, pseudoscientific alarmism, and outright lies.

For modern Democrats, every political loss, no matter how inconsequential, threatens democracy, if not the earth's very existence. H. L. Mencken famously quipped, "The whole aim of practical politics is to keep the populace alarmed (and hence clamorous to be led to safety) by an endless series of hobgoblins, most of them imaginary." Well, as we'll see, for the contemporary Democratic Party it's hysteria and apocalypticism all the way down.

"BlueAnon." That's what conservatives on social media have taken to calling this collection of elected officials, professors, reporters, columnists, fabulists, rando Democrats, and Chicken Little. The moniker is as good as any, but it also offers us a useful juxtaposition.

The name "BlueAnon" plays off the far-right cult of "QAnon," an insane conspiracy that revolves around an anonymous individual or group known as "Q." As far as I can make out, the movement believes that a cabal of satanic, cannibalistic child molesters, operating a Washington, DC, pizza parlor, are running a global child sex-trafficking ring.

Listen, I'm pretty tough on the left, but that's a bit too far, even for me. Still, Democrats ensure us that conspiratorial movements like QAnon are gaining a "foothold" in the GOP. Its "themes," they say, are already a central concern for conservatives. As far as I can tell, there have been perhaps a handful of QAnon-adjacent candidates running for Congress—if that. I've learned far more about QAnon from reading left-wing outlets than from any conservative sources. And it's not particularly close.

I'm not alone. In 2020, in the midst of the media's obsession with the cult, polls found that less than half of Republicans had ever even heard of QAnon. In truth, I don't think I've ever met anyone who's openly professed to be a QAnoner, and I spend a lot of time around conservatives. That doesn't mean adherents don't exist, but it speaks to just how fringy and unacceptable it is even among very conservative people, let alone more mainstream Republicans.

In contrast, ask yourself how many Democrats believe conservatives are plotting to institute a Republic of Gilead, or scheming to revive the Confederacy. How many believe that the Russians stole the 2016 presidential election? How many believe "book bans" were thriving in red states, or that one can't "say gay" in Florida, or that Republicans were planning their own Nuremberg Rallies, or that the Supreme Court is secretly run by a cabal of oligarchs, or that the world is going to be a giant fireball in twelve years.

Despite perceptions of the right as fringe and conspiracy-minded, the American left is far better at creating, disseminating, and internalizing conspiracy theories. To understand why, begin by comparing the aesthetic and tonal quality of QAnon and the conspiracies spread by the modern left. The right's ham-fisted theories are often crude, palpably screwy, and largely inconsequential to policy. But the left's conspiracies and hoaxes are laundered through mass media, polished off with high production values, calibrated for maximum plausibility, and draped in a patina of legitimacy.

Most of the right's conspiracy theories are spread by deranged characters and marginal social media voices. Some are more popular than they should be, yes. But the left's deception is broadcast by trusted television hosts, politicians, public health officials, journalists, former federal intelligence officials in suits who appear on MSNBC, CNN, and NBC News armed with impressive degrees and résumés.

The biggest difference between Alex Jones and Rachel Maddow is the haircut.

How did we get here? When I began writing political opinions around twenty years ago, there were still loads of debates across the ideological spectrum. Blogs had recently popped up. Unconstrained by the physical restrictions of paper or the blessing of gatekeepers, the blog age offered an explosion of interesting takes covering mainstream policy, culture, and a host of hyperspecific topics.

"Democratized" media, as it was soon called, also meant an army of amateurs could fact-check, debunk conspiracy theories, and keep establishment media organizations honest. Bloggers, most famously, took down the then-mighty CBS newsman Dan Rather, who had pushed fake documents regarding George W. Bush's time in the Air Force reserve service on *60 Minutes*. This takedown occurred only a few months before the 2004 presidential election. It was a significant moment.

All of that was great. After that, online interactions became faster, and shorter, and dumber, not to mention a lot meaner. As social media grew in prominence, "news cycles" were atomized by the 24/7 barrage of stories, images, and opinions. The incentives of social media are warped, undermining thoughtful interactions and supercharging anxiety. It is the perfect petri dish for conspiracy theories.

For starters, spreading a lie in 280-character missives takes negligible work or skill. Any twit clout-chaser can please the mob. An expediently edited or a contextless quote or a misrepresentation of hypothetical musings, or even a poorly worded sentence, can attract thousands looking to confirm their priors. Social media makes it easy for attention-chasers to cobble together events and package them into effective disinformation. Almost instantaneously, they are spread wide and far. The louder, more dishonest, and more idiotic your theories, the better the response.

Social media also altered how political parties and journalists function. "Too good to check" became the unstated ethos of the modern political media—especially if it was directed against the right. The media is supposed to be tempering partisan fearmongering and debunking the conspiracy theories of the masses. The opposite is happening.

Today, the swamps of social media are where television producers find segment fodder and editors go for their insights and reporters congregate to fine-tune their bias. This is where the historians, intellectuals, and experts vie for "attaboy" retweets from their deranged followers, rather than seeking deeper comprehension of the world.

Whether they are credulous lightweights or devious participants, reporters feed the beast, if that beast helps Democrats. Today there is barely any countervailing force to stop BlueAnon from doing its work.

Republicans, of course, aren't so lucky. With awe-inspiring and pedantic precision, an army of reporters and "fact-checkers" sift through every utterance by every GOP candidate, condemning even the slightest deviation from the most literal truth.

Most conservative conspiracies—whether they are spread by randos on Facebook or by former presidents—are smothered in fact-checks from major media organizations, even if it turns out the conspiracy theory was, in fact, true (truths are often smothered alongside lies, but that's another story).

So, when Donald Trump contends an election is "rigged," rest assured that every major media institution—not to mention a contingent of conservatives—will jump into action to push back against his claims. When Democrats make similar contentions, as they have with gusto for decades, no matter how dubious or outlandish or easily disproved their theories, virtually every left-wing institution will be mobilized to give it a hearing, if not legitimacy.

There have been so many ginned-up moral panics over the past few years that it's difficult to keep track of them all. Once exposed, they tend to dissipate into the ether while we all move on to the next frenzy. One panic simply compounds the next, to create a continuum of paranoia. And anyway, by the time the Covington kids or Jussie Smollett hoaxes were debunked, BlueAnon had moved on to the next panic or the next smear. It is impossible to keep up.

Don't expect any mea culpas, because dishonesty is the point. The more successful the conspiracy theory, the more those who engage in it are rewarded with prestigious jobs and more attention.

The other driving forces in BlueAnon are the increasingly radicalized ideology of the left and the reality they face.

Many on the left seem to be under the impression that because they've earned a social science degree from a prestigious school or live in an urban environment or vote Democratic, they are immune from conspiratorial thinking. As you'll see in the coming pages (or any time you turn on MSNBC), that is clearly not the case. Some of the biggest whack-jobs in the country are perched in the political science departments of our local universities or on the editorial boards of major newspapers.

Some, alas, are running the country.

The "progressives," socialists, Marxists, and "social justice" warriors who now infest the Democratic Party believe that the government can control outcomes for hundreds of millions of people. They believe in the potential of an omnipotent, omnipresent, and omnibenevolent state to solve every political, social, and even personal problem anyone may face. In this utopian delusion, they envision a government that can bring about universal fairness, and override human nature.

So, it makes all the sense in the world that the left believes their political adversaries have the magical power to control the mechanisms of the world as well. It's the nature of progressivism to view the world in zero-sum terms, where all that really matters is who has the power. In this world, Americans are either victims or oppressors—the latter buttressed by the alleged rampant injustices of capitalism and racism and scheming forces lurking in the shadows.

Traditionally, it's the dispossessed—or those who think of themselves as powerless—who are most prone to believing and promoting conspiracy theories. Somehow the modern left, which controls or influences virtually all major American institutions—corporate media, the academic world, the federal government—has pulled off the trick of running the country while playing the victim at the same time.

This is why some conservatives have correctly argued that the contemporary left's neurotic worldview is necessitated by the Democratic Party's many cultural victories over the past decades. Without BlueAnon, the left would run out of victims to "help" and enemies to slay. Many of the modern left's central issues would be rendered useless. Consequently, they create new traumas, condemn imaginary crimes, and warn of nefarious cabals.

BlueAnon convinces its constituents that they are without agency, lorded over by shadowy billionaires, aspiring fascists, and "minority rule." Every setback needs a conspiracy theory to make sense. Communicating through elusive "dog whistles" and propped up by "dark money," conservatives can only succeed if they ally with foreign adversaries and extremists to roll back "democracy," strip women and minorities of human rights, steal from the poor and give to the rich, and even destroy the earth.

Despite all this, we are constantly being warned that it's conservatives who are the unhinged conspiracy theorists.

Virtually the entire legacy media, editorial boards of major newspapers, cable news "experts," professors, our elites, pollsters, left-wing pundits, late-night talk-show hosts, and ordinary Democrats all contend, with great confidence, that conservatives are bonkers. One can't visit a mainstream political website these days without running across some hand-wringing article lamenting the rise of right-wing disinformation and misinformation.

Major news outlets assign entire teams of journalists to take deep dives into the creepy underbelly of the conservative web—message boards, Reddits, Twitter threads—to root out the latest nutty trends, making sure to give the right's fringe voices *far* more attention than they ever could have hoped to find otherwise.

Sociologists at prestigious universities cook up studies confirming that conservatives are more susceptible to conspiracy theories, while political "scientists" warn us that the trend isn't merely urgent but an "existential" menace to our every way of life.

Elected officials use all these warnings as a justification to propose illiberal regulations to tackle the alleged avalanche of right-wing lies. And those who run our federal agencies deputize themselves arbiters of Truth, and push censorship to cleanse the people of this scourge of falsehood.

Democrats have been convinced that Republicans aren't merely hateful but dangerously gullible, antireason, and antiscience. Any person who doesn't accept that every instance of inclement weather portends the end of the planet is branded a nihilistic knuckle dragger. Leftists stick sanctimonious signs on their front lawns to declare to passersby that in *their* house, unlike yours, "science is real."

As we'll see, there's just one big problem: it's mostly projection.

THE RISE OF
BLUEANON

THE VAST RIGHT-WING
CONSPIRACY WILL NEVER DIE

Yes, Virginia, there is a vast right-wing conspiracy.

—PAUL KRUGMAN

On January 27, 1998, First Lady Hillary Clinton appeared on NBC's popular *Today* show and declared that a "vast right-wing conspiracy" had concocted a rumor about her husband, Bill, carrying on an affair with a White House intern named Monica Lewinsky.[1]

Hillary, who was aware of Gennifer Flowers, Paula Jones, and several of Bill's other extramarital relationships, told millions of Americans watching that morning that the very idea of her husband engaging in a dalliance with a young woman was so absurd it could only have been cooked up by "mean-spirited" conservative adversaries (among them, apparently, her husband's own attorney general, Janet Reno, who was investigating the incident).

Clinton hadn't dropped the phrase "vast right-wing conspiracy" spontaneously that morning. The term had been test-driven by Democratic Party consultants a few years earlier as they tried to find ways to diffuse the seemingly endless scandals that were dogging the corrupt first couple.[2] In a 1995 White House counsel memo, Clinton staffers mapped out an imaginary "conspiracy commerce" that had turned "fantasy" into "fact." The process, they contended, began with partisans at conservative magazines and think tanks, where tawdry stories about the Clintons were invented. Those rumors were then laundered through government officials and major media outlets.

As the *Washington Post*'s David Maraniss noted in 1998, it was modus operandi for the Clintons to deflect accusations of wrongdoing by blaming them on a "reckless conspiracy launched by desperate opponents."[3] This formula, as we'll see, would become modus operandi *for the entire American left.*

Admittedly, as was the case with every president since George Washington, conspiracy theories attached themselves to the Clintons. The emergence of the internet guaranteed that those conspiracies spread faster and wider than ever before. The corrupt predilections of the Clintons imbued those theories with a bit more believability.

As it turned out, of course, the stories about Bill and Lewinsky were no "fantasy." That, however, did not deter Hillary from spending the next three decades cautioning the country about the treachery that had been launched against her and her husband. During her presidential campaign in 2016, the former first lady warned that the vast right-wing conspiracy was not only alive but more dangerous and "better funded" than ever. New "multibillionaires" like the Koch brothers, Hillary cautioned, were funding the effort because they wanted "to control our country" and "rig the economy so they can get richer and richer."

Clinton, who knew well that the libertarian Kochs—who supported, among many other issues, school choice for the poor and across-the-board tax cuts—opposed the candidacy of the populist Donald Trump, went on to say that there was "no doubt about who the players are, what they're trying to achieve. . . . It's real, and we're going to beat it."[4]

Alas, Hillary did not beat "it." What she did was launch the most successful conspiracy theory in American political history.

Despite perceptions, Democrats are no strangers to political conspiracy mongering. During the Trump era, George W. Bush would be portrayed as the honorable head of a once-rational Republican Party, but during his presidency Democrats regularly accused him of colluding to further fascistic policies; of fighting wars in the Middle East for personal, monetary gain; and of running international schemes to bring the nation into ruin.

Alleging that Republicans harbored dreams of resurrecting Nazi policies harks back to the early 1960s, at least, when Arizona senator Barry Goldwater took the Republican nomination. "The stench of fascism is in the air," then–California governor Pat Brown famously declared. The practice revved up after Ronald Reagan won the presidency. Democratic representative William Clay of Missouri warned that the Gipper was "trying to replace the Bill of Rights with fascist precepts lifted verbatim from *Mein Kampf*."[5]

By the time W. won the presidency, the entire Democratic Party and its institutions were calling or intimating that the Republican president was a "crypto fascist." Leftist megadonor George Soros wrote that the former Texas governor displayed the "supremacist ideology of Nazi Germany."[6] Democratic senator Robert Byrd of West Virginia said that Bush reminded him of Nazi propagandist Hermann Goering.[7] (To be fair, as a former Klansman, Byrd probably knew a thing or two about Aryan supremacists.) "Bush the Despot" was the headline of a piece penned by Bill Clinton aide and Hillary confidant Sidney Blumenthal in 2005.[8] An ad on MoveOn.org, then a powerful activist group, began with an image of Adolf Hitler morphing into President Bush with the tagline "What were war crimes in 1945 is foreign policy in 2003."[9]

In those days, comparing a politician to a Nazi was still sort of big news. It would soon become the norm.

By the mid-2000s, the Democratic Party began drifting toward progressivism, a movement predicated on the belief of zero-sum economy ideas, where shadowy men control the fortunes of powerless citizens. The hard left infused the Democratic Party with an even more pronounced conspiratorial outlook.

Though progressive Howard Dean lost the nomination in 2004 to the institutional pick, John Kerry, his rise in the party—he would become chairman of the Democratic National Committee—was a harbinger for this new style of politics.

In a 2003 interview with NPR's popular host Diane Rehm, Dean was asked what he made of President George W. Bush's "suppressing" the independent investigation into the 9/11 terror attacks.[10]

Rehm, a longtime left-wing host on the tax-funded radio broadcast, was herself a dabbler in conspiracies. Only a few years later, the host would famously ask the socialist Bernie Sanders if he benefited from "dual citizenship with Israel," a claim often used by antisemites to intimate a lack of patriotic loyalty.[11] When a confused Sanders responded that he was not in possession of any such citizenship, Rehm assured him that she was working off a "list" of influential Jews in America, no doubt procured from some shady corner of the web.

In any event, in this instance, Dean explained to Rehm that he didn't know for sure about the Saudis, but there were "many theories" being bandied about, and the most interesting one he'd heard was that President Bush "was warned ahead of time by the Saudis."[12]

Dean, you see, was just asking questions, his defenders explained.

It was unsurprising that a few years earlier Dean was the first major Democrat to float the concept that Bush ignored tangible, actionable warnings from the Saudis about 9/11—a story that probably originated at *World Socialist* magazine.[13] Perhaps that's where Dean, at the time the most left-leaning presidential political candidate in postwar American history, latched on to the belief.

More interestingly, Dean's comments garnered only scant media attention at the time, and not a single genuine denunciation from a Democratic Party leader. Dean "neither apologized nor repudiated himself for passing along this urban legend," wrote the late conservative journalist Robert Novak at the time, nor was he asked to do so.[14] Dean, as it turns out, was merely conveying the outlook of a significant bloc of the Democratic Party.

While researching this book, I noticed that most studies investigating 9/11 "trutherism" have connected the outlook to the extreme right wing. But that fact shouldn't distract us from the fact that trutherism was, and probably is, quite popular on the mainstream left.

When an Ohio University poll for Scripps Howard asked Democrats in 2006, "How likely is it that people in the federal government either assisted in the 9/11 attacks or took no action to stop the attacks because they wanted the United States to go to war in the Middle East?," 22.6 percent said it was "very likely" and another 28.2 percent said it was "somewhat likely."[15]

Or in other words, over half of Democrats believed, or were open to believing, that the president probably had foreknowledge of the 9/11 attacks.

A 2007 Zogby poll found that 42 percent of Democrats believed that Bush had participated in the death of over three thousand Americans on 9/11 or let it happen for personal gain.[16] That same year, then–Democratic congressman Keith Ellison, soon-to-be deputy DNC head, was *still* comparing the 9/11 attacks to the Reichstag Fire—the pretext for the Nazi takeover of Germany in 1933.[17]

The conspiracy theory about 9/11 did not recede with time. A 2016 Chapman University study would find that more than half of Americans still believed that the government was concealing what really happened in the 2001 attacks. Though the poll did not ask for party affiliation, it is almost surely the case, judging from history, that Democrats made up a larger percentage.[18]

Conspiracy theories about the Bush administration were incredibly popular in the 2000s. Let's not forget director Michael Moore's *Fahrenheit 9/11*, a compendium of many of the well-worn myths of the age. Released in 2004, it offers a pristine example of old-fashioned conspiracizing, bundling a batch of disparate incidents and half-truths to tell an unfalsifiable tale of intrigue.

The "documentary" wasn't screened for ex-hippies and anti-WTO Antifa types on campuses in Berkeley or Boulder, as similar leftist documentaries in the past. It was released widely by Miramax, at the time owned by the family-friendly Disney, and home to numerous indie hits. Just try to imagine an iconic American film company backing a movie about QAnon or the Rothschild weather machine. It would simply never happen.

Fahrenheit 9/11 begins by accusing Fox News of engineering Bush's victory by prematurely calling the 2000 election. Moore, who found fame with his anticapitalist film *Roger and Me*, then alleges Florida officials were guilty of voter fraud—though no such scheme had ever been uncovered, much less prosecuted.

The movie then dives into darker conspiracies surrounding the Bush family's connections to the Saudi Arabian theocracy. The Bushes' oil concerns, Moore argued, were secretly funded by various Sunni Arab families, including the bin Laden family through intermediaries. The president, we learn, did not invade Afghanistan to avenge 9/11, but to enrich himself by building a natural gas pipeline to the Indian Ocean. And Osama bin Laden, believe it or not, was in on it.

Moore wasn't alone. Numerous other works of pseudojournalism would emerge in the 2000s along these lines. Russ Baker, who had written for the *New York Times* and *Washington Post*, penned the bestselling *Family of Secrets*, alleging that the Bush family were also participants in the Watergate scandal and the assassination of John F. Kennedy. They got around.

Bush the warmonger both targeted Muslims and protected Islamic terror groups—which, let's just say, was a heavy lift. *Fahrenheit 9/11* is on par with something an imaginative conspiracy theorist on YouTube these days might pull together on his iPhone. The difference is that far from being ignored by critics or the public, it was a massive success.

Fahrenheit 9/11 was not only the top-grossing movie its opening weekend, making $23.9 million in the United States and Canada—more than most documentaries make in their entire existences—but it became the third most successful documentary in history, making over $221 million.[19]

The country's best-known critic at the time, Roger Ebert, gave the documentary three and a half stars out of four, writing that Moore "brings a fresh impact to familiar material by the way he marshals his images." The film was the first documentary to win the Palme d'Or in Cannes since oceanographer Jacques Cousteau won for the classic *The Silent World* in 1956. As of this writing, the film holds an approval rating of 82 percent on Rotten Tomatoes.

When Moore won the Oscar for his agitprop documentary *Bowling for Columbine*, he called Bush a "fictitious president" who had unleashed a war "for fictitious reasons" in Iraq, and got a standing ovation from the crowd.[20]

Filmmakers and artists still occasionally flirt with 9/11 trutherism. In the original cut of *NYC Epicenters: 9/11–21–2021½*, released in 2021 on HBO, Spike Lee gave prominent airtime to Truthers, treating them as equals to scientific experts. "The amount of heat that it takes to make steel melt, that temperature's not reached," the famous director told the *New York Times*.[21] The same people who would feign horror at "birtherism," the claim that Obama was not born in the United States, were participants in movements that put that conspiracy to shame.

The main difference, one that will continue to dominate American media, was that Democrats were not asked repeatedly to dismiss these partisan fantasies or answer for them—despite its popularity among their constituents.

The left's conspiratorial nature was tempered somewhat during the Obama years, since the left was again in charge.

Then again, when the populist libertarian Tea Party movement emerged as a political force, it was quickly framed as "AstroTurfed"— which is to say an orchestrated campaign made to look like a grassroots effort that actually had its string pulled by wealthy conservative puppet masters. There was little evidence that the organic demonstrations had anything to do with big funders, though big funders would try to jump on the bandwagon as the movement succeeded.

The Tea Party was regularly accused of acting "like terrorists," as then–vice president Joe Biden reportedly put it.[22] Nancy Pelosi lied that the movement was "carrying swastikas and symbols like that to a town meeting on health care."[23] Bestselling author and *New York Times* writer Thomas Friedman called the Tea Party the "Hezbollah faction"[24] of the GOP, and his colleague Joe Nocera advised the conservatives to "put aside their suicide vests."[25]

Unlike some of the Black Lives Matters or anti-Israel protesters, Tea Party activists had not once engaged in an act of political violence, much less terrorism.

During the Obamacare debates, Democrats framed opposition— which polls showed was most of the nation at the time—as a movement backed by Big Pharma (which had helped write Obamacare) intent on keeping the poor in destitution.

One progressive Democratic House member, Alan Grayson, held up a sign that read, "The Republican Health Care Plan: Die Quickly," during a House floor speech.[26]

No Democrat, as far as I can tell, refuted this characterization.

● ● ● ● ●

The big conspiratorial topic during the Obama years was "birtherism," the belief that Barack Obama wasn't a natural-born U.S. citizen and thus was ineligible to be president. The left-wing media was perpetually fascinated that conservatives believed this allegedly racist story. There was endless polling and hundreds of pieces written about the harmful nature of birtherism and what it said about conservatives and the nation. Elected Republicans were incessantly implored to mobilize and quash the claim.

In truth, birtherism was given outsize importance. Yes, in 2011 Donald Trump, still nominally a member of the Reform Party, made it an issue. Until then, and later, no notable Republican of any consequence pushed birtherism. Senator Lindsey Graham called it "crazy." Senator Marco Rubio said he was "more concerned with issues that are happening back here on planet Earth."[27] The then-editor of the influential RedState.com, Erick Erickson, banned "truthism" from the site's community.[28] Popular radio talk-show hosts like Mark Levin and Glenn Beck called it a myth. In 2008 GOP presidential candidate John McCain was booed for dismissing birtherism at a town hall meeting.[29] In 2012 candidate Mitt Romney said "the citizenship test has been passed."[30]

What most Americans might not recall is that like numerous other conspiracies adopted by the right, the roots of "birtherism" can be traced to the left.

The story probably goes back to Obama's days in Chicago. It was likely Hillary Clinton's supporters who began the widespread fueling of the claim, circulating anonymous emails contending that opponent Barack Obama had been born in Africa and not the United States.[31] James Asher, former McClatchy Newspapers Washington bureau chief, claims Hillary's hatchet man Sidney Blumenthal "strongly urged me to investigate the exact place of President Obama's birth, which he suggested was in Kenya. We assigned a reporter to go to Kenya, and that reporter determined that the allegation was false."[32] (Blumenthal denied ever speaking to Asher about the issue.)

The media also conveniently forgets that the left liked to ratchet up similar questions about presidential eligibility. In 2008, Democrats began to make a big deal out of GOP presidential candidate John Mc-Cain's birth to two American parents in the Panama Canal Zone. NBC News justice correspondent Pete Williams claimed that the Arizona senator's candidacy was a "serious question with no clear answer."[33] The *New York Times* and *Washington Post* published numerous pieces about the nonissue.

Much the same thing occurred in 2016, after Texas senator Ted Cruz pulled off a surprising win in the Iowa Republican caucuses. Because of his birth in Calgary, Alberta, to a Cuban father and an American mother, suddenly the senator's eligibility became a big topic of conversation. Donald Trump took up the Cruz birther conspiracy, as well.

Only days after Cruz's win in Iowa, numerous stories about his eligibility appeared in major media outlets. Harvard Law School held a forum for two constitutional scholars to debate whether Cruz should be disqualified from the presidency.[34]

There were very clear answers, however: the Texas senator was as eligible as any other American citizen, including Barack Obama.

There is, incidentally, really nothing inherently wrong with asking questions about candidates. However, once those questions are answered, it is time to move on. It is almost surely the case that if a media-sanctioned iteration of birtherism would have emerged had either of those Republicans won, considering the left's history of leaning into those questions when it suits their purposes. Almost surely, considering the disposition of modern Democrats, the answer is yes.

DEMOCRATS HAVE NEVER LOST A PRESIDENTIAL ELECTION, AND THEY NEVER WILL

You can run the best campaign. You can even become the nominee. And you can have the election stolen from you.
—HILLARY CLINTON[35]

For all their shrilling about "democracy" and election denialism, it should not be forgotten that the contemporary left has yet to accept the legitimacy of a presidential loss in the twenty-first century.

What am I saying? Democrats have barely accepted the legitimacy of any presidential election loss in the past fifty years. Past, present, or future, it doesn't really matter, BlueAnon simply can't live with the thought of Americans denying them power.

In March 2023, for instance, the *New York Times* published a *long* profile about a Texas Republican political operative named Ben Barnes.

Now in his mid-eighties, Barnes is alleged to have successfully sabotaged the reelection campaign of President Jimmy Carter back in 1980 at the behest of Ronald Reagan's campaign.[36] The retired politico told the *Times* he could "vividly" recollect being sent on a secret mission to the Middle East by his mentor, John B. Connally Jr., the former governor of Texas and then-Reagan advocate who "was running for secretary of state or secretary of defense."

As the *Times* helpfully pointed out, "Mr. Carter's best chance for victory was to free the 52 Americans held captive [by Iranian revolutionaries in Tehran] before Election Day."

So, off went Barnes, purportedly to meet with "a host of regional leaders to deliver a blunt message to be passed to Iran: Don't release the hostages before the election. Mr. Reagan will win and give you a better deal." According to this little-known functionary, the plan worked. As the *Times*' Peter Baker explained, Carter's camp had "long suspected that Mr. [William] Casey or someone else in Mr. Reagan's orbit sought to secretly torpedo efforts to liberate the hostages before the election."

Once the *Times* embraces a story, it becomes canon on the American left. Thus the Barnes story was immediately regurgitated by scores of columnists and leftist intellectuals.

"Ronald Reagan's 'October Surprise' Plot Was Real After All," read the headline at popular progressive *Jacobin* magazine.[37] "Lawmaker Confirms 'October Surprise' Plot to Sabotage Jimmy Carter's Reelection," a *New York* magazine piece recounted.[38] "Revealed: the secret plot that brought down Jimmy Carter," wrote the *Telegraph*.[39] PBS ran an entire segment trying to convince themselves the idea was conceivable.[40] "It's All but Settled: The Reagan Campaign Delayed the Release of the Iranian Hostages," said the *New Republic*.[41]

Pundits and journalists spread the story across social media, as well. James Fallows, who is not some fringe Substacker but rather an award-winning writer for the (once) prestigious *Atlantic* magazine, took to the web to contend that "OF COURSE" the Iranians, who were anti-Carter and pro–Ronald Reagan, had tried to manipulate the results.[42]

Carter was cheated out of the presidency. Even Reagan, one of the most popular presidents in American history, was only victorious because of a seditious plan to steal the election. The preordained leftward trajectory of American political life, consequently, was altered forever by the scheme. Another election stolen from its rightful party.

Times *readers may* not have been aware that Barnes's story was knocking around in the media for decades. Leftist fictions do not die; they are merely repackaged. As the historian Daniel Pipes notes, the first person to theorize that Reagan engineered an "October surprise" by colluding with Iranian revolutionaries was the infamous conspiracy theorist Lyndon LaRouche. Just after the election in December 1980, his magazine *Executive Intelligence Review* cited *Iranian* sources and "top level intelligence sources in Reagan's inner circle," who claimed that former secretary of state Henry Kissinger was the dealmaker.[43]

LaRouche, incidentally, is typically portrayed by historians and media as an extension of right-wing nuttery. His politics, however, never followed any coherent (or sane) ideological arch. LaRouche, in fact, began his political life as a Trotskyist. His first presidential run was under the U.S. Labor Party banner in 1976. As proponents of nationalizing education and health care, among other decidedly left-wing positions, LaRouchites did quite well among Democratic constituents during the 1980s.[44] So successful was his small army of proselytizers that national Democrats began to worry they might steal a consequential number of votes in certain districts.[45]

In any event, the Reagan-stole-the-1980-election theory would then be filtered up "a media food chain," as Hillary Clinton might say, making the big time in 1991 when the same *New York Times* allocated *nearly the entire editorial page* to a piece authored by a former naval officer and foreign policy expert named Gary Sick, who contended that "individuals associated with the Reagan-Bush campaign of 1980 met secretly with Iranian officials to delay the release of the American hostages until after the U.S. election. For this favor, Iran was allegedly rewarded with a substantial supply of arms from Israel."[46] Sick expanded on his "covert political coup" theory in a book titled *October Surprise: America's Hostages in Iran and the Election of Ronald Reagan*, which was published that year.

Let's remember that George H. W. Bush was then president, and hanging this plot on his former boss would be politically beneficial for Democrats.

That said, in the 1990s there were still some mainstream journalists who valued professional ethics over partisan activism. Even left-leaning publications like the *Village Voice*, *New Republic* (at the time, still a respected center-left journalistic outfit), and others debunked

Sick's story. *Newsweek*, which had over three million readers at the time, concluded, after "interviews with government officials and other knowledgeable sources around the world," that "the key claims of the purported eyewitnesses and accusers simply do not hold up."[47]

On top of all that, there were not one but *two* congressional inquiries into the claim. A House committee, chaired by Democrat Lee Hamilton, found that there was "wholly insufficient credible evidence" of any communications between Reagan campaign officials and the Iranian government and "no credible evidence" that Republicans desired a delayed release of the hostages.[48] Another 1992 Senate investigation found that "by any standard, the credible evidence now known falls far short of supporting the allegation of an agreement between the Reagan campaign and Iran to delay the release of the hostages."[49]

Then, like now, however, the veracity of the conspiracy theory wasn't the point. The point was feeding the perception that something was wrong to taint the election in the eyes of voters.

It worked. By 1994, a study by pollsters at the academic journal *Political Psychology* found that 55 percent of respondents believed it was "definitely" true or "probably" true that "Ronald Reagan and George Bush collaborated with the Iranians so that the American hostages would not be released until after the 1980 elections." Only 34 percent of those asked believed it was "definitely" or "probably" false.[50]

Now, perhaps one day some intrepid reporter will uncover a memo that proves Barnes's contentions were real. I highly doubt it. Because, like all good conspiracy theories, a story that is impossible to prove is also impossible to disprove. That is why journalists have an obligation to corroborate claims before spreading them.

As it stands, the *Times* spent little space grappling with alternative possibilities to the stolen-election speculation. It does not explain why Reagan would pick a Texan with so little clout or foreign policy experience to take on this astonishing task. It does not ponder why Sunni leaders in Egypt or Saudi Arabia or the Jewish politicians of Israel would trust, much less pass along, this extraordinary offer. It does not wonder why, if Barnes successfully dissuaded theocratic Iranian revolutionaries from releasing American hostages to help Reagan win, Connally was not offered secretary of state or secretary of defense jobs.

It is worth stressing the exceptionally poor quality of the *New York Times*' journalism—because it is the same kind of shoddy "reporting" that is the earmark of BlueAnon.

Not only did the *Times* fail to provide a single contemporaneous witness to substantiate Barnes's forty-three-year-old tale, but the paper did not provide a letter, not even scribbles on a notepad, or any voice recordings, nor bank record nor canceled check to corroborate the plot. The *Times* piece was loaded with conjecture and journalistic verbiage. It is the same formula it uses for an array of conspiracy theories, including the Russia Collusion hoax.

It is essentially impossible to imagine a major establishment newspaper running some far-fetched evidence-free conjecture about a Democratic president engaging in what amounts to sedition. Yet the *Times* opened its pages, spending thousands of words, relaying accusations that had no merit or proof. Because, as we'll see, virtually *any* left-wing fantasy about an election being subverted by Republicans will merit, at the very least, a hearing from major left-wing journalistic institutions.

Then again, the revisionist stolen 1980 presidential election merely joins the stolen 2000 presidential election and the stolen presidential 2004 election and the stolen 2016 presidential election in the continuum of mythological events that have snatched elections from their rightful victors. The left can't countenance losing. It is impossible for them to accept that voters, in full possession of their agency, faculties, and good sense, made a conscious decision to reject "progress."

It's gotta be something else.

2000

Despite his destructive legacy, left-wing revisionists like to place former vice president Al Gore in the pantheon of great statesmen, as a man who stepped aside to save the country from a prolonged, divisive battle that would undermine the public's trust in elections. Gore's story is often retold as a juxtaposition against Republican inflexibility and denialism of the 2020s.

It is a fable. Gore only walked away from the presidency after the Supreme Court deprived him of any other plausible, legal path to try to claim victory in Florida. Like Trump, he was left with no other choice.

At the time, the entire left was captured by an array of conspiracies—fed and nurtured by Democrats and a pliant media. The vice president, it should be remembered, relied on a slew of bizarre claims when refusing to concede the 2000 election, setting a precedent of attacking the integrity of the electoral system for personal gain, and then dragging the nation through an absurdly acrimonious constitutional crisis that was not grounded in any reality.

Despite ostensibly conceding, it should be remembered, Gore has never definitively accepted his loss. In 2002, he alleged he "would have won" if every vote in Florida was counted and that he "absolutely" believed he would become president after the ordered recount. Even as late as 2017, Gore was saying, "Actually, I think I carried Florida."

The reality is that the courts *did* allow counting the Florida votes to finish in 2000. In every count, Bush won. It was Gore who then demanded selective recounts in the most heavily Democratic counties—without offering any genuine legal cause other than its being too close for his liking.

Imagine the reaction from the media if Trump demanded that Georgia or Pennsylvania recount *only* certain districts that possibly benefited him in 2020.

Democrats soon settled on the infamous "hanging or dimpled

chads" hysteria, and the media went about finding allegedly confused voters who purported wrongly cast ballots, a claim that would never, and could never, be verified—though media also spread the unprovable rumor that Floridians, confused by the ballot, had accidentally voted for third-party candidate Patrick Buchanan.[51]

At the time, Gore's lawyer Mark Herron instructed Democratic recount observers how to challenge Republican-heavy absentee ballots from U.S. military overseas.[52] Ron Klain, the Gore campaign's general counsel and later Joe Biden's chief of staff, led the charge in trying to exclude military votes.[53]

As this went on, Gore and media outlets worked to delegitimize the results, knowing full well that, outside an unconstitutional revote, there would be no way to know. It was only then that Gore decided to throw it to the courts. That's when *seven* U.S. Supreme Court justices agreed that there was an Equal Protection Clause violation when attempting to use different standards of determining the validity of votes. Then five of the justices decided that the law still mattered, finding that no constitutional grounds existed for ignoring state law allowing recounts to go past a December 12 deadline.

Only when all those legal options were exhausted, when there was no court to petition, and there was nothing left to gain, did Gore, like Trump, finally walk away.

Even if the U.S. Supreme Court had allowed a hand recount to go on, using the loosest standards, counting partial punches and dimpled ballots and so on, Bush still would have won. When the *Miami Herald* and *USA Today* recounted the vote, they found that Bush expanded his 537-vote margin to 1,665.[54] The National Opinion Research Center—which recounted the votes for the Associated Press, the *New York Times*, the *Wall Street Journal*, and others—also found that Bush would have won.[55] In every official count and nearly every recount completed by the media, Gore lost.

o   o   o   o   o

Despite all this overwhelming evidence, to this day most Democrats will tell you Gore *really* won 2000. Hillary Clinton, like numerous other high-profile members of the left, likes to say that Bush was "selected" rather than elected president.[56] And Clinton, who would later help concoct explosive fairy tales about the 2016 election, was going on about how the Supreme Court "took away a presidency" in *Bush v. Gore*. "The only way [Republicans] could win the election was to stop the voting in Florida," she lied.[57]

In both 2013[58] and 2016[59], Joe Biden said he thought Al Gore won 2000.

The stolen-election conspiracy is treated as objective fact among left-wing journalists. Pundits like Jonathan Chait, who later speculated that Donald Trump might have been an embedded KGB asset since 1987, is a champion of the genre: "Yes, Bush v. Gore Did Steal the Election," he wrote in 2012.[60] But he is hardly alone. Basically, every major newspaper editorial board, and every left-wing columnist on their staff, still makes similar claims. Even today, you are unlikely to find any Democrats who would concede that Bush fairly won the 2000 presidential race.

No one calls these people "election deniers." Rather, this revisionist history has become reality for millions.

2004

Perhaps by virtue of it being historically close, one could forgive those who bought the rickety idea that Gore was robbed by the courts in 2000. People, however, tend to forget—or ignore—that there was plenty of genuine election "denialism" over George W. Bush's 2004 victory against John Kerry as well. Whether it was sentient Diebold machines and nebulous claims of "voter suppression," this was no fringe effort. After losing, Kerry would himself continue to raise questions about the outcome, contending that Americans were "denied their right to vote; too many who tried to vote were intimidated."[61] After numerous investigations, there was no evidence to back this claim.

In those days, candidates delegitimized elections through proxies, rather than risk looking unstatesmanlike. Mark Crispin Miller, author of the bestselling *Fooled Again: How the Right Stole the 2004 Election, & Why They'll Steal the Next One, Too* (*Unless We Stop Them*), maintained that Kerry, his close friend, believed that "the election was stolen."[62]

Others waged an open campaign to delegitimize the results. In 2005, House Democrats authored a report contending that "numerous, serious election irregularities" occurred in Ohio's presidential vote.[63] Then–California senator Barbara Boxer and representative and cochair of the DNC Stephanie Tubbs filed an objection to the certification of Ohio's electoral votes.

That year, thirty-one House Democrats voted to reject the electoral vote total, including well-known national leaders like the future chair of the Committee on Homeland Security Bennie Thompson, Barbara Lee, Maxine Waters, Raúl Grijalva, James Clyburn, and now-senator Ed Markey—nearly all of whom would later spread the Russia Collusion hoax and other preposterous speculations about their partisan opponents.[64]

These kinds of legal objections would be framed as an effort to "overturn the election" when Republicans used them in 2020.

In 2004, Democratic presidential candidate Howard Dean, then leading in national polls, theorized that the CEO of Diebold, a Republican donor, might well manipulate machines to discount Democratic voters. "Whether you can program a chip or not is up for debate. I think you probably can and have a vote for Al Gore count as a vote for Pat Buchanan," Dean explained.[65]

Claims of cheating during the 2004 election were preemptively leveled, which, as we'll see, is now a regular component of left-wing conspiracy commerce. By 2006, Dean, then–Democratic National Committee chairman, was putting on hearings to cast doubt on the vote tally in Ohio.

To this day, not a single case of a vote having gone uncounted or tampered with or ignored or canceled by machines or anyone else has been found. Then again, who knows, perhaps in a few decades the *New York Times* will run the claims of an octogenarian who claims to vividly remember his vote being stolen in 2004.

No one called it the "Big Lie" back then.

At the time, the effort to stop the results was covered merely as the normal workings of democracy. Oh no, Minority Leader Nancy Pelosi argued that challenging the vote was "fundamental to our democracy" and "appropriate" to have the "legitimate concerns" regarding the "integrity" of the election.[66] What would be framed as insidious attacks on the foundations of "democracy" in 2020 were referred to as an "important service for American democracy" by then-senator Tom Harkin. Terry McAuliffe, then-chairman of the DNC and future governor of Virginia, commissioned a "comprehensive investigative study on election practices in Ohio" to address "legitimate questions and concerns."[67]

The "Liberal Lion," Ted Kennedy, and powerful senator Frank Lautenberg also alleged "systematic voter disenfranchisement" and faulty voting machines.

Democrat Danny Davis, who has praised racist conspiracy theorist Louis Farrakhan, claimed the 2004 election contained widespread "fraud." Future Democratic presidential candidate Dennis Kucinich, who once appeared to flirt with 9/11 trutherism,[68] maintained that "dirty tricks occurred across the state."

Jerry Nadler, still a leading Russia Collusion conspiracist, said there were "irregularities with respect to the electronic and other voting machines."[69] Dozens of other congressmen would make almost identical claims despite there not being a shred of evidence proving anyone's vote was denied or altered.

Again, a significant number of Americans fell for it. A 2005 Fairleigh Dickinson University poll found that 23 percent of respondents believed that President George W. Bush's supporters "committed significant voter fraud" to win the 2004 presidential election in Ohio.[70] Among Democrats, 37 percent said it was likely true.

The myth of the stolen 2004 election would be rooted in the mind of the left as a political continuum of GOP misconduct. Hillary Clinton, who today pretends to abhor election "denialism," argued that there were "legitimate" questions about the "accuracy" and "integrity" of the 2004 election.[71]

Democrats have been eager to accept full-blown conspiracy theories to explain their losses. For years, they had fostered an environment where it was perfectly acceptable to not only question the authenticity of elections but to concoct lurid tales of intrigue to explain them. The biggest one was yet to come.

THE GREATEST HOAX IN
AMERICAN HISTORY

*This must be the product of a great conspiracy
on a scale so immense as to dwarf any previous
such venture in the history of man.*

JOE MCCARTHY, 1951

Hey genius, Russia hacked a candidate in the 2016 election.
—REP. ERIC SWALWELL, 2023

The Russia Collusion hoax had it all. Political intrigue. International espionage. Tawdry affairs. Celebrities. Sedition. Republicans behaving badly.

Well, it had it all *apart* from any substantive evidence corroborating its central contention that Republican presidential candidate Donald Trump colluded with the dictator Vladimir Putin and the Russians to steal the 2016 election from Democrats.

Which seems like an important oversight.

Nevertheless, the Russia Collusion hoax sparked an unparalleled angst that gripped our political universe for nearly four years. There were the weekly media meltdowns and moral panics. There were the fantastical accounts of clandestine foreign powers manipulating the vote and burrowing themselves into our most cherished institutions.

At first, even normally skeptical Americans weren't sure what to make of the crush of alleged scoops about Putin's influence on our brittle democracy. Sure, it all sounded a bit far-fetched, but one could never be sure. Though it might sound counterintuitive, the more spectacular and sweeping a conspiracy theory, the more difficult it is to disentangle and debunk. Besides, Trump was no ordinary candidate. He was a man prone to hyperbole, outlandish contentions, and unconventional foreign policy positions.

Nor was the Russia Collusion hoax spread by easily dismissible fly-by-night websites or gaggles of tinfoil-hat-wearing social media personalities. The fiction was passed on by our most trusted institutions. A major political party was behind the hoax. Former CIA directors and high-ranking intelligence officials regularly confirmed its veracity. Once-respected journalists reported on each new revelation with a passion and urgency not seen since Watergate.

When it was all said and done, tens of millions of Americans were convinced that the Russians not only altered their votes in 2016 but infiltrated one of the country's major political parties. From then on, "democracy" was in a constant state of peril.

It would take a *long* book to properly unwind the convoluted origins, life cycle, and afterlife of the Russia Collusion hoax. Instead, let's look at how the election of Trump broke the brains of Democrats and infected every institution on the left.

After eight years of Barack Obama, Democrats struggled to wrap their minds around the reality of losing the White House to anyone. For those who believe government is the wellspring of all decency, losing to a Republican was painful enough. But surrendering power to this crass, unapologetic, populist celebrity was simply unfathomable. So, Democrats were desperate for an explanation.

∘ ∘ ∘ ∘ ∘

Though it would be later forgotten in the fog of the perpetual histri-onics of our news cycles, no major Democrat fully accepted the va-lidity of Trump's victory in 2016. Not really. Not from the start. Not his opponent, Hillary Clinton, who argued Trump was an "illegitimate president."[1] Not the future vice president Kamala Harris, nor former presidential candidates John Kerry, Al Gore, and Jimmy Carter, who said "Trump didn't actually win the election in 2016—he lost the elec-tion, and he was put in office because the Russians interfered."[2] The late civil rights hero John Lewis did not accept the results, nor did the late Senate majority leader Harry Reid, who said there was "no ques-tion" that Russia altered vote totals during the 2016 election.[3]

Even *before* the Russia Collusion had fully formed, the entire Dem-ocratic Party was delegitimizing the 2016 results. And rather than de-mand accountability from the conspiracists, as would be the case in 2020, the media entertained every one of the left's far-flung theories.

Democrats initially struggled to settle on a justification to tell the public that Trump's election was bogus. Sure, they blamed "fake news" and Fox News. They always did. This time around they also attributed the loss to left-wing media showering Trump with too much coverage. They blamed systemic racism and "voter suppression." They blamed imaginary electoral shenanigans. As they did in 2000 and 2004, "ex-perts" sat on cable news panels and deliberated on the possibility that the Democratic Party candidate "may have been denied" tens of thou-sands of votes in battleground states like Wisconsin.[4] It was bunk.

One of the more popular early excuses for losing the 2016 election revolved around the suspicion that right-wingers had infiltrated the FBI and engineered a Trump victory.

In 2015, Congress discovered that Hillary Clinton was operating a pri-vate, secret computer server to send official communications while in the State Department so she could circumvent transparency—possibly to hide favor-trading related to the Clinton Foundation. Two inspectors general asked the Justice Department to open an inquiry into the presidential candidate. So, the FBI was given little choice. From the primaries onward, an FBI investigation hung over her campaign.

Numerous left-wing columnists, including the *New York Times'* Paul Krugman, argued that the feds had "rigged" the 2016 results by investigating Hillary's private email server. (In a few years, contending that 2020 election was "rigged" would have you ejected from decent company.) The FBI, wrote the Pulitzer Prize–winning columnist, exerted its considerable influence and "spread innuendo" to "influence the election."[5] Clinton herself, reverting to nineties form, referred to the investigation as "another conspiracy theory."[6]

Like most accusations Hillary calls "conspiracy theories," the facts checked out.

In summer 2016, FBI director James Comey held a press conference scrupulously detailing Hillary's numerous evasions of the laws governing the handling of classified information. Comey probably let the former secretary of state skate, maintaining the FBI couldn't prove her intent, to save himself the trauma of indicting someone almost everyone believed would be the next president. Perhaps that was for the best. Clinton, he explained, was "extremely careless" in "handling of very sensitive, highly classified information."[7]

In 2024, President Joe Biden would also be allowed to skate on his decades-long mishandling of classified information that he had been hoarding since the 1970s. And though special counsel Robert Hur had found that Biden had "willfully retained classified information" after his vice presidency, he let the president off as he was too elderly and too feeble-minded to ever be convicted by a jury—an assertion that even those in denial would have to admit when watching Biden during the first presidential debate of the 2024 race.[8]

Trump, on the other hand, wasn't given a pass for similar infractions.

Hillary later lied about her efforts to evade transparency, maintaining she was merely guilty of sending emails about "Gefilte fish."[9] According to the FBI, however, Clinton had broken security protocol on at least 600 occasions, sending 110 emails with clearly marked classified information—36 of those emails contained merely secret information, and eight of those email chains contained "top secret" information.[10] The FBI also found that Hillary should have known that many topics under discussion in correspondences were classified, even if they were not obviously marked.

"We assess it is possible that hostile actors gained access to Secretary Clinton's personal e-mail account," Comey explained at the time. Even the *Times* conceded that the communications were almost surely intercepted by foreign powers.[11]

Moreover, Clinton's staff attempted to destroy all the evidence potentially related to her illegal server—as innocent people are wont to do. Comey noted in testimony that Hillary's staff had "cleaned their devices in such a way as to preclude complete forensic recovery."

To top it off, a few days before the election, on October 28, Comey confirmed that the FBI found classified emails on the computer of the sex-addict erstwhile husband of Clinton's top adviser, Huma Abedin. Former congressman Anthony Weiner would soon spend eighteen months in prison for sending obscene material to a minor from that very computer.

It quickly became an article of faith among Democrats that a "Comey letter" to Congress a week before the election had triggered the downfall of Democrats. The reality was that Comey had no choice but to inform Congress that there was new evidence because he already promised congressional investigators—under oath—that he would let them know if such were to emerge. And that's what he did. What Democrats demanded was that Comey withhold evidence to help Hillary. Blaming a letter rather than Clinton's unlikable supercilious nature, malleable positions, and terrible campaign strategy would feed the impression that Hillary's inevitable victory was compromised by a cabal of plotters.

Let's face it, the FBI-did-it take was weak tea. BlueAnon needed something more explosive, more mysterious, and more chilling to destroy the public's trust in the validity of the 2016 election. What it whipped up would create a political spasm like no other in modern political history. It would alter domestic politics, destroy the right's trust in important institutions, and remake the Democratic Party into an outfit increasingly reliant on conspiracy for results.

THE DOSSIER

The dossier has been a convenient foil, their false flag.
—DAVID CORN[12]

On January 11, 2017, only a few days before Donald Trump was sworn in as the forty-fifth president of the United States, BuzzFeed, then a flashy new entrant into political journalism, published a photo depiction of a thirty-five-page memo headlined "Republican Candidate Donald Trump's Activities in Russia and Compromising Relationship with the Kremlin."

The contents included what is known as the "Steele Dossier," an opposition research document that claimed to prove that Donald Trump plotted with Russian president Vladimir Putin to "steal" the 2016 election. As BuzzFeed explained, the memo was "circulated at the highest levels of the U.S. government" and had "acquired a kind of legendary status among journalists, lawmakers and intelligence officials."[13]

Within the year, we would find out the memo originated from the Democratic National Committee and Hillary Clinton's campaign, which paid a research firm called Fusion GPS and former British intelligence operative Christopher Steele to compile the dossier of uncorroborated raw "intelligence"—some of it derived from Kremlin sources.

Kompromat, unsavory information used to blackmail or extort public figures, is a longtime Russian specialty. The belief that the "dossier" was a fact-based document compiled to extort the new president for policy favors would become the prevailing view of the left. And, as with any disinformation, the Steele Dossier featured a smattering of truth—yes Donald Trump had done some business in Moscow—to imbue the document with believability, allowing conspiracy theorists to maintain that it was mostly "true."

The *true* parts didn't really matter to BlueAnon. What mattered was scurrilous and unverified parts. One of the most popular snippets of the dossier depicted the future president asking Moscow hookers to engage in a "golden shower" on the bed of a luxury hotel suite that supposedly had once been occupied by the Obamas.

BlueAnon spread this story by engaging in a little game they like to play where they pass unverified innuendo about Republicans into the public record, worrying about corroboration later. CNN ("Mueller investigated rumored compromising tapes of Trump in Moscow"[14]), the *Washington Post* ("Real or 'fake news'? Either way, allegations of lewd tape pose challenge for Trump"[15]), the *New York Times* ("Lordy, Is There a Tape?"[16]), and virtually every lefty outlet gave the "pee tape" story enough attention to ensure everyone in America knew about it.

Soon, however, BlueAnons would begin dressing up the amateurish "intelligence" in professional journalistic verbiage and leak its contents in misleading bits. The media continued to act as if it had confirmed accusations before reporting on them. This was untrue.

One of the more explosive stories in the Steele Dossier, one that in many ways buttressed many of the most filmic theories of the left, maintained that Trump's personal attorney Michael Cohen secretly traveled to Prague in the summer of 2016 to meet Russian aides of

President Putin to arrange hush payments for hackers who broke into Democratic Party computers. There was nothing illegal about such a meeting, but it *felt* seditious to the press. And if true, it confirmed that a plot was afoot.

The Prague trip was reported on by *every* major media organization, though none had independently verified whether Cohen ever set foot in Czechia. Cohen, who, to be fair, wasn't competent enough to pull together his own travel arrangement much less the biggest coup in human history, told the media he never made the clandestine trip and then denied the trip had occurred, under oath in front of Congress, claiming he was in Los Angeles at the time with his son. The University of Southern California confirmed he was on campus during this time.[17] The Czech government said they had no record of Cohen entering the country.

No matter!

The story lingered for years. In 2019, after BlueAnon had largely moved on to fresh intrigues, McClatchy revived the story, reporting that Cohen's phone pinged a cell tower near Prague and that Russians were overheard at some point discussing the trip in 2016. This was then repeated by every major news organization without independent verification. And this too was untrue.[18]

Though the imaginary Cohen trip set the table for the press, the Steele Dossier had other toxic and long-term repercussions in Washington.

We later learned that the Foreign Intelligence Surveillance Act (FISA) applications sought by the FBI to spy on the Trump campaign were almost "entirely" predicated on the fabulist Steele Dossier, according to an inspector general investigation.[19] We learned that agents also left out contradictory, exculpatory evidence when kicking off the spying against Carter Page, a minor Trump campaign worker, which opened the door to spying on almost the entire Trump organization. We learned that most applications for a FISA warrant in the case featured "significant inaccuracies and omissions" and at least one was based on "fraudulent" evidence.[20] We learned that partisan Obama administration officials "unmasked"—which is to say, identified formerly anonymous people in intelligence reports—those who worked for the Trump campaign.[21]

After Trump's 2016 win, Obama holdovers and opponents of the new president within the government began leaking misleading snippets of the Russia investigation to a largely pliant media, which prompted the hysteria that dominated American news coverage for the next four years. Joe McCarthy would have blushed at the effort.

It should be noted that the foundations of the Russia scare were laid even before the dossier was made public. The buildup to panic began in 2016, when media began reporting that American intelligence agencies ascertained Putin was partial to Donald Trump's candidacy. This contention seemed true-ish enough. In the same way Iran and Hamas would be partial to a Biden administration. The GOP candidate offered sympathetic remarks about the Russian president and the prospects of peace with that authoritarian nation. As we'll see, many of these comments, though delivered in Trump's typically indelicate manner, were not especially unusual.

Besides, the Russians were always interested in causing mayhem in the United States. And, thanks to the participants and the media, they succeeded in ways Putin probably never imagined possible.

A *few days* before Election Day, for instance, Slate published a story tying the Trump Organization's email server to those of Russia's Alfa-Bank, a connection that purportedly was a way to send secret messages and funds between the two camps without public scrutiny. Such an arrangement, needless to say, would indicate a devious plot that involved payoffs.

Many Americans learned about this shocking arrangement from the Democratic Party candidate herself. "Computer scientists have apparently uncovered a covert server linking the Trump Organization to a Russian-based bank," Hillary Clinton tweeted.[22] Jake Sullivan, then a senior adviser on the Clinton campaign and now President Joe Biden's national security adviser, noted that the story "could be the most direct link yet between Donald Trump and Moscow."[23] It wasn't true. A later FBI investigation found there were no improper links between the two.[24]

Both Clinton and Sullivan must have been well aware that the accusation was complete garbage. Because, as we would learn later, the *Clinton campaign* were the ones who planted the story. The Clinton campaign, in fact, had already sent the accusation to the FBI, which rejected it as implausible.[25] Franklin Foer (as of this writing, a journalist in good standing at the *Atlantic*) almost certainly took the information straight from Fusion GPS, the dossier's author, and simply wrapped the allegations in the lingo of investigative journalism: before publishing the piece, Foer sent it back to Fusion GPS so it could look over the piece for "omissions and errors."[26]

No real journalist would act in this manner. Yet this process became the norm.

There is something of a maxim in journalism—or, at least, there used to be when reporters still did their jobs: if a story is perfect, it's almost surely a fake. During the Russia Collusion hoax *every* story seemed perfect and yet on most days the entire establishment media chased them with earnest, bated breath. Rather than challenging, debunking, or contextualizing the leaks that were landing in their inboxes, BlueAnon lackeys acted as conduits for untruths and half-truths and myth, reinforcing them with performative journalistic jargon and sensationalist headlines.

The tone of accompanying commentary was nearly always histrionic and melodramatic. So many tweets from reporters began with the word *Wow!* that, after a while, one could preemptively discount whatever words followed as a likely fairy tale. Reporters assumed, or acted as if they assumed, every new revelation was merely bringing them closer to the ultimate truth. These journalists were either in on the hoax or they were credulous dupes. Either way, they played their part.

"The walls were closing in" became a trope for Democrats, repeated each time a new gotcha story about Russians appeared. The walls were always closing in.

On June 12, 2017, the political media melted down after *Fortune* magazine reported that Russia Today, the state mouthpiece for the Kremlin, had hacked and taken over C-SPAN coverage. The station soon confirmed the report.

It turned out to be a false alarm. After an investigation, C-SPAN found that it was an internal routing error.[27]

In June 2017, citing multiple anonymous sources—the norm during the Trump presidency—CNN confirmed that former FBI director James Comey was going to tell a congressional committee under oath that Trump lied when claiming that Comey had told him on three occasions that he hadn't been under investigation. It was a bombshell. This vital piece of the puzzle confirmed that the president had evaded any action against Russian interference even after being advised it was happening. The only reason he would do that was to protect himself.

Despite all the animated breaking-news chyrons, the opposite turned out to be true. Comey testified that he *had* told Trump three times he was not being investigated.

On June 22, 2017, three CNN journalists were forced to resign (perhaps the last time anyone has paid any price for passing along Russia hoax content) after reporting that Congress was investigating a "Russian investment fund with ties to Trump officials." Finally, evidence that the new president was bought.[28] The problem was that the reporters relied on a single anonymous source. It turned out to be false. CNN retracted the story. From then on, media outlets would become increasingly reluctant to correct or withdraw claims.

On December 1, 2017, the internet blew up again when the chief investigative correspondent for ABC News, Brian Ross, broke a story that former national security adviser Michael Flynn would be testifying that Trump ordered him to contact the Russians *during* the election. If this didn't point to Russian collusion, nothing would. The Dow Jones Industrial Average tumbled 300 points after ABC broke the news.

As it turned out, Flynn testified that Trump asked him to connect with Russian officials during the transition period—a completely normal thing for presidents to do.[29]

On December 9, 2017, leading BlueAnonist Manu Raju reported in an "exclusive" that Donald Trump Jr. had advanced access to DNC emails that were hacked by Russia and published by the site WikiLeaks.

Now, that was *a big story*. "Candidate Donald Trump, his son Donald Trump Jr. and others in the Trump Organization received an email in September 2016 offering a decryption key and website address for hacked WikiLeaks documents, according to an email provided to congressional investigators," wrote CNN. The email, the outlet reported, was dated September 4, 2016, before WikiLeaks published letters from the DNC hack. This was definitive evidence that the Trump Organization was working with Russians to steal democracy.

Within an hour, in fact, NBC News' Ken Dilanian, another top Russia Collusion pro, had "independently confirmed" this blockbuster scoop, one of the biggest in American political history.

The problem, as it turned out, was the email was not dated the fourth but the fourteenth of September—a date when the DNC hacks were already widely available to anyone who wanted to read them. Raju had, in a still-unexplained "mistake," found two completely independent sources who both gave him the exact same wrong date. Dilanian, in another remarkable happenstance, had also got the same wrong date from another independent source. Crazy, right?

On July 26, 2018, CNN reported that Trump's personal lawyer, Michael Cohen, would be willing to tell Special Counsel Robert Mueller that the president knew in advance of the June 2016 Trump Tower meeting between his campaign and a Kremlin-linked lawyer who was allegedly selling dirt on Hillary Clinton. This too was quite the exclusive.

They finally had Trump. The story, bylined by Carl Bernstein of Watergate fame and former Obama administration political appointee Jim Sciutto, cited numerous "sources" with knowledge of the supposed bombshell. The *Washington Post*, chasing the same story, soon outed Cohen's lawyer, the preternaturally mendacious Lanny Davis, as the source of the contention. Davis, one of Bill Clinton's most unctuous defenders, was forced to walk back the claim, conceding that he "should have been more clear" and that he "could not independently confirm what happened," and then he sort of apologized.[30]

Anyway, it never happened.

These are just a few examples of the dozens of supposed innocent "mistakes"—as media defenders would call them—that BlueAnon engaged in. The mistakes always—always—skewed in the same direction. It didn't take a genius to figure out that reporters were regurgitating stories from the same cadres of "independent sources." No matter how many times media organizations were burned by these sources, they kept pumping out the fake news. On and on it went.

Every big Russia Collusion story, even though most were misleading or untrue or overstated, compounded the public's perception that American democracy was appropriated by a foreign entity with the help of a fascistic administration. Media "missteps" wouldn't trigger a turn toward more judiciousness or professionalism, but the opposite. Reporters simply ratcheted up the coverage to even more ludicrous heights. And, as with any good conspiracy theory, every denial elicited a slew of new questions.

The *New York Times* and *Washington Post* both won Pulitzer Prizes for National Reporting in 2018 for now-disproven contentions that

Trump had colluded with Russia to interfere in the presidential election. The ironic part is that it's quite possible that the information they used to make those claims came from Russian information included in the Steele Dossier.

KGB ASSETS

Trump returned from Moscow fired up with political ambition.
—JONATHAN CHAIT

As each layer of a conspiracy theory is exposed as a lie, believers expand the scope of the plot to explain the inconsistencies. The story thus becomes increasingly complex. It ensnares more participants and institutions. The drama is amped up, or the story loses steam. But the payoff always remains right over the horizon.

What began as a story of Trump colluding with Russians to retrieve oppo info about his political opponent would morph into an astonishing tale of a Manchurian candidate who was "installed" by a foreign regime. Or as leading BlueAnon conspiracist Jonathan Chait of *New York* magazine alleged: there was "evidence" that "Russian intelligence carried out a successful plan to pick the government of the United States."[31]

Remember the last time you went down to the polling station and, relying on your own free will, cast a ballot for the presidency? That was, apparently, a figment of your imagination.

Before Trump and Putin met at the G-20 summit in 2018, Chait penned his masterwork—perhaps the single most thrilling piece of Russia Collusion fiction ever written—"Will Trump Be Meeting with His Counterpart—or His Handler? A plausible premise of mind-boggling collusion."[32] In over eight thousand words, Chait speculates on whether Trump, a celebrity billionaire who'd been in the public eye for over forty years, was cultivated as an asset for the Kremlin since 1987.

The tale is adorned with all the hallmarks of the genre, stringing together opaque events and out-of-context statements to create a narrative of "mind-boggling" deception. Modern cranks often mask their recklessness with questions. Lots and lots of questions. Yet, after years of tenderizing the public's perceptions with tales of Russian infiltration, hacks, and skullduggery, even glossy American magazines showed no qualms publishing pieces that only a few years earlier would have been found in photocopied zines that some Noam Chomsky enthusiast had stapled together in a basement dorm room.

Never deterred, when investigations turned up nothing on the collusion front, Chait doubled down, claiming that he had suspected there was a "10 or 20 percent" chance that the president had worked for the Kremlin for decades, but that if he had to guess, he would "put the odds higher, perhaps over 50 percent."[33]

One of the ways to expand the intrigue was to cast the entire Republican Party as saboteurs in this treacherous scheme. As with any good conspiracy theory, those *rejecting* the accusations were merely proving they were in on it. So when, for instance, White House spokesperson Sean Spicer correctly noted that there was "no evidence" that Russia had "influenced the election," the DNC called him a "shill for Putin."[34] Soon every Republican would be working for Putin.

Rachel Maddow, at the time the most popular cable news talk-show host outside of Fox News (and some nights, the most popular), often suggested that members of the administration were doing the bidding of Russians. "We are also starting to see what may be signs of continuing influence in our country," Maddow explained to her audience in March 2017. "Not just during the campaign, but during the administration. Basically signs of what could be a continuing operation."

The "operation," as it turned out, was completely imaginary. Yet it was the anchor for thousands of hours of cable news coverage.

When former Exxon CEO Rex Tillerson was named secretary of state by Trump, Maddow explained that his appointment was "a dream for Putin." Stories about the "deep ties" between Exxon's former CEO and Russia began to appear across the establishment media.[35] Every Trump administration member, in fact, was vetted to check if they had any meetings with people carrying a Russian name. Trump's first attorney general, Jeff Sessions, was basically branded a traitor and forced to recuse himself from anything related to the Russia Collusion conspiracy theory because it was revealed that he had once met with the Russian diplomat while a senator.[36]

Before Trump, it was standard for political and industry leaders to meet with Russians—especially if you were a CEO of a major international company or worked in Washington. Before Trump, mollycoddling Russia was a Democratic Party specialty.

When Joe Biden went to Munich in 2009, delivering the Obama administration's first major foreign policy speech, he argued that it was "time to press the reset button" after eight years of purported American antagonism toward Russia. The speech was framed as a return to diplomatic normalcy after the tumultuous Bush years, rather than a surrender to a dictator.[37]

The Obama administration also spearheaded the effort to reward Moscow by giving it access to the World Trade Organization. Biden told Putin's dupe Dmitri Medvedev that Russia's access to the WTO was "the most important item on our agenda."[38] In 2012, Obama was caught on a hot mic telling Medvedev that he would have more "flexibility" on missile defense after the 2012 presidential election.[39]

Can you imagine the thermonuclear media meltdown if Trump had done the same?

By that time, incidentally, Obama had already canceled long-promised missile-defense systems to our allies in Poland and the Czech

Republic. It was the Trump administration that approved the sale of a Patriot missile system to Poland. For that matter, it was Trump who, finally, approved the sale of defensive lethal weapons to Ukraine. And it wasn't during a potential invasion.

Democrats didn't merely mock Republican presidential candidate Mitt Romney in 2012 as an out-of-touch amateur for maintaining that Russia was our top geopolitical threat, they sent a smug Biden to appear on the Sunday morning news shows, where he described the Putin kleptocracy as a burgeoning ally and partner. Though "we have disagreements with Russia," Biden noted, they were "working closely with us" on a slew of issues. "This is not 1956," he scoffed.[40]

The same people who cheered on the Obama administration's peace-loving turn transformed every innocuous interaction with a Russian by a Trump associate into an act of treason.

Leftist pundits like to mock Trump for his often incoherent and swirling speech patterns. So, when the president spoke lucidly about his foreign policy positions, Maddow wondered why Trump was "curiously well versed" in "specific Russian talking points," insinuating that he had taken direction.[41] With the sarcastic caption "No Puppet No Puppet" featured prominently behind her.

After an American missile attack on Syria, Maddow's colleague, lockstepping partisan Lawrence O'Donnell, told her that it was "impossible" to rule out the idea that "Vladimir Putin orchestrated what happened in Syria this week—so that his friend in the White House could have a big night with missiles and all of the praise he's picked up over the past 24 hours."[42] She agreed.

Barack Obama and Joe Biden, incidentally, both bombed Syria on numerous occasions.

In another monologue, Maddow gave Republican Senate majority leader Mitch McConnell his Russia Collusion–era nickname: "Moscow Mitch." In the real world, McConnell supported a slew of sanctions against Putin, and was not only more hawkish than Trump but more hawkish than anyone in the Obama administration when it came to Russia. "Moscow Mitch" would be one of the leading champions for funding Ukraine in their war against Russia. Yet the derogatory nickname was earned for blocking "election security legislation," which would have nationalized elections but, more importantly, had nothing to really do with Putin.

"Moscow Mitch" became widely used by the likes of Nancy Pelosi and spurned Trump bestie Joe Scarborough. Hyperpartisan *Washington Post* columnist Dana Milbank wrote a piece calling the longtime Cold Warrior a "Russian asset."[43] Then again, the *Post* ran an opinion piece by partisan hatchet man Paul Waldman contending that "the entire Republican Party is becoming a Russian asset."[44] The contention probably came as a great surprise to a hundred million or so Americans.

The Russia Collusion hoax induced once-rational people to lose their minds, inhibitions, and often their moral compass. Once-respected constitutional scholar Laurence Tribe argued, before Trump had even stepped into the White House, that impeachment should begin on "Inauguration Day." Trump's crime was yet to be determined. But only *eight* days after his inauguration, Tribe settled on the idea that, in little over a week, the new president "must be impeached for abusing his power and shredding the Constitution more monstrously than any other president in American history."[45]

The extent of Tribe's deranged ravings are too copious to properly catalog here, but let's just say that his popular Twitter account birthed a slew of imaginary intrigues, among them the suggestion that Trump bribed members of Congress with Russian money to pass GOP initiatives.

At one point, Tribe, a Harvard law professor, directed his hundreds of thousands of followers to listen to "the incomparable Louise Mensch," a notorious conspiracy theorist who had only recently reported that "the [nonexistent] Marshal of the Supreme Court" had notified President Trump that secret impeachment proceedings were already underway.

While some lost their minds, other once-respected figures were willing participants in the BlueAnon racket. Take former director of national intelligence James Clapper, a man who famously lied to Congress about the government's warrantless mass-surveillance program.[46] "I think if you compare the two that Watergate pales, really, in my view, compared to what we're confronting now," Clapper explained in a June 7, 2017, interview.[47] On December 31, 2017, Clapper said that Putin is a "great case officer, he knows how to handle an asset and that's what he's doing with the president."[48]

In another interview with CNN, Clapper claimed that there was a strong possibility Trump was a "Russian asset," "whether witting or unwitting."

I mention the dates because in 2020, after Republicans released all the interviews from the House investigation into Russian interference, we learned that in July 2017, just as Clapper was running around accusing the president of being an asset to a foreign adversary, he was telling congressional leaders that he "never saw any direct empirical evidence that the Trump campaign or someone in it was plotting/conspiring with the Russians to meddle with the election."[49]

In 2020, Clapper maintained that he was deeply concerned about all the "anecdotal evidence." The fact that a former head of the United States' intelligence services felt comfortable accusing the president of sedition on the strength of hearsay says something about his lack of professionalism and seriousness.

Few, however, did more to buttress BlueAnon lunacy than a little-known California congressman named Adam Schiff.

In early 2018, not long after taking control of the House Intelligence

Committee, Schiff confirmed what every Democrat wanted to hear: Congress had not only uncovered evidence of a criminal plot by the president's 2016 campaign, but now had an "abundance" of incriminating evidence in its possession. It was, of course, huge news. But it also turned out to be a spectacular lie.

Special Counsel Robert Mueller, with a staff of partisan Democrats, spent roughly two years digging through accusations of coordination between the Trump campaign and the Russian government to steal the 2016 presidential election. Despite the best efforts of his staff to find Trump's alleged crimes, they came up with nothing. There were thousands of articles and columns during Mueller's twenty-two-month investigation about the coming storm. Yet there had not been one indictment related to the 2016 election.

Nor would a twenty-five-person investigative staff that worked for Schiff and the Democrats find anything resembling collusion. It was not for lack of trying. The left did not even pursue impeachment proceedings related to this supposed scandal of the century.

Yet Schiff, who powered dozens of embarrassing media misfires during this time that caused irreparable damage to the reputation of the press, felt no pressure to explain. On multiple occasions, Schiff declared he was in possession of an "abundance" of irrefutable "direct evidence" corroborating collusion with Putin.

In more serious times, such barefaced deceit would be a small calamity for the reputation of a politician. In the Trump era, however, spreading mind-blowing fictions would only boost your prospects, and it transformed Schiff into a hero. The most valued action in the Trump era was fantastical partisan fan service. The wilder the accusation, the better.

No one in the media even bothered to inquire about the discrepancy until *The View*'s Meghan McCain brought it up in an interview with Schiff, who told the TV host that the proof was in "plain sight" the whole time—which was the opposite of what he'd told us before.

If this is true, and there is evidence that the president committed treason, why didn't House Democrats initiate impeachment proceedings? This is still a mystery.

ATTACK OF THE RUSSIAN BRAINWASHING SUPERBOTS

Twitter Bots Boosted Donald Trump's Votes by 3.23%: Study
—TIME

In 2020, Showtime released the trailer for *The Comey Rule*, a film based on the alleged moral struggles of the on-again, off-again Resistance hero, former FBI director James Comey. In it, one anxious official asks his colleague if it was possible that Russians had infiltrated American democracy.

The response, quite hilariously, is "Ever spend much time on Facebook?"

The groundless fear of Russian bots launching fake accounts that had the power to upend American democracy was one of the most transparently preposterous panics of the era. Story after story declared that the 2016 presidential contest was infiltrated by rogue foreign accounts on social media that could brainwash the naïve user. The number of times reporters and pundits at formerly reputable news organizations dropped terms like "election hacking" to explain the phenomena was incalculable.

At best, Russia *tried* but failed to interfere in the election on the margins. They have done this for decades, incidentally. So had China, Cuba, and Iran, and probably other geopolitical enemies looking to cause divisions in America.[50]

Endeavoring to interfere in a foreign election is a violation of international norms, and it should be investigated and retaliated against. But part of living in a free, roiling, messy, and democratized society means being bombarded with missives from all kinds of elements—even ones we can't stop. And this fact was used by BlueAnon to convince millions that they had been stripped of a victory.

Only a couple of weeks after the 2016 election, the *Washington Post* kicked off the panic with an exposé uncovering "more than 200 websites" that were "routine peddlers of Russian propaganda during the election season, with combined audiences of at least 15 million Americans." The piece added: "stories planted or promoted by the disinformation campaign were viewed more than 213 million times."

That sure sounds like a lot of times. Until one realizes that there are somewhere around *eight* billion views on Facebook, *per day*.[51] Still, it seemed at the time like there were eight billion stories warning Americans about how Facebook was stealing their souls and compelling them to vote for a Republican. "Did Fake News on Facebook Help Elect Trump? Here's What We Know," explained NPR. "What Facebook Did to American Democracy" and "All the ways Trump's campaign was aided by Facebook, ranked by importance" were other entries in this genre.

In 2018, the editors at the *New York Times* pulled together an interactive tool to help readers figure out whether they too were hoodwinked by Russians into voting for Trump. "See Which Facebook Ads Russians Targeted to People Like You," the story promised, allowing readers to pinpoint exactly which ads may have targeted them on social media.[52] As a victim of Putin mischief, I was quite curious to see how the dictator had tried to hoodwink me into voting Republican. After entering my age, area, and interests, fudging the information slightly to make myself a complete Red State normie, I came face-to-face with the alarming truth. "Accounts linked to Russia showed these 3 advertisements to people like you on Facebook or Instagram," the *Times* informed me.

Three.

Because "people like me," which is to say, middle-aged Americans who live near big population centers and are consumers of political news, can, apparently, be bullied into voting against our beliefs simply by glancing at a trio of ads that pass through our social media feeds.

In any event, the messaging deployed by Vladimir Putin to prod me into offering my allegiance to Trump was layered with a subtle complexity that was likely undetectable to the average person. For example, one of the ads, pushed by a front group with the ambiguous name "Trumpsters United," used a stock photo of American flags and asked viewers "to remember those who lost their lives and for their families and loved ones." The other two ads, both from an account labeled "Being Patriotic," rallied fans of manufacturing jobs to Trump.

How can anyone be expected to resist this brand of messaging?

The ads, of course, were indistinguishable from the thousands of other partisan appeals that hit our feeds and inboxes during the election season. The most visible of these advertisements garnered 260 reactions and 27 comments, total. It was dumb.

Millions of Americans were led to believe, and accepted, that a handful of these *terrible* memes—and I mean some of the most amateurish and puerile online efforts imaginable—were enough to overturn a presidential election in one of the most educated nations on earth. But Trump voters *must* have been duped. Why else could anyone vote for him? Yet, as hard as I searched to unearth a single American voter who had been brainwashed by Facebook, I came up empty. Probably because no such person exists.

It wasn't always Putin either. Even commonplace electoral efforts were retroactively transformed into scandalous efforts. In 2018, a new "scandal" involving British company Cambridge Analytica blew up in the news. "The revelations of the apparent skullduggery that helped Donald Trump win the 2016 presidential election keep sending shock waves across the political landscape," noted Bloomberg.[53]

Well, it's partially true. Everyone was talking about it. The story consumed most of the mainstream media's focus for a week (an eternity in the frenetic Trump years). The conspiracy theory involved a firm, partially owned by the conservative Mercer family, that apparently persuaded millions of Americans to vote Republican by targeting them with political ads. Shocking, indeed.

As Cambridge Analytica contractor Christopher Wylie breathlessly told CNN, the company employed "psychological warfare weapons" to "exploit mental vulnerabilities that our algorithms showed that [Facebook users] had."

Those who have covered politics for more than five minutes were surely aware that this unnerving rhetoric was merely describing normal online microtargeting, which has been used by hundreds, if not thousands, of firms before.

Nevertheless, to feed these anxieties, media started throwing around exotic words like *psychographics* to insinuate that conservatives invented a way to bore into the deepest recesses of the collective soul.

Reframing traditional political efforts as devious, high-tech endeavors that could turn the feeble-minded into Trump voters became a popular BlueAnon genre. One of the best examples was a much-discussed McKay Coppins 2020 piece in the *Atlantic*, "The Billion-Dollar Disinformation Campaign to Reelect the President," in which the author uses eight thousand unnerving words to paint commonplace political operations as dark, undemocratic, and groundbreaking.[54] But there were scores of similar pieces.

The effectiveness of Cambridge Analytica's targeting, as it turned out, was as questionable as its business practices. Many experts thought the company ineffective and its data useless.[55] Republicans merely used the firm to open the door to the Mercers' checkbook. The Trump campaign, in fact, had dropped Cambridge Analytica for more precise data at the Republican National Committee, reportedly never using any of the "psychographic" information.

Even if the campaign had utilized psychographics, its efforts would have differed little from previous digital campaigns serving the interests of Democrats. In fact, Facebook allowed the Obama campaign to harvest data in much the same way in the past. The only consistent position BlueAnon seems to take these days is that the mechanisms it uses to keep power are innocent and professional, while the very same practices are tools of authoritarianism when the opposition utilizes them.

Then again, no Russian Twitter troll farm or Facebook ad campaign has done more damage to the confidence Democrats have in national elections than BlueAnon hysteria.

NO EVIDENCE? NO MATTER

Mueller Report Finds No Evidence of Russian Collusion
—NATIONAL PUBLIC RADIO

"It's one of the most egregious journalistic errors in modern history," Axios's Sara Fischer wrote of the media's regurgitation of the Steele Dossier in 2021, "and the media's response to its own mistakes has so far been tepid."[1]

Well, it all depends how you look at it, right? For one thing, it's generous to assume that most of the media merely erred in spreading the disinformation. Then again, though BlueAnon destroyed the reputation of several vital American institutions with conservatives (and perhaps many independents), when viewed as a political operation it was a first-rate success.

In a December 2016 poll, taken only a month after the election, an *Economist*/YouGov poll found that 52 percent of Democrats believed Russia "tampered with vote tallies."[2] This result was cultivated when we had only begun to hear how the Kremlin's gremlins had subverted our democracy. By the fall of 2018, in the heyday of Russia-panic-mongering, another YouGov poll found that 67 percent of Democrats believed it was "definitely true" or "probably true" that "Russia tampered with vote tallies in order to get Donald Trump elected"—even though there was not a shred of evidence pointing to a manipulation of votes.[3]

By this time, incidentally, the bipartisan Senate Intelligence Committee report on Russia's interference featured a full subsection titled—in all caps—"NO EVIDENCE OF CHANGED VOTES OR MANIPULATED VOTE TALLIES."[4]

When Special Counsel John Durham examined the origins of the FBI's investigation of links between Russian officials and Donald Trump's 2016 presidential campaign, he concluded that the FBI had not only failed to corroborate the Steele Dossier, but it also regularly ignored existing, sometimes dispositive, evidence to keep the investigation alive. The only indictments in the entire debacle were handed to someone connected to the Hillary Clinton campaign who had allegedly lied to the FBI.

In a 2022 poll by right-leaning Rasmussen, 72 percent of Democrats still believed it's likely the 2016 election outcome was changed by Russian interference.[5] Most media stopped polling the question. They had moved on to new speculation by then.

Any sort of "reckoning" for BlueAnon would mean retractions, followed by investigative deep dives into how scores of big scoops turned out to be partisan chum. Those who perpetuated the Russia Collusion deception—and this means editors and pundits, politicians, bureaucrats—still hold premier jobs. Many, in fact, have been rewarded with better gigs. Is anyone at the *Washington Post* or *New York Times* going to return a Pulitzer Prize they won for coverage of the nonevent? Unlikely.

Most of the worst offenders would never concede that they were duped or participated in the hoax. Many tried to resuscitate the collusion hoax. When a largely inconsequential Russian informant in the Hunter Biden investigation named Alexander Smirnov was indicted for lying to the FBI, Democrats quickly tried to frame it as collusion. "It now appears as if the House Republican majority is being used by Russia to interfere in the 2024 election on behalf of Donald Trump," Democratic congressman Dan Goldman told Anderson Cooper on CNN.[6]

MSNBC's Joe Scarborough, a former Trump acolyte, was still clinging to these clichéd attacks in 2021, long after it was clear that no one had "hacked" any election much less stolen it. "I'm amused by so-called reporters who are—I don't know if they're useful idiots for Russia or if they're on Russia's payroll; I don't know, and I don't really care, but there are some gifted writers who spend all night and day trying to dig through, looking for instances of where the press screwed up on Russia stories, pushing this 'Russian hoax' fallacy."[7]

This is about as stark an example of projection as one could hope to find. Even after the entire sordid affair had been exposed as a fraud, reporters who attempted an accounting of the Russia Collusion–era mistakes would be attacked as dupes for Russia—or perhaps paid agents of Putin. A lack of evidence will never convince the true believer. It will induce him to expand his theory.

In truth, very few reporters spent any time, much less "night and day," digging into the problems with the story. When asked by Axios about the Steele Dossier, the two outlets that churned out some of the most sensationalistic content of the Trump era, CNN and MSNBC, wouldn't even comment.[8] The most charitable explanation is that reporters became such saps for Democrats that they were inclined to believe the most fantastical stories imaginable. The more plausible explanation, considering the lack of any genuine accountability and self-reflection, is that they were in on it.

In the end, despite the increasingly unbalanced accusations and the widely held perceptions of millions of Democrats, not a single associate of Trump was convicted of any crime in connection to colluding with a foreign power in the 2016 election. There was never any evidence that Trump worked with Russia in any capacity. And it had no more contacts with Putin than any other administration.

Yet the Democratic Party was fully on board. Without a media there to hold them accountable, they were freed of any need to temper their accusations. Even deep into 2024, Democrats like Congressman Dan Goldman were still spreading the conspiracy that Republicans "knowingly" assisted Putin "to install Donald Trump as president."[9]

"DISINFORMATION"

Hunter Biden story is Russian disinfo,
dozens of former intel officials say.
—POLITICO

Beginning with the 2016 presidential contest, the Democratic Party fully descended into the politics of hysteria. The collective psychotic break that followed Donald Trump's election was bolstered by an unethical political media and a corrupt investigation into the president, predicated on an opposition-research document filled with fictions, distortions, and, very likely, the very "Russian disinformation" that the left warned us about. But Democrats wanted to cripple the president. They succeeded.

Success breeds success. From 2016 on, the claim of "Russian disinformation" became an all-purpose excuse for dismissing inconvenient-but-true stories as deception, disinformation, and misinformation. One of the most consequential instances of BlueAnon exploiting the paranoia over Russia was the Hunter Biden laptop story.

On October 14, 2020, less than a month before Election Day, the *New York Post* published a series of articles that were based on emails obtained from the younger Biden's laptop, showing potential corrupt behavior from presidential candidate Joe Biden.

This is not the place to sift over the Biden Inc. scandals. But it is worth noting that the *Post* not only reported the story; it described, in great detail, how reporters had physically obtained Hunter's laptop and the evidence in it. The paper featured an on-the-record interview with the owner of the Delaware computer shop where Hunter had abandoned his computer. It shared pictures of Hunter's signature on a receipt and on-the-record sources with intimate knowledge of his interactions. Later, Hunter's emails—some detailing his debauchery, others trading off the name of his powerful dad—were authenticated by forensic specialists. The effort was undertaken with more professionalism and transparency than any of the Russia Collusion stories shared widely by the media.

Years later, when Hunter Biden was finally in court to answer for gun charges, the FBI admitted that the laptop was real.[10]

Yet virtually the entire censorious journalistic establishment, with the help of tech giants like Facebook and Twitter, limited the story's exposure by censoring it as potential "disinformation." Major media outlets refused to report on or authenticate the story, creating the impression that it didn't meet proper journalistic standards. The same reporters and editors who passed on the "pee tape" story and every unverified one-source tale of Russian infiltration into American life suddenly claimed they needed to verify all the information in the *Post* piece before mentioning it in their outlets.

By then, the media had become the main cog of the BlueAnon effort. There had always been bias, sure. Events and stories have often been ignored, of course. There have been loads of smears. But now most of the institutional media was openly colluding—and pressuring Big

Tech—to suppress stories that might damage their chosen presidential candidate.

To offer some more perspective, a month before the *Post* story, Jeffrey Goldberg, editor of the *Atlantic*, published a piece accusing Donald Trump of besmirching the American military by refusing to visit the Aisne-Marne American Cemetery near Paris in 2018—"It's filled with losers" and "suckers," the president had allegedly said—without offering a single on-the-record source or corroborating evidence.[11]

Every major outlet reported on the story, despite having no substantiation. "Trump's 'losers' and 'suckers' troops scandal is one final call to action for America," an MSNBC headline read.[12] Rather than independently validating the claims, newspapers like the *Washington Post* fact-checked Trump's contention that there were twenty-five witnesses who disputed the *Atlantic* piece.[13] (The number of people who disputed the "suckers and losers" story turned out to be fourteen. Which seems like a lot. Media kept reporting on it as if it were undisputed fact.)

The Hunter laptop featured correspondences that implicated Joe Biden, who had forcefully maintained he hadn't even discussed Hunter's foreign dealings, as a participant in his son's business.[14] And still House Intelligence Committee chairman Adam Schiff, who'd been spoon-feeding compliant media a torrent of disinformation for four years, maintained that the Hunter Biden emails were from the "Kremlin."[15]

More than fifty former senior intelligence officials—some of whom have been deceiving the American public for years, such as Jim Clapper—signed a letter maintaining that the *Post*'s story "has all the classic earmarks of a Russian information operation."[16] Those cunning Russians had somehow induced Hunter Biden to leave his laptop filled with incriminating pictures of him engaged with prostitutes, emails with business deals, and texts at a Delaware computer repair shop.

Really, what couldn't the Russkies do?

We later learned that future Biden administration members told potential signees about the letter, promising it would be used as a "talking point" to "push back on Trump" during the final presidential debates. None of these people had genuine evidence that the contents of the *Post*'s story were planted, but they signed on anyway. And, as planned, when the topic was brought up during a presidential debate, Biden claimed the Hunter story was a "Russia plant." CNN wondered if "Trump spread Russian disinformation during the debate?" by bringing up the laptop.[17] He had not.

Director of National Intelligence John Ratcliffe would point out soon after the debates that Hunter's emails are "not part of some Russian disinformation campaign." Another senior intelligence official told the *Washington Examiner*, "What Ratcliffe said is 100% correct. There has been no intelligence community assessment or information that the IC has gotten to suggest in any way that the Hunter Biden laptop story is a Russian disinformation operation."[18]

In 2024, after Hunter admitted that the laptop was real in open court, Clapper was asked if he would retract his contention about the *Post*'s story. His one word answer: "No."[19]

It mattered not. The media has invented a new standard for this occasion, because the media is now a major subsidiary of the BlueAnon project. The Russia Collusion hoax laid the groundwork for the Democrats' near-complete transformation into a party reliant on fear to advance its goals. The deep suspicions could be used to both condemn the left's enemies and dismiss charges from them.

Conspiracy was now the preeminent tool of the American left. Sometimes one wonders if they have any other trick.

WHAT'S THE WORST THAT COULD HAPPEN?

The more we learn about 2016 election the more ILLEGITIMATE it becomes. America deserves to know whether we have a FAKE President in the Oval Office.
—CONGRESSMAN HAKEEM JEFFRIES, FEBRUARY 16, 2018[20]

We will never bend the knee to the election deniers who poison our democracy.
—MINORITY LEADER OF THE U.S. HOUSE OF REPRESENTATIVES HAKEEM JEFFRIES, OCTOBER 14, 2022[21]

Considering all the left's talk about preserving democracy these days, it's worth noting that the centerpiece of BlueAnon's agenda in 2020 and 2024 was also to preemptively cast doubt over the results—should Democrats lose.

Democrats are no more likely to accept losses. Two months before Election Day in 2020, a *USA Today* poll found that 1 in 4 voters weren't prepared to believe the outcome as "fair and accurate." Among them, 28 percent of Biden's supporters said they did not believe a Trump victory would be "fairly won," while 19 percent of Trump's supporters said the same about a potential Biden victory.[22] A significant minority of American voters, and a larger share of Democrats, did not believe the next election promised to be legitimate if their candidate lost. Neither side is accepting the results of elections.

Feelings of doubt, by the way, grow if you lose. It is almost surely the case that a second Trump term in 2020 would have seen the flowering of a thousand new conspiracy theories on the left, just as it had in 2016.

Hillary Clinton's advice to Biden before the 2020 votes were counted, in fact, was to refuse to concede defeat that night no matter what happened—a comment that was meant not only to delegitimize the results of 2020 but to insinuate that the presidency was unfairly denied her as well.[23] It will almost surely be the same advice Biden or any other Democratic presidential candidate is given in 2024.

Before the 2020 presidential election, the *Washington Post's* Outlook section asked readers: "What's the Worst That Could Happen?" The worst was *really* bad. Trump could win.[24] Or, as one commenter noted, "Who wins if Trump pulls off his coup? Putin and corporations."

In the piece penned by Rosa Brooks, a Georgetown University law professor and cofounder of the Transition Integrity Project, numerous potential outcomes of the presidential race were explored, but in "every scenario except a Biden landslide, our simulation ended catastrophically," the report noted. The United States, she went on, was confronted with "a big popular win for Mr. Biden, and a narrow electoral defeat," an outcome destined to spark "violence" and a "constitutional crisis" that led to a "highly politicized" Supreme Court stealing the election.[25]

This was a widely held belief on the left. "It's worth pointing out that *almost* no one thinks Trump will actually win more votes," MSNBC's Chris Hayes told his followers before the election. "I think if he wins the electoral college and loses the popular vote *again* you're looking at the worst legitimacy crisis since secession."[26]

This is like declaring a Super Bowl illegitimate because your team had more running yards and still lost. There is no legitimacy crisis because there is no such thing as a "popular vote."

Democrats trump up political paranoia by treating completely valid mechanisms of American governance as corrupt and catastrophic when it does not serve their immediate purpose. After all, a "big popular win for Mr. Biden, and a narrow electoral defeat" is defined as a spotless and fair election by the Constitution. We have federalized elections—as do most free nations.

•   •   •   •   •

No one is stealing an election by playing by the rules. The constant talk about "popular vote" by BlueAnon nurtures suspicion among those ignorant of basic civics that there is something undemocratic going on.

Republicans, like all winning candidates, focus their campaigns on the Electoral College—the *only* way to win. That means forgetting votes in big states and concentrating on the entire country. For numerous small-*r* republican reasons, the Constitution diffuses centralized power in DC. Democrats want a couple of big states lording over the country, and the fact that this doesn't happen—because we live in a system built specifically to stop it from happening—is now a "crisis." Yet Democrats act as if something has been stolen from them.

Direct democracy does not exist here. The real crisis is pretending that it does.

Anyway, how did Democrats plan to react?

In the Transition Integrity Project war game powerful Democratic Party strategist John Podesta, playing the role of Biden, refused to concede the race. Instead he alleged "voter suppression" and then persuaded Democratic governors of Trump-won states *to send pro-Biden electors* to the Electoral College to vote for the Democrat. This is exactly what Democrats later claimed was an authoritarian plot to steal the election. But there was more. States like California, Oregon, and Washington would then threaten to *secede from the union* if Trump took office. Then the Democrat-controlled House unilaterally names Biden president.

"At that point in the scenario," the *New York Times* reported, "the nation stopped looking to the media for cues, and waited to see what the military would do."[27]

It was a game, true. But if history was any indicator, it was clear that Democrats were ready to oust Trump in every way imaginable. Why should we believe the 2024 presidential race will be any different?

Constituents of the Democratic Party are bombarded with rhetoric that preemptively challenges the results of every coming election.

In January 2020, during Trump's first impeachment trial, Representative Adam Schiff argued that the impending presidential election was no place to decide the presidency, since Trump's "misconduct cannot be decided at the ballot box, for we cannot be assured that the vote will be fairly won."[28] Then–House Speaker Nancy Pelosi agreed, saying that "Let the election decide" was a "dangerous position" because Trump is already "jeopardizing the integrity of the 2020 elections."

How's that for democracy?

In 2024, Democrats in Colorado and Maine attempted to take Trump off the ballots before the Supreme Court stopped them. No trial. No due process. The lawfare attacks leading up to the 2024 election were meant to create the same impression. In the eyes of most Democrats, the presidential election was lost by Trump before the first ballot was cast. And each time a Supreme Court decision didn't go the left's way, Democrats would accuse the courts of helping Donald Trump steal an election.

Even if one concedes that Trump was wrong to throw suspicion on the electoral system, you are compelled to wonder why Democrats weren't accused of engaging in "denialism." While Trump's "Big Lie"—a term meant to evoke Nazi imagery, because everything these days is meant to evoke Nazi imagery—is endlessly documented and debunked by the left, BlueAnon's "denialism," entrenched in all its institutions, is amplified and legitimized by helpful media outlets.

During the 2022 midterm election, Joe was asked by reporters whether voters could trust the electoral system, and twice the president contended that a "fair election" was unlikely unless the Senate was blown up and the Democrats were allowed to pass an election power grab. "I think it would easily be illegitimate," Biden said. "The increase in the prospect of being illegitimate is in proportion to not being able to get these reforms passed."

Weird, because only two years earlier, Americans were told by "top election experts" that 2020 was "the most secure in American history."[29] What great event had occurred under Biden's watch that suddenly put the legitimacy of elections in grave danger? We do not know, because political journalists do not stalk every elected Democrat and demand their solemn attestation to the sanctity of the next election. Far from it.

No, Democrats have been working to convince their constituents that there is no legal way in which Trump could win again in 2024. Numerous politicians and high-profile columnists have laid the groundwork making the case that Trump is an insurrectionist. Their argument hinges on the histrionic, paranoid contention that *any* GOP victory, large or small, portends the end of "democracy."[30]

THE PLOT AGAINST AMERICA

The Republican party wants to turn
America into a theocracy.
—ROBERT REICH

In most partisan battles these days, the left will throw around the term *dark money*. It is meant to evoke thoughts of ominous, unsavory, and criminal behavior. It is meant to insinuate that fully legal, anonymous contributions by citizens to political causes are antidemocratic and corrupt. It is one of the most misleading neologisms of modern political rhetoric.

These days, the term *dark money* is used by both sides of the political spectrum, but if you follow establishment media outlets, you might be under the impression that anonymous giving from wealthy donors is nearly exclusively a right-wing funding mechanism.

As it turns out, the top fifteen politically active nonprofit organizations aligned with the Democratic Party spent more than $1.5 billion in the last presidential cycle in 2020, while the top fifteen politically active nonprofit organizations aligned with Republican Party issues spent approximately $900 million.[1] The Sixteen Thirty Fund, the leftist "dark money" clearinghouse, was the single biggest funder of "dark money" PACs in the 2020 cycle, meting out $60 million to Democrats' political action committees in federal races and over $200 million to other groups pimping for Democrats. As is their right.

BlueAnon's selective angst over the supposed evils of unregulated money in politics can probably be traced back to the Supreme Court's *Citizens United* decision, which reaffirmed the right of all Americans to form groups and practice their right of free expression without reporting to the state.

When the decision was handed down, President Barack Obama rebuked the Supreme Court justices *during* his State of the Union address that year, warning that the decision "reversed a century of law that I believe will open the floodgates for special interests—including foreign corporations—to spend without limit in our elections."[2]

From then on, as we'll see, paranoid attacks against the judiciary would become the norm. Obama's attack wasn't only unprecedented, meant to frighten voters; it was also untrue. The court hadn't overturned a century of law (though the age of a law bears absolutely no relevance to its constitutionality). *Citizens United* reversed portions of a law that was less than a decade old, which forbade Americans from contributing as much as they wanted directly to *the funding of speech, not to politicians.* Corporations were still banned from donating directly to candidates, as they had been since 1907.

Yet one suspects that, if you asked an average Democrat about the specifics of the case, they would be unaware of these distinctions. The belief that corporations control the outcomes of elections—stripping the ordinary citizen of agency—is highly popular among all voters. It is foundational to leftist apprehension about the system.

As it turns out, what happened after *Citizens United* was, in many ways, the opposite of what Obama prophesied. Small-dollar donors would be more in demand. Socialist Bernie Sanders, who ran competitive races for the Democratic Party primary in both 2016 and 2020, raised more money from small donors than any candidate in history.[3] Donald Trump raised more small donor money than anyone in history in 2016.[4] And the Republican candidate will likely break that record in 2024.

The axiom that money wins all elections is disproven every cycle. Of course, funding is helpful to a campaign, but it is only part of the equation. There are no guarantees. Hillary Clinton was immeasurably better funded than Trump in 2016. Not a single CEO in the Fortune 100 even donated to Trump's campaign that year.[5] In 2020, billionaire Tom Steyer spent $200 million trying to win the Democratic Party nomination and walked away with a single delegate.[6] Steve Forbes spent $69.2 million on two runs for the GOP nomination and won only a handful of delegates.[7]

Former New York City mayor Michael Bloomberg donated $1.2 billion of his own money to fund a four-month presidential campaign in 2020.[8] That was more than the combined campaign expenditures of every Democratic Party hopeful that year.[9] It was far more than the National Rifle Association—one of Bloomberg's favorite targets—has spent on political lobbying in its entire existence.[10] Big Pharma, the top lobbying group in Washington, spends around a fifth of what Bloomberg did every year.[11]

Of course, the expectation that private citizens must publicly attach their names to every donation or act of expression (especially if they're conservatives) is an imaginary standard. Private citizens have no such duty, as "Publius"—Alexander Hamilton, James Madison, and John Jay, better known as the authors of the Federalist Papers—could tell you. "Anonymity is a shield from the tyranny of the majority, it exemplifies the purpose behind the Bill of Rights and of the First Amendment in particular: to protect unpopular individuals from retaliation . . . at the hand of an intolerant society," the Supreme Court noted in *McIntyre v. Ohio Elections Commission.*

All of which is to say that *Citizens United* wasn't radical; it was a return to the norm.

The clamoring for "funding transparency" is often meant to drive the idea that unsavory characters operating in the shadows are undermining democracy, driven by leftists who are frustrated at their inability to vilify and chase conservative donors out of public life. Progressive groups have become quite adept at destroying the reputations and businesses of those who fund Republican Party causes. Which is why it seems probable too that many wealthy conservatives avoided contributing to political causes if they were forced to deal with ugly public attacks on their businesses and families. The left's big donors never have such worries.

Indeed, any moderately successful conservative organization can expect to find itself the target of BlueAnon conspiracy theories revolving around "dark money."

Take the NRA, which leftists have regularly referred to as a "terrorist organization" and have accused of abetting school shootings and gun violence.[12]

If the NRA disappeared tomorrow, another group would take its place because there are millions of gun owners in the United States. Nearly 50 percent of American households have a firearm. But the only way BlueAnon can explain the existence of the NRA is to claim that it is propped up by shady oligarchs.

These days, "taking on the NRA" has become one of the most common acts of faux bravery among Democrats. The stand is predicated on the imaginary hold that the paranoid left believes the NRA has on Republican legislators. If the NRA were as powerful as its critics contended, the civil and constitutional rights of gun owners would never be challenged. If the NRA spent the kind of money its critics insinuated—or even as much money as its many detractors do—it would be one of the most powerful organizations in American political life.

In the real world, the group's expenditures are minuscule in comparison to other major lobbying efforts and far less than antigun groups. It is true that the NRA spent a lot of money opposing Hillary Clinton in 2016, as she repeatedly promised to destroy the organization and pass illiberal gun restrictions. But the NRA's entire 2018–19 lobbying efforts amounted to under $2 million.[13] In 2023 it spent 1.7 million. The NRA is only influential because it represents, either through direct membership or ideological kinship, a lot of American voters. Most NRA funding comes from small donors, which is in fact quite "democratic."[14]

During the Trump years, like almost every other conservative institution, the advocacy group, which was founded not long after the Civil War, was accused of being a front group for Russian plutocrats. "The Trump-Russia-NRA Connection: Here's What You Need to Know," explained *Rolling Stone*.[15] Headlines like "The NRA Received Donations from Russian Nationals" to "NRA Discloses Additional Contributions from Russian Donors" set the stage to push this claim, all of which probably sounded damning for anyone who didn't have the time to investigate the claims. Russian "nationals," which amounted to twenty-three "Russian-linked" individuals—some of them American citizens living in Russia—had contributed around $2,300 total, mostly in membership dues, over three years' time. Approximately $525 of that sum came from "two individuals."[16]

Two.

Now, I'm not going to sit here and tell you that $2,300 is nothing, but one imagines that if the NRA was going to sell out its country—and there is zero evidence this was the case—the organization would have asked for substantially more to do it.

Nor, incidentally, is supporting Trump an act of sedition, though you might not know it from BlueAnon. But this is the kind of overwrought "journalism" that feeds the perception about democracy being snatched from voters by greasy foreigners. When the entire Russia Collusion hoax fell apart, the story disappeared.

Ironically, one of the organizations that BlueAnon likes to pretend is scheming to destabilize and destroy the United States is the originalist legal foundation, the Federalist Society for Law and Public Policy Studies.

Those who trust mainstream press coverage may come away with the impression that the Federalist Society works behind the scenes as all-seeing puppeteers who can manipulate America's political fortunes. In truth, the group has around seventy thousand members, chapters at nearly every law school in the country, as well as around ninety other colleges, where thousands of public events and debates have been held over the years. Among the notorious right-wingers who have appeared in front of the group are Supreme Court justices Elena Kagan[17] and Ruth Bader Ginsburg.[18]

The Federalist Society is so secretive that on its extraordinarily accessible website a person can find out about the group's originalist judicial philosophy, watch videos of debates and lectures, and peruse a list of staff members and the board of directors. Anyone with even the slightest acquaintance with contemporary constitutional disputes or American politics has heard of the Federalist Society. There is nothing secretive about its mission. It might be one of the most transparent organizations in DC.

None of that has stopped BlueAnoners like Sheldon Whitehouse from treating the Federalist Society as a Star Chamber, "funded by dark money and designed to remake our judiciary on behalf of a distinct group of very wealthy anonymous funders."[19]

In one of his numerous speeches on the matter, "The Scheme Speech 5: The Federalist Society"—no, I'm not making that title up—the senator pulled out all the stops, including juvenile visual aids, to paint the advocacy of the group as something disreputable and mysterious. The "dark money sluice gates into the Federalist Society provide the perfect means of influence," Whitehouse explains. "Money talks. Dark money whispers."[20]

Because the contemporary progressive left's views of the judicial system is wholly consequentialist—meaning, the ends are the only thing that matter—any principled judiciary that occasionally veers from those ends is belittled as fraudulent. Paranoid leftist Alexandria Ocasio-Cortez tells millions of social media followers that the Supreme Court is "boosted by some billionaire who secretly thinks voting rights should only belong to landed gentry."[21] When the Supreme Court sided with Donald Trump and handed down a narrowly tailored decision on presidential immunity in the summer of 2024, the congresswoman promised to file articles of impeachment against every justice she disagreed with.[22]

Amazingly, AOC knows exactly what donors secretly think. In a way, I wish she was right! Considering how many of America's uberwealthy vote for and promote left-wing causes, it actually would be nice if conservatives had "some billionaires" to support good organizations like the Federalist Society.

As we've seen, one of the ways in which BlueAnon fuels political paranoia is by painting entirely standard actions by Republicans as shifty and corrupt. In the summer of 2023, the *Washington Post* published a breathless piece that perfectly encapsulates how "journalism" spreads disinformation on the issue of "dark money." The headline: "Gov. Ron DeSantis Used Secretive Panel to Flip State Supreme Court."

So, how did the cagey Florida governor pull off this Machiavellian coup?

First, DeSantis "narrowly" won the governorship in 2018 . . . by, you know, campaigning and winning more votes than his opponent. Revolutionary! When Republicans "narrowly" win elections, journalists like to imply that the resulting conservative achievements are quasi-illegitimate. After all, if you don't win by a wide margin, you're obviously an enemy of democracy (in 2022, DeSantis went on to win by a wide margin).

Second, rather than handing judicial nomination decisions to Democrats and their allies, the Republican governor decided to pick his own replacements for three Florida Supreme Court seats—after sitting justices were compelled to step down due to the state's *mandatory* retirement age, a requirement passed by a referendum of the *voters*, not the governor.

The dastardly scheme does not end there. DeSantis did all this with the guidance of noted legal advisers to help him find competent candidates whose judicial outlooks aligned with his own. But here's the *Washington Post* describing this normal, constitutional process:

> *The hard-right turn was by design. DeSantis seized on the unusual retirement of three liberal justices at once to quickly remake the court. He did so with the help of a secretive judicial panel led by Leonard Leo— the key architect of the U.S. Supreme Court's conservative majority— that quietly vetted judicial nominees in an Orlando conference room three weeks before the governor's inauguration.*

You see, DeSantis was not fulfilling campaign promises, but rather taking a "*hard*-right" turn "by design." The governor of Florida doesn't depend on advisers like every other politician does; he empowered a "secretive judicial panel" that "quietly" "seized" on "unusual" moments. All these loaded words insinuate insidious motives and corrupt behavior. Have you ever read a national story about the left-wing "takeover" of a state court, much less apprehension about a far-left "supermajority" or lack of diversity in viewpoint in New York or California? The only "viewpoint" any court should care about is upholding the law.

BlueAnon also targets Leo, whose legal activism is described by the *Washington Post* as an effort that "pushed conservative and libertarian judges onto the nation's courts through multimillion-dollar influence campaigns fueled by secret donors." You would think Leo was, like Dr. Evil, running an organization out of some secret lair situated in a hollowed-out volcano in the Pacific.

What the *Post* meant to say was that Leo led an advocacy group that openly argues for originalist constitutional ideas and solicited help from donors—like virtually every other political organization and movement in DC. This advocacy, established on sound historical and legal principles, and decades of scholarly work, has been successful. That is Leo's real sin.

By the way, a vast number of leftist advocacy groups—including groups working to delegitimize and pack the Supreme Court—live off "dark money." None of them advocate for a principled, nonpartisan judicial philosophy. None of them share their true goals with the public. Many of them exist to create and spread conspiracy theories.

Here's how it works:

A scandal that can't withstand even the slightest examination is cooked up by a wealthy anti-court oppo group. Groups like Demand Justice, headed by former Hillary Clinton and Barack Obama aides, as an example, dropped millions in "dark money" dollars defaming Brett Kavanaugh during the Supreme Court confirmation fight.[23]

The story is then sent to a front group posing as a media outlet (often funded by the same people). The best known among these is ProPublica, which has mastered a kind of Potemkin journalism, dressing up nonstories with neutral-sounding journalistic verbiage, useless graphs, and grainy pictures. ProPublica pumps out endless "investigations" on the scourge of "Dark Money," "right-wing takeover of the courts," and fake scandals involving Supreme Court justices.

The conspiracy theory, now packaged and ready for prime time, is then shopped to accommodating partisan outlets to create the appearance of widespread, organic reporting. Beneath the journalistic language, each new story is dumber than the last. In the past few years, for example, we have learned that Clarence Thomas vacations with rich friends, shares meals with former clerks, is married to a woman with her own opinions, and belongs to an organization of wealthy families that gives college scholarships to thousands of poor kids.

All originalist justices have been targeted, but there is a special disdain for Thomas, who's committed the grievous sins of defying the racial stereotypes of the left and showing contempt for a media that has been trying to destroy him for more than thirty years.

None of the stories, however, show anything remotely approaching a conflict of interest by anyone. More importantly, none have ever shown any justice altering or deviating from their long-held judicial philosophy to help anyone benefit, much less themselves.

COUPS, PUTSCHES, AND INSURRECTIONS

There are conservative marches in the
South with swastikas all the time!
—CONGRESSMAN DAN GOLDMAN (D-NY)

Whenever I ask Democrats to justify their Nazi analogies with evidence, they bring up the events of January 6, 2021—even though, as we'll see, Democrats had been calling Trump, and Republicans, Nazis for years before the Capitol riot ever occurred.

Now, there's plenty of blame to go around for January 6: the post-election hysteria created by many Republicans, the reckless speech from the president and other politicians, and the inadequate security around the Capitol all come to mind. The preponderance of the blame, though, lays with perhaps a few hundred extremists, fellow travelers, and opportunistic troublemakers who ended up disrupting Congress's certifying of the election.

While it was an embarrassing day for the nation, and a dangerous one for the many innocent people engulfed in the mayhem, January 6 wasn't the "worst attack on our democracy since the Civil War," as Joe Biden has preposterously, and repeatedly, claimed.[24]

Nor did it veer anywhere in the vicinity of being as dangerous as the terror attacks of 9/11, as MSNBC hosts and others on the left have argued.[25]

Nor did the rioters, as the chairman of the January 6 committee, Bennie Thompson, risibly argued, come "dangerously close to succeeding" in upending "American democracy."[26] And contra erstwhile Republican Adam Kinzinger, there's zero evidence that "self-governance" itself was threatened by those who entered the Capitol.

January 6 was not a "coup" or a "putsch," as others have maintained.[27] It wasn't even an "insurrection"; not in any real sense. The rioters did not have the backing of any courts or the military or any governmental power, or even a political party.[28] Neither the rioters like the QAnon Shaman, who sauntered around the halls of Congress with his Norse battle helmet, nor any of the other fringe nuts who participated that day had any plan, much less any capacity, to take over the government.

Nor is there any evidence that Donald Trump, who used irresponsible rhetoric that day, was scheming—or knew how to scheme, or knew anyone who knew how to scheme—to implement a coup d'état. The electoral votes had already been counted. Vice President Mike Pence had already spurned Trump's request to reject the results. No court was going to overturn an election or stand with the imbeciles wandering around Congress. And no one in the armed forces was going to help occupy Congress.

It was a riot. Or, as the writer Christopher Caldwell more forgivingly called it, "a political protest that got out of control."[29] Only two sets of people would gain anything from feeding the mythology that rioters had the wherewithal to overthrow the United States government: Democrats and right-wing extremists.

. . . . .

Yet, the left exploited January 6 to create a permanent state of irrational fear over political violence. Fear of extremists. Fear of terrorism. Most of all, fear of Republicans. That was the dominant purpose of the endless overwrought coverage, anniversaries, and investigations into January 6. The United States House Select Committee on the January 6 Attack, set up by Democrats ostensibly to scrutinize the causes of the event, spent years spreading hysteria for political purposes, offering nothing constructive on the security lapses that day.

From nearly the moment the riot began, Democrats began spreading conspiracy theories about Republican legislators.

House Democrats Steve Cohen and John Yarmuth both told the media that they witnessed Republicans outside the Cannon House Office Building with groups of people three days before the riot.[30] Others said outright that elected Republicans were giving tours to would-be insurrectionists inside Congress. Representative Mikie Sherrill (D-NJ) claimed to see "members of Congress who had groups coming through the Capitol . . . a reconnaissance for the next day."[31]

The Capitol Police never substantiated any of these claims. Congresspeople walk around with constituents all the time.

More consequentially, BlueAnon has spent every day since January 6 conflating the actions of rioters with those of peaceful marchers. The preponderance of Republicans who protested that day over the results of the 2020 presidential election did not participate in any violence or illegality. By the time the QAnon Shaman was walking the halls of Congress, BlueAnon had already built something of a symbiotic relationship with extremists.

While cosplaying Nazis and radicals basked in the preposterously outsize coverage given them by journalists, the journalists in turn used the haters to denigrate Republicans and frighten Democrats. Pro-Trump "right-wing organizations" are "training up in the hills somewhere" ready to pounce, claimed Democratic Rep. Maxine Waters on MSNBC in 2024.[32] It was nothing new.

In November 2016, the National Policy Institute, a white supremacist organization (if one *really* stretches the definition of "organization"), put together a "conference" (ditto) in Washington, DC. Reading the fraught tone of the coverage of this irrelevant gathering, a person might have believed that they were witnessing an ominous turning point in history, much like the Nuremberg marches in Nazi Germany.

"Energized by Trump's Win, White Nationalists Gather to 'Change the World,'" read one NPR headline.[33] The new president's victory had given the white supremacist movement a "jolt," we were informed, propelling this once-inert ideological faction into the mainstream.[34]

One could see numerous commonalities between these budding fascists and Republicans proper, NPR insinuated. Richard Spencer, the group's leader, used the term *lügenpresse*, a Nazi-era phrase that described criticism of the media. It didn't take NPR readers a giant leap to recall that Republicans—especially Trump—were also aggressively, and sometimes hyperbolically, critical of the press.

Anyone who bothered to take a deeper dive into the story would have learned that perhaps three hundred people showed up to the event that day, "split nearly evenly between conference attendees and protesters of the conference outside."[35] Unmentioned was the fact that perhaps another one hundred press were on hand. Let's be generous and say that 150 white supremacists from around the country attended the event.

That's not nothing, but it is close to nothing.

To put the media's intense coverage of this gaggle of white supremacists into perspective, remember that hundreds of thousands of people show up every year for the peaceful anti-abortion March for Life in DC, and it isn't afforded even a fraction of the media coverage. Every week, thousands of groups holding a broad array of eccentric interests—say, Flat Earth Society conferences that are held every year—attract hundreds of attendees for their events.[36] Yet here it was, the "jolt" that promised to forever alter the American political landscape; the white supremacists attracted 150 people in a nation of 330 million.

The summer after the fascist conference, a few hundred khaki-clad Nazi flag-bearers descended on the college town of Charlottesville, Virginia, at the infamous "Unite the Right" rally—ostensibly a protest over the proposed removal of a General Robert E. Lee statue from Lee Park. The event *dominated* media coverage. One would have thought the very soul of the nation was at stake. Nearly every news story connected the events to the new populist GOP. One might have been under the impression that the Republican National Committee had deployed the Wehrmacht to the Virginia town.

Terry McAuliffe, then Virginia governor, declared a state of emergency to ensure there would be maximum attention focused on the right-wing nuts. And the gross display by far-right attention-seekers did exactly what it was meant to do, getting the entire media to act as if it were the dawn of Nazi America. Conservatives around the nation were asked to condemn the marchers—which they did—as if there were an ideological kinship between the two groups. Which, of course, was the point.

In a time of healthy and useful media coverage, such an event would be treated in passing as a politically irrelevant and ugly moment. Yet it was the dominant topic on news for days, weeks even. PBS (with the help of the left-wing activist group ProPublica) produced a documentary to mark the occasion. The event is still regularly referred to by the media as if it were another 9/11. Yet by the two-year anniversary of that march, perhaps two dozen racists showed up in Virginia, and not a single person for the next anniversary.[37]

. . . . .

In 2024, Joe Biden would make the fear of democracy being overturned the central claim of his campaign. In his opening statement during the first presidential debate, the president lied that Trump had called tiki-torch cosplay Nazis of Charlotteville "very fine people," and claimed, without any evidence, that the former president had said "Hitler has done some good things."

The BlueAnon fixation on white supremacists often led them to (inadvertently) comical expressions of anxiety.

"She went from a liberal non-voter to burning books with white supremacists," read a CNN piece headlined "How women fall into America's white power movement."[38] *Time* magazine described "The White Supremacist Origins of Exercise in the U.S." Also, very scary. Watch out in the gym, because "fitness trends have gone extreme—literally," warned MSNBC.[39] Physical fitness has always been central to the far right. In *Mein Kampf*, Hitler fixated on boxing and jujitsu . . ." "'Fascist fitness': How the far right is recruiting with online gym groups," added the *Guardian*.[40] "Why White Supremacists Are Chugging Milk (and Why Geneticists Are Alarmed)" was a real headline in the *New York Times*.

The tone of these stories was reminiscent of alarmist 1980s ABC *After-School Specials*.

Media soon began to warn that white supremacism had become so prevalent that it was even infecting minority populations. The *New Yorker* detailed an alleged "Rise of Latino White Supremacy." It's a frustrating piece that asks—or at least tries to ask—an interesting question: "Why are there nonwhite white supremacists?"

Why, indeed.

None of this is to contend that there aren't any bulked-up Latino racists chugging raw milk. Ragtag groups of Nazis, skinheads, Klansmen, and

other—often ideologically incoherent—extremists have been marching in America for decades. Need it be said, bigotry is real. Violence
is real. But white supremacists and other such extremists represent
a microscopic faction of our political makeup. More importantly,
they wield no real power and no influence—not in the GOP or anywhere else. They have no future. That is why they rely on stunts—and
BlueAnon-fueled mistrust—to imbue them with a false sense of importance.

There is no funding infrastructure for those who support white
power. There is no religious denomination, or any notable political
faction, that gives white supremacy any theological or ideological legitimacy. There are no white supremacist lobbyists. Despite the claims
of Democrats, there are no white supremacist organizations in DC. In
this free nation, any political party is free to participate in the process,
yet the reach and power of racist groups is still minimal.

If BlueAnon wasn't constantly telling you about them, most people
probably wouldn't know they existed, including most conservatives.

Placing inordinate importance on covering every act of random violence
in the nation—no matter how ideologically muddled—is an effective
way to create the perception that we are on the cusp of a civil war.
Every act of right-wing violence, even the most tenuously connected
to contemporary politics, is a major event that threatens "democracy."
Those acts, say a mass shooting by a man who has said bigoted things
online, are inevitably blamed on the rhetoric and actions of the conservatives, making them part of the "right."

For years, conservatives were blamed for every nut job who shot
up a Planned Parenthood. The National Rifle Association, and every pro-life organization in the country—nay, every pro-lifer in the
country—was called to do some soul-searching about their positions
and rhetoric. The panic over extremists is meant to impel conservatives to self-flagellate, whether it is over the January 6 rioters, or Alex

Jones, or the white supremacists of Charlottesville. BlueAnon wants conservatives to tie themselves to the extremists.

The reverse is almost never the case.

When "pro-Palestinian" rioters, who put on Charlottesville-type marches virtually every week in 2024, throw objects at police or mobs of anticapitalists destroy downtowns in anti-WTO demonstrations, no one asks progressives to denounce their socialist leanings.[41] When a Bernie Sanders fan takes a gun to Alexandria, Virginia, and attempts to murder an entire congressional delegation, as happened in 2019,[42] or a man tries to assassinate Supreme Court justice Brett Kavanaugh, as happened in 2020,[43] there are no "national conversations" and no one in establishment media demands Democrats temper their rhetoric. There are no panics over the menace of left-wing violence.

Left-wing Antifa rioters and BLM members engaged in the most expensive and prolonged domestic destruction in American history from 2016 to 2020, and Democrats were never asked in any serious way to condemn it.[44] There are no documentaries commemorating the violence, and no congressional inquiries into the root causes of the problem.

This skewed treatment of ideologically motivated violence creates the perception that one group is more violent than the other.

BlueAnon relies on double standards, creating the perception that one side is inherently violent and its movement combustible, while diminishing the other side's aggression as "mostly peaceful." Recall that in 2017, protesters against Trump turned violent in the nation's capital and clashed with police, damaged vehicles, destroyed property, and set fires across the country. Over 217 people were arrested in Washington, DC. And no one was worried about this attack on democracy.

In May 2020, Secret Service agents sheltered Donald Trump in a White House bunker for hours as hundreds of protesters began overwhelming police, some throwing rocks and bottles and trying to break down police barricades.[45] This was never an attack on "democracy" in the eyes of the left. It was, perhaps, even an expression of democracy itself.

BlueAnon tries to distance itself from the far left's most destructive elements, but sometimes it creates fantasies about their heroics. Media personalities like CNN host Chris Cuomo compared the Antifa leftist rioters to GIs storming the beaches of Normandy on D-Day.[46] In *Teen Vogue*, a Dartmouth College historian explained that the movement "grows out of a larger revolutionary politics that aspires toward creating a better world, but the primary motivation is to stop racists from organizing."[47] Actually, Antifa was inspired by Antifaschistische Aktion, a German communist group funded by the Soviet Union.[48] But that's another story.

Sometimes when left-wing violence breaks out, say in Portland, Oregon, and Kenosha, Wisconsin, the right is still blamed. "As right-wing groups increasingly move to confront protesters in U.S. cities, demonstrators are assessing how to keep themselves safe," the *New York Times* editorial board explained.[49] When riots broke out in cities across America in 2020, Adam Schiff blamed Trump and (who else?) the Russians for "willfully fanning the flames of this violence."[50] MSNBC's Joy Reid, who was recently given a prime-time show on one of the country's major news networks, believed that the riots were false-flag operations perpetrated by "armed white nationalists" deployed as part of a nationwide strategy to help reelect Trump.[51]

When Trump sent National Guard troops to quell Portland "protesters" who were attempting to firebomb the federal courthouse the entire Democratic Party's media complex mobilized to fearmonger.

MSNBC's John Heilemann told the network's audience that Trump had dispatched the police for a "trial run" on how to use "force" to "steal this election."[52] In a piece titled "Trump's Occupation of American Cities Has Begun," Michelle Goldberg of the *New*

York Times contended that "fascism" is already here.[53] House Speaker Nancy Pelosi called the police "stormtroopers" who were "kidnapping protesters."[54]

All these contentions were ugly, hyperbolic allegations meant to encourage unhealthy partisan anxiety before an election. In the end, a single man had been detained in Portland; he refused to speak without his lawyer and was released a little more than an hour later without any charges. This was not an isolated incident. An emerging story was merely another opportunity for reporters and columnists at once-respected publications to jump to bloodcurdling conclusions.

These were conspiracy theorists who were on a par with the fringiest right-wingers. And yet, they were given a hearing by the mainstream left.

DEMOCRACY, ALWAYS IN PERIL

The Constitution is kind of trash.
—ELIE MYSTAL, ON *THE VIEW*[55]

When BlueAnon isn't fearmongering about Republicans destroying norms and "democracy," they're typically undercutting public trust in the very ideals they claim to protect.

Of course, for the modern progressive, "democracy" no longer adheres to the idea of a constitutional order. "Democracy" can signify anything the partisan left decides at any given moment. This reimagining of American governance has irreparably disintegrated any shared understanding of long-existing norms. Though it does allow the left to accuse anyone who stands in the way of their partisan efforts of being an enemy of "democracy."

So, for instance, if Republicans oppose the nationalizing of the entire economy through the Green New Deal to avert a "climate crisis," they are accused of attacking democracy. According to Congressman Jamie Raskin, you see, "we've got to save democracy in order to save our species."[56]

Then again, if Republicans *oppose* emptying the Strategic Petroleum Reserve to temporarily flood the market to keep gas prices low to help Democrats win elections, they too are strangling democracy. "We find ourselves in a situation, where keeping gas prices low is key to preserving and strengthening the future of our democracy," MSNBC host Chris Hayes argued.[57]

What if Republicans don't help pack the Supreme Court? Yup. It means the end of "democracy," explained W. Kamau Bell—who is something called "a sociopolitical comedian."[58] Senator Elizabeth Warren concurred, writing a *Boston Globe* op-ed advocating to expand the Supreme Court "to protect America's democracy and restore faith in an independent judiciary committed to the rule of law."[59]

A bill proposed by House Democrats in 2021 expanding the Supreme Court by adding four seats to create a thirteen-justice left-wing court was also needed to, you guessed it, "save democracy," according to the authors.[60] In reality, the effort is meant to circumvent the deliberative constitutional process and the division of power. The court would be turned into a de facto legislative body that would keep expanding in perpetuity whenever another party took power.

It is worth noting that when President Franklin Delano Roosevelt unveiled his court-packing scheme in 1937, the Democrat-controlled Senate Judiciary Committee wrote that it was a "measure which should be so emphatically rejected that its parallel will never again be presented to the free representatives of the free people of America."[61] The modern Democrat, however, does not see it that way.

Sometimes, when things aren't going their way, BlueAnon will stoke apprehension by framing long-respected constitutional norms as tools of oppression.

"The Electoral College Is an Instrument of White Supremacy—and Sexism," a writer noted in Slate after the 2016 election.[62] In 2020, the *Washington Post*, nervous about another Trump victory, demanded that the nation "abolish the electoral college."[63] "Mr. Trump's election was a sad event for the nation," notes the *Post*, and "his reelection would have been a calamity."

Again, the fact that the Electoral College doesn't align with the "popular vote" isn't alarming—*it is the point*. The college was created by the founders because they did not believe in a direct democratic national vote. It isn't a "loophole" or a workaround, it is a bulwark against centralized power. The Electoral College exists to diffuse the very thing the *Post* claims is most beneficial: the "overbearing majority," as James Madison put it. Yet BlueAnon has convinced Democrats that a mechanism that stops a few big states from lording over the entire nation is undermining self-determination.

BlueAnon often frames the messy reality of our democratic system as troublesome or fascistic. During the presidency of Barack Obama, the left often groused about the alleged crisis posed by a "dysfunctional" or "broken" Congress, which in leftist jargon is roughly translated to mean "Democrats aren't able to do whatever they like."

As expected, after Donald Trump won the 2016 presidential race, another recalcitrant Congress (this time run by Democrats who relied heavily on the filibuster) was no longer framed as dysfunctional but rather as a "resistance" upholding the vital separation of powers. After Democrats retook the White House in 2020, the Republican Congress—elected by the people in the same way—were again menacing "democracy."

In 2022, Joe Biden, a stalwart defender of Senate norms in his younger years, declared the institution a "shell of its former self,"[64] lamenting that the GOP had used the filibuster over one hundred times in the past year to blunt the will of the people. Unsaid was the inconvenient fact that Democrats had done so over three hundred times the preceding four years.[65]

Democrats see no problem using the thinnest of fleeting majorities to shove through massive generational federal "reforms" without any national consensus or debate when it serves their purposes. When Democrats were pushing to pass the massive Build Back Better Act (later ludicrously rechristened the Inflation Reduction Act) or various "voting rights" bills,[66] many media members, including major editorial boards at outlets like the *New York Times*, painted the filibuster as it if were an antiquated, racist institution undermining progress.

"For Democracy to Stay, the Filibuster Must Go," the Gray Lady argued.[67]

"Voting rights organizations, Democratic lawmakers, and even artists like Joe Jonas and Billie Eilish are urging the party to take this step for a bill of this magnitude," one story noted.[68]

Even one of the Jonas Brothers is on board, so you know this is serious.

Meanwhile, in *USA Today*, a former Justice Department prosecutor, saying he was "done with the filibuster," claimed, "if the Senate's intractable minority is allowed to continue to prevent all legislation to protect our democratic system, we will run out of time. Efforts in the states to curb voting rights and ensure rule by a shrinking white minority will be able to take effect without any check."[69]

The subtitle of the article says "This sounds apocalyptic and maybe a little crazy. It is not," which is pretty much what a conspiracy theorist says when he's about to tell you something, well, apocalyptic and crazy.

As it turned out, thirty-nine Senate Democrats, eleven of whom had signed a passionate letter *defending* the filibuster only a few years earlier, demanded its elimination during the Biden presidency. In 2018, powerful Democrat Dick Durbin argued that abolishing the filibuster "would be the end of the Senate." By 2021, with Biden in charge, the high-ranking Democrats maintained that "the filibuster has a death grip on American democracy."[70]

This kind of jaw-dropping double standard is the norm. In 2005, then-senator Barack Obama passionately argued that the filibuster was imperative for the Senate to "rise above an 'ends justify the means' mentality because we're here to answer to the people—all of the people—not just the ones wearing our party label."[71] By 2020, Obama argued, not that he had changed his mind on the efficacy of the filibuster, but that the mechanism was a racist "Jim Crow relic" that needed to be eliminated "in order to secure the God-given rights of every American."[72]

Sure, it was just shameless and transparent, cynical hypocrisy. It also promoted suspicion among Democrats ignorant of basic American civics—alas, many of them these days—that the system empowered a "minority" to lord over them even when they "win" elections.

Deceptive headlines catering to this illiteracy dot the media landscape: "Popularity Is Optional as Republicans Find Ways to Impose Minority Rule,"[73] "Minority Rule Cannot Last in America,"[74] "Is American Democracy Sliding Toward Minority Rule,"[75] "'Tyranny of the Minority' Writers Say Constitution Not Strong Enough to Protect Democracy,"[76] and "Republicans Are Moving Rapidly to Cement Minority Rule. Blame the Constitution" are just a small sampling.[77]

All these pieces treated institutional federalism, a bedrock principle of limited government, as innately authoritarian. All of it was meant to foster the paranoid belief that the state was stripping people of self-determination, when the opposite was true.

When the *Atlantic* laid out "The Democrats' Last Chance to Save Democracy," it lamented the "*democratic* deficits in the Senate and the Electoral College," as if the existence of states and the Electoral College weren't purposely instituted to diffuse consolidated federal control. Blunting the federal government's power over states and the state's power over individuals isn't "minority rule," it's one of the most indispensable ways to ensure that a diverse number of people in a big nation are allowed to govern themselves. Which, of course, is the real problem for BlueAnon.

In years past, any high school educated American could have pointed out that the United States was no kind of "democracy," but rather a republic with a constitutional order that checked majoritarianism. Today anyone who mentions that indisputable fact is mocked as being hopelessly naïve or a crypto-racist. It's no accident. The most basic belief in the American system is often depicted as a conspiracy against the citizenry.

When bestselling author and Yale University philosophy professor Jason Stanley hears the riffraff going on about "natural law," which is to say the tenets of our Constitution, he hears "a dog whistle to white Christian Nationalism."[78] "This July 4, let's declare our independence from the Founding Fathers," the *Washington Post*'s Paul Waldman argued, griping about the Constitution, including the idea that every state should have two senators.

It is entirely possible, even probable, that modern progressives don't view their abuses of power as illiberal or authoritarian. For them the process is irrelevant and so they do not comprehend the gist of a neutral principle. It's about the ends, period—encouraging suspicion and skepticism about our governing norms is now a BlueAnon specialty.

THE HANDMAID'S TALE

*Mike Johnson, theocrat: the House speaker
and a plot against America*
—GUARDIAN[1]

In the summer of 2023, an intraparty skirmish broke out among congressional Republicans, resulting in Kevin McCarthy being ousted as Speaker of the House.

The kerfuffle, fought over some now-forgotten petty grievances of members, had little bearing on the future of policy, or even the philosophical outlook of the Republican Party. Yet, as with every political event involving the GOP, BlueAnon quickly framed this *vote* over leadership as a menace to the future of "democracy."

"Vote to oust McCarthy is a warning sign for democracy, scholars say," read one *Washington Post* news story.[2] Democrats often engage in these kinds of selective appeals to authority, seeking out groups of "experts" or "scholars" who will elucidate on how Republicans are ruining everything.

In this case, one of the experts was Daniel Ziblatt, the author of a tract critical of traditional American republicanism, called *Tyranny of the Minority*. No doubt there were plenty of other "scholars" out there who saw the House voting on a new Speaker as merely a humdrum political event. But interviewing them would have ruined a perfectly good headline.

That said, the claim was also weird because not long before McCarthy's ouster, Democrats like Adam Schiff warned that the moderate Speaker of the House was also a "threat to our democracy."[3]

When it appeared that Republicans had settled on naming Jim Jordan as speaker, Minority Leader Hakeem Jeffries cautioned that the longtime Ohio congressman was also "a clear and present danger to our democracy."[4]

Finally, when the GOP landed on Mike Johnson for the job, Liz Cheney, by now a passionate ally of Democrats, told CNN that Johnson posed a "significant threat" to democracy.[5]

You see the problem here, right? The only way to save "democracy" was for Republicans to pack up all their things, shut up, and go home.

To add to all the apprehension, Johnson was an openly religious Christian—more so than most, even. This was sure to trigger a slew of distraught claims about the impending theocracy. *Playboy*'s former senior White House correspondent, Brian Karem, wrote that Johnson's leadership ensured that Congress would turn into a "discount version of the apocalyptic orgasm the holy rollers have dreamed of for years." In a piece headlined "MAGA and Christian nationalism: Bigger threat to America than Hamas could ever be," Karem unleashes a torrent of panic-stricken warnings about completely traditional positions and beliefs held by the new Speaker. Johnson posed a bigger threat to us, he contended, than Hamas—you know, the terrorist group that slaughtered over thirty Americans on October 7, 2023.[6]

Churches are struggling to fill the pews and yet BlueAnon was acting as if the ninth Crusade had descended upon Washington.

Thomas B. Edsall of the *New York Times*, one of the paper's chroniclers of the American right, noted that Johnson was "the embodiment of White Christian Nationalism in a tailored suit." Johnson, wrote the columnist, "is the first person to become speaker of the House who can be fairly described as a Christian nationalist, a major development in American history in and of itself."[7]

The preposterous panic over "Christian nationalism" would reach something of an apex in March 2024 when *Politico* writer Heidi Przybyla appeared on MSNBC's *All In with Chris Hayes*. Donald Trump, she explained, had surrounded himself with an "extremist" cabal of "conservative Christians," who were misrepresenting "so-called natural law" in their attempt to roll back abortion "rights" and other leftist policy preferences.

What makes "Christian nationalists" different, she went on, was that they believe "our rights as Americans, as all human beings, don't come from any earthly authority."[8]

These contentions were probably really confusing to anyone who had taken American civics 101, because Przybyla's description of "Christian nationalism" comported perfectly with the case for American liberty offered in the Declaration of Independence. The idea that man has inalienable, universal rights, in fact, goes back to ancient Greece, at least. The entire American project is contingent on accepting the idea that the state can't give or take certain God-given freedoms.

To the modern progressive, this is a bizarre and ugly idea spread in the shadows by monied interests with bad intentions.

BlueAnon did immediately go to work digging up as much as they could on the little-known congressman. "Mike Johnson's Ties to Christian Nationalism Revealed" was a scoop from *Newsweek*.[9] Hold on to your hat because the investigation exposed that Johnson didn't believe in things like "coincidences," but rather that God "raises up those in authority." Or, in other words, the man subscribed to notions shared by millions of other Christians—not to mention Jews and Muslims and probably others—about God ruling the universe.

There was more, however. "Why Is Mike Johnson Flying a Christian Nationalist Flag Outside His Office?" asked the *New Republic*, linking to a "report" from *Rolling Stone* that found the new Speaker displaying an Appeal to Heaven flag outside his office door. Johnson, *Rolling Stone* reported, had "ties to the far-right New Apostolic Reformation— which is hell-bent on turning America into a religious state." However, the "key" to his "Christian Extremism" was hanging right there outside his office.

In the summer of 2024, the *New York Times* whipped up a similar attack on Justice Sam Alito, whose family apparently flew an Appeal to Heaven flag outside the family beach house.[10] Democrats demanded that the justice recuse himself from any cases involving Donald Trump because some protestors on January 6 had allegedly hoisted the same flag.[11] The same flag had also flown at Civic Center Plaza outside San Francisco City Hall for sixty years with "zero controversy." That is, until officials removed it after the *New York Times* story.[12]

One didn't need to be a vexillologist to unfurl this mystery. They simply needed to use Google. The Appeal to Heaven flag—sometimes known as the Pine Tree flag—was a Revolutionary-era banner originally used by frigates commissioned by George Washington, then commander in chief of the Continental Army. It traces its origins to John Locke's refutation of the divine right of kings. That sounds about as thoroughly American as any flag. This one is still used by certain Massachusetts governments. Ron Swanson, the fictional libertarian on the NBC show *Parks and Recreation*, had a replica on his desk. But BlueAnon transformed a harmless display of patriotism into something cultish, weird, even chilling.

Now, obviously, there are Christian nationalists out there. And, for years, Democrats have oscillated between treating orthodox Christians as icky weirdos and lecturing them about how they've entirely misinterpreted Jesus's lessons. According to the left's self-styled theologians, Jesus was a big proponent of compelled redistribution of wealth, socialized medicine, and abortion. Yet these days, as fewer Americans go to church and most social conservatives have migrated to the GOP, the left has settled on treating most orthodox Christians as fifth columnists.

It was during the election of George W. Bush, "born again" as an evangelical Christian in 1985, that the panicked rhetoric about the coming theocracy really kicked off. In his 2006 bestseller, *American Theocracy*, Kevin Phillips masterfully weaved together scores of unnerving strands that proved a cabal of evangelicals had infiltrated the government and were working to create a Christian state. "Christian nationalism" was lurking in the halls of power.

We are still waiting for the "Bush Theocracy" to emerge.[13] Nowadays, though, subscribing to any brand of socially Christian credo makes one a theological supremacist in the eyes of the progressive left. "Most Republicans Support Declaring the United States a Christian Nation" was the scary headline of a recent piece in *Politico Magazine*.[14] "Christian nationalism, a belief that the United States was founded as a white, Christian nation and that there is no separation between church and state, is gaining steam on the right," explained two professors from the University of Maryland's Critical Issues Poll.

In the age of Trump—not exactly a latter-day Cotton Mather, it should be pointed out—the power of the Christian nationalist was growing, according to "experts."

It took only a little digging to realize that this long piece condemning Republicans as modern-day Crusaders was based on a highly dubious two-question (online) poll that asked participants if they would "officially declare" the United States "a Christian nation."[15]

First off, pollsters do not define what "declare" means. And nowhere does the poll mention anything about a "white" Christian nation or a

"Christian nationalist" state or anything about stripping other faiths of their religious freedoms or overturning constitutional protections. If participants were asked about those issues, the numbers would have almost surely turned out very different.

This, though, was the modus operandi of BlueAnon. Not only is the questioning deceptive—a setup, really—but the two professors then retroactively defined what they believed a "Christian nation" entailed and then attributed a politically loaded understanding of the term to an entire political party. It was as if a conservative pollster asked a bunch of leftists if they were fans of "taxing the rich," and then defined that position as being in favor of a communist dictatorship.

None of this is to say that there aren't *any* conservatives who support theocratic or illiberal philosophies. But there's nothing shocking or radical about Republicans "declaring" the United States a "Christian nation." Many of the foundational principles of the nation were bound up in Christian ethics. The nation was almost exclusively Christian at its founding; it is still predominately so in matters of faith. These are objective realities.

Nor is there anything extreme or theocratic about allowing Christianity to inform one's political principles. I know this because, as noted, leftists will often ask me, "What would Jesus do?" (Probably not conduct partisan push-polling, is one of my guesses.) Yet, to bolster these bogus findings, the professors contend that "prominent Republicans" across the nation have been mainstreaming Christian nationalism.

They offer us three people to prove this point. First, the backbencher Representative Marjorie Taylor Greene, who is mostly "prominent" because she's often nutty and thus a favorite straw woman of political journalists. Then comes former, long-forgotten Pennsylvania gubernatorial candidate Doug Mastriano, who apparently once said that "separation of church and state" is a "myth," at a "QAnon meeting." Johnson too once called the separation of church and state "a misnomer."

Now, I don't know much about Mastriano, and I can't track down the context of this comment, or this alleged QAnon meeting he attended, but let's concede for the sake of argument that the GOP candidate did these things. Social conservatives have correctly argued that "separation of church and state" isn't mentioned in the Establishment Clause, and some have convincingly argued that the idea has been appropriated, almost exclusively, to strip religious institutions of state funding, push God from the public square, and attack religious liberty.

Religious liberty, once a bedrock belief of the American populace, is now highly "controversial" (the media's euphemism for "conservative" issues; every political issue, after all, is controversial). To stress the alleged insincerity of the social conservative position, journalists will almost always place quotation marks around perfectly factual phrases like "religious freedom." Outlets like CNN skip any pretense of impartiality and put phrases like "so-called" in front of foundational doctrines of liberty, like the "conscience rule" that allows health care workers who cite moral or religious reasons to opt out of providing certain medical procedures, such as abortion, sterilization, and assisted suicide. This way it is no longer a debate about issues, but about the social conservative's furtive efforts to use traditional American customs and laws to institute theocratic rules.

This shading of issues is increasingly prevalent in political discourse and meant to create the impression that faithful Christian beliefs are at odds with the norms of American governance—when really, they are only at odds with the newly adopted cultural mores of the progressive left. Even the mention of God was framed as odd and alarming.

When BlueAnon believed that Florida governor Ron DeSantis was blossoming into a presidential prospect, the media began noticing that he was "flirting" with Christian white nationalist ideology. Now that was big news. Here is how the *Miami Herald* explains it:[16]

The Republican governor, a strategic politician who is up for reelection in November, is increasingly using biblical references in speeches that cater to those who see policy fights through a morality lens and flirting with those who embrace nationalist ideas that see the true identity of the nation as Christian.

Here again we see journalists coloring completely normal behavior as devious and dangerous. The *Herald* reports that DeSantis, a Catholic, recently dropped a biblical reference while speaking to an audience at a private Christian college, Hillsdale. Nothing about "white" people or theocracies, mind you. The *Herald* says that Christianity has been a "recurring theme" for DeSantis and other GOPers. If you're shocked that Christian politicians see the world through the prism of their faith or infuse religious imagery into their rhetoric, I have some more news for you: essentially every major politician in American history has integrated Scripture into speeches and imagery. That includes Hillary Clinton, Barack Obama, and "devout Catholic"—as the *New York Times* claims—Joe Biden, for starters.

The anti-Catholicism of the American past was predicated on an aversion to new immigrants, anxieties about the pope, and a general long-standing theological distrust among High Church denominations. These days, the distrust is meant to impress on Democrats that faithful Catholics are incapable of doing their jobs because a new kind of papism is at odds with our national laws—namely on the issue of abortion, the foundational tenant of the left's "democracy."

"Do you consider yourself an orthodox Catholic?" Senator Dick Durbin asked future Supreme Court justice Amy Coney Barrett, when she was still a nominee to a federal appeals court.[17] Durbin knew that the Notre Dame Law School professor was a strong prospect for the high court and a devout Catholic. The implication was that her positions were incompatible with her job.

Barrett's Catholicism came up numerous times during those hearings, and in even more troubling ways. "When you read your speeches, the conclusion one draws is that the *dogma lives loudly within you*," the late Dianne Feinstein declared (emphasis mine). "And that's of concern when you come to big issues that large numbers of people have fought for years in this country."

The only "big issues" for a court nominee should be related to the law. But the only dogma on the agenda that day were the left's concerns regarding abortion. So it was time to reignite apprehension about the alleged theocratic temperament of Catholics.

Al Franken, then in the Senate, asked Barrett about speaking honoraria she received from the civil rights organization Alliance Defending Freedom (ADF), comparing the group to genocidal Cambodian communist Pol Pot.[18] "I question your judgment," the star of *Stuart Saves His Family* lectured the constitutional lawyer and mother of seven.

ADF and other similar civil rights groups had long been smeared as saboteurs of democracy for defending religious freedom—most famously the case of Jack Phillips in Colorado, who refused to create a unique cake for a gay wedding. MSNBC's Sarah Posner, who described Johnson as the "most unabashedly Christian nationalist Speaker" in history, claimed the ADF wanted to "eviscerate the separation of church and state."

Creating the impression that legal outfits like the Alliance Defending Freedom were extremists was an ongoing BlueAnon effort. Activist groups like the once-respected Southern Poverty Law Center branded organizations like ADF and the Family Research Council as "hate groups," adding their names to a list with violent white supremacist organizations and other justifiably repulsive groups.

Conflating organizations that work to protect the civil rights of the devout with extremists was meant to give the impression that it all belongs to the same broader movement to destroy the foundations of a (small-l) liberal state. Nothing could be further from the truth. ADF has participated in seventy-four Supreme Court victories, directly in fifteen victories in front of the Supreme Court.

Yet the peception that traditional Catholic Americans were radicalizing would become so engrained in Democratic Party circles that the Biden administration set up an operation to spy on churchgoers and flush out connections to "the far-right nationalist movement."[19] At least one FBI agent was sent out to spy on Catholics who were worshipping at churches and chapels in the Richmond, Virginia, area, but there were also agents on the case in Oregon and California—and perhaps more places we have yet to discover.

Then again, anti-Catholic bias can go from serious to almost comical. When Democratic senators Kamala Harris and Mazie Hirono learned that Donald Trump's nominee for the U.S. District Court for the District of Nebraska, Brian Buescher, was a member of the charitable Knights of Columbus, they jumped into action, labeling it an extremist organization. The Knights of Columbus, though it fails to adhere to the new progressive moral canon, is nothing but a benevolent society. Anyone who's had any interaction with the charitable Knights knows they are some of the least scary people imaginable.

And, alas, Catholicism, unlike progressivism, has never inhibited anyone from faithfully executing his or her constitutional duties. Barrett's real sin, as it were, was that she took the oath of upholding the Constitution far more seriously than any of the people questioning her.

GILEAD

Better never means better for everyone....
It always means worse, for some.
—COMMANDER, *THE HANDMAID'S TALE*

"Mike Johnson Sparks 'Handmaid's Tale' Comparisons After Becoming Speaker," *Newsweek* helpfully noted not long after the Louisiana congressman ascended to the Speakership.[20] Accusing the GOP of building a society reminiscent of the fictional nation of Gilead in Margaret Atwood's *Handmaid's Tale* has become a favorite subgenre of BlueAnon.

By the time Johnson's Pine Tree flag was detected by the eagle-eyed press, most politically active Americans had probably heard something about the Hulu television series based on the 1985 science fiction novel. In the book, fascistic Christian fundamentalists seize power after a terror attack and create a patriarchal state where women are not only forbidden from owning property, or reading, or wearing their own clothing, or having their own ideas, or making any choices, but they are also thrown into a biblically determined caste system. The Handmaids, women who are identified as corrupted, are compelled to bear the children for chaste couples.

Sounds horrific, right? Much like George Orwell's *1984*, the book is a favorite point of analogy in contemporary politics. Unlike *1984*, however, it offers not even a single remotely valuable lesson about the modern political experience or life in the United States, where women are freer today than any women have ever been in history.

Nevertheless, *The Hill*, *Washington Post*, *People*, *New Republic*, and *New York Times*, to name just a few outlets, have published pieces offering fretful comparisons between social conservatives and the patriarchal fascists of Gilead.

While the novel exhibits a deep misunderstanding of Christianity and Americans, for that matter, the aesthetics of *The Handmaid's Tale*—the subservient women dressed like nuns under the constant watchful eyes of dour white men—provides powerful imagery to feed the darkest fantasies of the American left. When pollsters at Morning Consult decided to ask voters "Is 'The Handmaid's Tale' rooted in reality?," 17 percent of all respondents—29 percent of Democratic men and 26 percent of Democratic women—believed it was "grounded in truth and could become a reality someday."[21]

When Brian Stelter of CNN's *Reliable Sources* asked actress Ann

Dowd, who plays Aunt Lydia in the series, to comment on how close the United States is to a Gilead-like state (this is a real example of "begging the question," incidentally), she replied, "We're a heck of a lot closer than we were in season one, which is terrible." Dowd continued: "When I saw what was going on in Georgia [which restricted abortion to before a heartbeat could be heard], I thought, 'This can't be real.' It stunned me."[22]

Let's face it, most actors are incurious dolts. One might remember the actress Cameron Diaz telling Oprah Winfrey before the 2004 Bush-versus-Kerry election, "if you think that rape should be legal, then don't vote."[23]

As it is, twenty years later rape is still illegal, though the scaremongering about Republicans and rape is still going strong.

We see it when BlueAnon lies about Republican health care bills ("Rape and domestic violence could be pre-existing conditions," CNN says[24]) or when one of the Daily Beast's resident conspiracy theorists, Wajahat Ali, takes an obscure Idaho case and wonders, "Is the GOP's War on Women Now Pro-Rapist?"[25]

When the GOP is not *pro*-rape, though, it's *pro*-murder.

For decades, leftists have argued that pro-life social conservatives don't care if women perish by the thousands. Former Planned Parenthood president Leana Wen predicted, "We face a real situation where *Roe* could be overturned. And we know what will happen, which is that women will die. Thousands of women died every year pre-*Roe*."

We know no such thing. The reality was that *Roe v. Wade* was overturned and some states passed stricter limitations on abortion, while many passed more permissive abortion laws. What did not happen were thousands, or, for that matter, any deaths.

Pro-abortion advocates have long fabricated stories and statistics to emotionally manipulate and scare women. It began with the infamous Walter Cronkite 1965 documentary on the issue, *Abortion and the Law*, which *greatly* exaggerated the number of back-alley abortions and deaths from botched abortions, numbers that were incessantly repeated thereafter by the media to shape public opinion. The documentary claimed, under the veneer of scientific expertise, that a million illegal abortions were performed every year (more than are *legally* procured today) and that 5,000–10,000 women died from botched procedures. Experts who later looked at those numbers could never re-create them.[26] Even counting secondhand reports, only a small fraction of that number could be found. Back-alley abortions were incredibly rare. They were largely a myth.

If it's not legalizing rape or killing women, BlueAnon claims that conservatives want to steal your birth control. In 2023, Slate warned that "birth control" is next in line for anti-abortion Republicans."[27] Representative Kathy Manning argued that "Congress must codify the right to contraception before it's too late." As she wrote in *The Hill*: "The public needs to be made aware of the right-wing extremists' war on contraception and outright assault on Americans' fundamental rights, personal freedoms, and well-being. In their efforts to satisfy their fringe MAGA base, the GOP has made clear they do not and will not represent the 90 percent of Americans in favor of contraception."

It would be understandably disconcerting if Republicans were working to "deny women"—is it only women who use contraception?—access to birth control, as Senator Elizabeth Warren often warns.[28] Hillary Clinton, who based the near entirety of her 2016 presidential campaign on the fact that she happened to be born a woman—"Her turn," as it were—regularly dropped this accusation as well. Republicans, she said, want to stop making "contraception available to women who want to control their own bodies."[29]

Now, it is true that some Christians have justifiable faith-based reasons to oppose taxpayer-funded contraception. Catholics like Joe Biden are also allegedly opposed to contraception. But the political debate has always been over whether the government should be allowed to coerce insurance companies, and thus consumers, to pay for that contraception. This is why, years ago, the Obama administration sued groups like Little Sisters of the Poor: to force them to undermine their basic tenets of faith.

No Republican congressional bill, however, has ever proposed banning contraception. A number of Republican bills, in fact, both in states and in Congress, have proposed making birth control over-the-counter.[30]

The modern progressive has been convinced that if something hasn't been provided to them for free by the state, then it's as good as banned. But if opposing federally funded condoms is outlawing contraception, then refusing to pay for your Whopper is a ban on Burger King.

Moreover, Democrats like to conflate contraception and abortifacients, which some Republicans want to limit. One is prophylactic, a method or device that is used to prevent conception; the other is used to end the life of a conceived human being. Whatever your beliefs on the topic, they are substantively different.

This is not the place to litigate the abortion debate, but let's put the issue into some context: according to decades-long Gallup polling on the issue, around 45 percent of women believe that abortion should be legal only in certain circumstances, while another 15 percent believe it should be illegal in all circumstances.[31] There is a wide range of views among those women about the legality of the procedure and when life is worth protecting. The simplistic concept that opposing unfettered abortion, from conception to birth—the widely held policy position of the modern Democratic Party—is inherently "antiwoman" or authoritarian or dystopian is a BlueAnon talking point, not a reality.

It is certainly not antidemocratic to be pro-life.

As we've seen, every political setback for Democrats is transformed into an attack on the pillars of democracy, even when it *strengthens* the ability of people to decide their fate. That is certainly the case when it comes to abortion.

Let's recall, first, that the same institution that wrote the *Dobbs* decision, which overturned a constitutional right to an abortion, also unilaterally legalized abortion nationwide in the first place with the *Roe v. Wade* decision. That decision was decided by a court that was wholly made up of men, whereas the court that handed down *Dobbs* had multiple women, one of whom ruled in favor of overturning *Roe*. The difference between the rulings is that the *Dobbs* decision empowered the public *to vote* on an issue that was unmentioned anywhere in the Constitution.

That did not stop Harvard from putting together a conference about abortion and "the crisis of American democracy."[32] The powerful George Soros organization Open Society Foundations warned that "Overturning of Roe v. Wade Is an Assault on Women and Democracy Globally."[33] Outlets like Bloomberg ran pieces arguing that "Abortion Rights Falter as Democracy Slides."[34] The *Los Angeles Times* explained, "How the end of Roe turned into a threat to American democracy." The piece, written by two law professors, contends that overturning *Roe* undermined democracy because polls show that most people favor legal abortion—as if courts are bound to the majority rather than the law.

The *Washington Post* published a piece contending that "[Justice Samuel] Alito's *Dobbs* decision will further degrade democracy." In it, the author combines a batch of conspiracies to defend the courts instituting laws rather than the people: "Most of the states exalting over this decision are busily de-democratizing themselves by gerrymandering and restricting voting rights in order to restrict minority representation and powers." "The language of democracy, freedom and self-determination is always at risk of being turned to exclusionary," it claimed.

Those words, ephemeral and devoid of tangible legal reasoning, tell us nothing. Nothing in the "language of democracy" says anything about unborn children being aborted.

It is merely another childish emotional outburst meant to feed leftist paranoia.

MISOGYNISTIC STAR CHAMBER

Misogyny has become central to the Republican mission.
—JUDE ELLISON SADY DOYLE, NEWSWEEK

BlueAnon has also convinced millions of Democrats that a cabal of sexual predators run the highest court in the land.

I know what you're thinking: *I thought fear of sexual abusers in the government was a QAnon conspiracy theory.* Obviously, you haven't been listening to the experts.

During Brett Kavanaugh's elevation to the Supreme Court, CNN's lascivious chief legal analyst, Jeffrey Toobin, who was later fired for masturbating during a Zoom meeting, claimed 40 percent of the high court had "been credibly accused of sexual misconduct."[35]

This was the theme across all major media and the Democratic Party. "We have two alleged sexual predators on the bench of the highest court of the land, with the power to determine our reproductive freedoms. I still believe Anita Hill. And I still believe Dr. Christine Blasey Ford!,"[36] Representative Ayanna Pressley yelled at a protest of Supreme Court nominee Kavanaugh.

All of this is an excellent reminder that the left's unproven accusations, no matter how risible or rickety, are often embedded in history.

Not a single credible accuser had ever corroborated Hill's contentions—and Thomas had scores of subordinates working for him in government before his nomination to the court. The FBI investigated Hill's claims—though she was reluctant to cooperate[37]—and failed to uncover any evidence to substantiate her accusations.[38] After the hearings, FBI agents sent an affidavit to the Senate stating that Hill had omitted portions of her story in her FBI interview and offered testimony that contradicted what she had told them.[39] This part of the story rarely gets mentioned when the media recount her supposed heroics. And yet, in documentaries and books and media coverage, Hill is treated as a hero and Thomas as a criminal. The victim-oppressor complex is impervious to truth.

Christine Blasey Ford's accusations against Kavanaugh were even more tenuous.

There is still no evidence other than Ford's own word that the psychology professor had ever even *met* Kavanaugh in the 1980s, much less been a victim of sexual assault. She could not name a specific place or time of the alleged assault. And other than a handful of people (including Ford's husband) who claimed she told them her account decades after the fact, there had not been any witness that could corroborate Ford ever met or knew Kavanaugh, much less prove her account of the events.

Her former best friend, in fact, noted that she herself did not have "any confidence" in Blasey Ford's story,[40] who offered conflicting accounts of numerous important aspects of her allegations, had also deleted her entire social media history, which reportedly showed partisan motivations.[41]

Blasey Ford's unfalsifiable accusations of sexual assault were blasted out across the nation with complete certitude. Democrats put it into the Congressional Record. Pundits treated her accusations as objective fact as they lamented the ongoing "war on women." They destroyed a man's reputation. And nothing but an absolute confession of wrongdoing and a surrender would stop Democrats from accusing Kavanaugh of being a sexual predator.

Blasey Ford's accusations would have been laughed out of any court of law, and in more decent times, any newsroom. They should have been laughed out of Congress.

The opposite happened.

Big Media became accomplices. When teams of reporters were unable to find proof proving Blasey Ford's claims, outlets began pumping out story after story about the allegedly sexist 1980s culture that Kavanaugh grew up in, the allegedly sexist schools he attended, and the allegedly sexist people he knew. He was guilty by association. The media created a vivid picture of a world of oppressive culture in which monsters like Kavanaugh oversaw the fate of women as if they were slaves to their whims.

"Doesn't Kavanaugh have the same presumption of innocence as anyone else in America?" CNN's Jake Tapper asked Democratic senator Mazie Hirono during the hearings.[42] "I put his denial in the context of everything that I know about him in terms of how he approaches his cases" was her unexpectedly honest answer. Plainly put, Hirono's worldview contends that because Kavanaugh—who earned the highest rating from the American Bar Association during his time on the DC appellate court—holds a record of originalist jurisprudence, it's likely that he's also a sexual pervert and rapist.

This was all bad enough. But the legacy media soon began to spread every scurrilous accusation of anyone who claimed to know Kavanaugh.

The *New Yorker* published an interview with a woman named Deborah Ramirez, in which she claimed that during the 1983–84 school year at Yale University, when she and Kavanaugh were freshmen, he exposed himself to her during a drinking game in a dorm suite.[43] Ramirez offered no eyewitness support for her story that allegedly took place at a well-attended party.[44] So, what did the *New York Times* do? It published a piece detailing the culture of alcohol abuse at Yale as a way to implicate Kavanaugh through secondhand accounts.[45]

"Who is Julie Swetnick, the third Kavanaugh accuser?" read a *four*-bylined headline in the *Washington Post* in October 2018.[46] Among other things, Swetnick was "an experienced Web developer in the Washington area who has held multiple security clearances for her work on government-related networks." CNN also wondered:[47] "Who is Julie Swetnick, the third woman with allegations about Brett Kavanaugh?" "Julie Swetnick Is Third Woman to Accuse Brett Kavanaugh of Sexual Misconduct," answered the *New York Times*.[48] "Kavanaugh accuser Julie Swetnick speaks out on sexual abuse allegations" was NBC News' contribution. And so on and so forth.[49]

Well, Swetnick, who accused the Supreme Court nominee of being present at a gang rape, not unexpectedly turned out to have serious credibility issues: in one lawsuit, for example, she'd been accused by an ex-employer of falsifying her job application.[50] And though not every major outlet acted irresponsibly in spreading her story, most did (and consciously so). Shyster lawyer Michael Avenatti, the guy who trotted out these accusers—as of this writing serving nineteen years in federal prison for extortion and stealing millions—was a fixture on CNN for weeks.[51] In a book about the Kavanaugh controversy, *New York Times* reporters Robin Pogebrin and Kate Kelly claimed to have uncovered another victim . . . one who reportedly *couldn't even recall the incident herself.*[52] The two were interviewed by basically every major outlet as experts on the matter, without any pushback. This is the standard that legacy media uses when leveling accusations against those who stand in the way of progressivism.

Accusing Thomas and Kavanaugh of being "alleged sexual predators" is a slander that is built on warped perceptions about men and the court. It is meant to undercut the authority of legal process and to intimidate justices (and future nominees) who take the "wrong" side on the issue of abortion. For contemporary Democrats, the court exists primarily to safeguard the only constitutional "right" that really matters to them.

Kavanaugh was nominated by the duly elected president and confirmed by the duly elected Senate in the same constitutional manner that every Supreme Court justice in history has been nominated and confirmed.

It should be noted that even before the future Supreme Court justice Brett Kavanaugh had faced any uncorroborated accusations of sexual assault and gang rape, Senator Sheldon Whitehouse, Rhode Island Democrat, was zeroing in on some vital issues.

"Have you boofed?" he asked the judge.

"That refers to flatulence, we were sixteen," Kavanaugh incredulously responded. "You want to talk about flatulence at age sixteen on a yearbook page, I'm game."[53]

Oh, Whitehouse was *definitely* game.

Deciphering the clandestine nature of Kavanaugh's scribblings from 1985 was the center of the Democratic Party's—and thus the media's—attention weeks before the Blasey Ford allegations were made. Kavanaugh, who until then had a sterling reputation as a lawyer and family man, was the kind of DC creature who could easily be painted as an entitled, devious, predatory man. He was the manifestation of a pent-up paranoia about the patriarchy's depravity and power.

So much so that liberal commentators called in the big guns. "Why the FBI Should Investigate 'Boofing'" was the headline of an editorial of Washington's self-styled paper of record, *Politico*. "For its investigation to be comprehensive, the FBI must also get to the bottom of what 'boofing' means," wrote Brian Fallon and Christopher Kang, two leftist activists who in the coming years would lead efforts to delegitimize and destroy the court.[54]

The justice was forced to explain what "Ralph Club" meant. The annoyed jurist explained that he had a weak stomach and often could not handle spicy food; it was not vomiting caused by excessive drinking. The most murky and devious words in the yearbook surrounded something called "devil's triangle," referring to a note in Kavanaugh's now-infamous Georgetown Prep yearbook.

Then suddenly the left let their imagination take over. "Take devil's triangle," explained a Slate writer. "While it's remotely possible that Kavanaugh and his friends used an idiosyncratic definition, the euphemism typically refers to a threesome with two men and one woman."[55]

In a piece headlined "What We Know About the Allegations Surrounding Brett Kavanaugh,"[56] Philip Bump, as was his wont, took a deep dive into the scandal. "The suggestion" that Kavanaugh and his then-friend Mike Judge "might have been drinking heavily is bolstered by references on Kavanaugh's yearbook page to drinking. Judge also wrote a book called 'Wasted: Tales of a Gen-X Drunk,' in which he makes reference to a character named 'Bart O'Kavanaugh' who vomited and passed out after drinking," Bump concluded.

BlueAnon did yeoman's work in convincing so many Democrats that women are on the cusp of being thrown into servitude, or that conservative men who drank in high school were predisposed to engage in acts of misogynistic criminality. That was dumb enough. But convincing people that men, as a sex, had some kind of binding ideological viewpoint was both corrosive and genuinely sexist.

I'm a middle-aged "white man"—the epitome of the patriarchy—and I don't agree with most white men on anything. Why? Because being a man (or white) does not predetermine your political disposition. It is a biological reality. Convincing millions of people otherwise might be one of BlueAnon's most consequential achievements.

There are, of course, certain issues that concern women more than men, and vice versa. All men are not members of a lockstepping cabal. And most men do not think or act as an amorphous group of human beings when it comes to politics or much else. Many men, including myself, would rather see a government with hundreds of Amy Coney Barretts before a single conspiracy theorist like Sheldon Whitehouse.

THE FASCIST STATE

The Republican Party would have the American
flag and the swastika flying side by side.
—JULIAN BOND

After Joe Biden's *disastrous* performance in the first presidential debate, Democrats went searching for distractions. And they found one in a year-old Project 2025, a suggested policy roadmap for a second Trump Administration pulled together by the conservative Heritage Foundation.[1]

Biden said that Project 2025 "should scare every single American."[2] Project 2025, the president warned, "is run and paid for by Trump people. It was a project built for Trump, and it's the biggest attack on our freedoms in history." A bigger attack than 9/11? The Civil War?

One Democratic strategist told the *Washington Post* that his party needed to "instill fear in the American people" over the proposal.[3] The Associated Press warns the effort champions a "dramatic expansion of presidential power."[4] "It's the blueprint for a fascist regime," Joy Behar explained on The View.[5] "Everything is very disturbing because it's a very dark, dark vision of what America could look like . . . it becomes a dictatorship and he becomes the king," added cohost Sunny Hostin.[6]

"Project 2025 is not a game, it's white Christian nationalism," the star of *The Avengers* and budding Christian theologian Mark Ruffalo warned his millions of followers. "It is the Sharia Law of the 'Christian' crazy people who aren't Christian at all but want to control every aspect of your life through their narrow and exclusionary interpretation of Christ's egalitarian, inclusive, and kindly teachings."[7]

Donald Trump and his surrogates distanced the candidate from the effort.

I read the thousand-page document, which was written by a bunch of think tankers, former administration officials, and right-wing policy experts. Though I couldn't uncover any fascistic Christian nationalist diktats, I did find many public policy suggestions that Democrats would surely dislike. Because, for starters, most of the Project 2025 "mandate" is just a wish list of long-held, run-of-the-mill conservative policy positions that have been around forever.

One of the most talked about Project 2025 proposals, for example, was the firing of as many as fifty thousand federal workers. You can like or dislike the idea, but personnel decisions of federal employees are well within the constitutional discretion of the president.

Another allegedly scary Project 2025 proposal suggests the elimination of the Department of Education and its "woke-dominated system of public schools." Conservatives have been promising to get rid of the Department of Education—which didn't even exist until 1979—since Ronald Reagan first ran for the presidency and never do.

Project 2025 also suggests prohibiting the FBI from "fighting misinformation and disinformation." Democrats claim this is authoritarian. Others rightly point out that the state shouldn't be in the business of dictating speech. But whether you like it or not, curbing the FBI's reach is *limiting* executive power not expanding. What kind of fascist reins in the state police?

Another supposedly bloodcurdling Project 2025 proposal, according to Democrats, is the conservative efforts to end the "war on fossil fuels." This, too, has been a mainstream GOP position since Democrats began openly promising to dismantle our energy sector.

For all the talk of the coming theocracy, Project 2025, you may be surprised to learn, does not feature a single mention of "Jesus" or "Christ." It does champion traditional social conservative positions on religious freedom, abortion, marriage, and so on.

The policy guide features eight mentions of "God" in the entire document, most of those noting our "God-given individual rights to live freely." Though this might be offensive to *Politico* writers, as we've seen, or fringe "New Right" intellectuals who've abandoned "liberalism," it is one of the foundational ideas of the Constitution and Declaration of Independence.

"Christian" is mentioned seven times by Project 2025. One, a warning about the left's threats to tax-exemptions on churches and religious schools. Another mention suggests doing more to protect minority "Middle Eastern Christians" in foreign policy. Another reference reminds us about the COVID-era authoritarians who shut down "churches on the holiest day of the Christian calendar."

Faith is also touched on in a section about attacks on religious freedom that "compel a Christian website designer to imagine, create, and publish a custom website celebrating same-sex marriage but cannot compel an LGBT person to design a similar website celebrating opposite-sex marriage." There is nothing extreme about that statement. It is true.

Now, obviously there are numerous other nods to socially conservative policy that comports largely with orthodox Christian positions—anti-porn initiatives and the like. Not everyone in the right-center coalition might agree with them—especially on abortion. Trump doesn't even embrace those. But MAGA extremism? Hardly.

Despite recent efforts to convince Americans otherwise, there is nothing weird or unique or theocratic about faith informing your political choices. None of Project 2025 undermines the rights of other citizens. The scare campaign aimed at Project 2025 was the culmination of a cynical campaign that fed partisan paranoia in an effort to hold on to power.

Less than a week before the 2022 midterms, bestselling "presidential historian" Michael Beschloss unleashed this unhinged panic-stricken warning on MSNBC:

> *Fifty years from now—if historians are allowed to write in this country and if there are still free publishing houses and a free press, which I'm not certain of—but if that is true, a historian will say, what was at stake tonight and this week was the fact whether we will be a democracy in the future, whether our children will be arrested and conceivably killed.*[8]

Left-leaning voters hear this kind of utter madness not only on social media or in comments sections, but from the mouths of credentialed experts on major network television and newspaper outlets.

In a just world, Beschloss would be holding up a homemade "World to End!" sign and grumbling to himself while wandering aimlessly around Times Square. Instead he is a guest on *PBS NewsHour* and NBC News, a trustee of the White House Historical Association and the National Archives Foundation, and sits on the board of the Smithsonian Institution's National Museum of American History. His status was bolstered because he was willing to offer painfully stupid counterhistories and share thermonuclear hyperbole.

Beschloss's talent was sniffing out the sinister scent of fascism *everywhere*. When Donald Trump appeared on the White House balcony after returning from a stint at Walter Reed National Military Medical Center in October 2020, Beschloss told Rachel Maddow that if one wanted "to go into history to look for something like this? Go into Italian history and look at Mussolini. This is the way dictators come to power."[9]

When dozens of Twitter users helpfully produced numerous pictures of modern presidents appearing on the very same balcony doing the very same thing, Beschloss was unbowed. By virtue of who Trump was, anything he did was fascistic, and any aesthetic proof would do.[10] Why? Because the United States was, according to Beschloss, perpetually "in existential danger of having our democracy and democracies around the world destroyed."

By the time presidential historians were warning that the GOP would be executing innocent children, Biden was already president. Even if we concede for the sake of argument that Democrats are the true defenders of the republic—and that certainly stretches the imagination—they could have lost both houses of Congress, and no GOP could have threatened democracy.

Then again, the idea that a midterm, any midterm, was the difference between democracy and national *infanticide* was an insane contention to begin with.

Any conservative commentator working at a legacy outlet—as far as such people still exist—making comparably malicious warnings about Democrats would find himself fired and relegated to the fringes of the media echo-sphere. When CNN's Jeffery Lord, perhaps the only Trump-friendly pundit on CNN (or anywhere on major TV outside of Fox News), mocked the leftist anti–free speech group Media Matters and its use of boycotts of advertisers of conservatives, by typing "Sieg Heil!" in a tweet, he was immediately fired.

Yet there was Hayes, an MSNBC host who spent years spreading absurd theories about democracy being stolen by Russians, nodding at Beschloss's outlandish comments. In years past, a self-respecting journalist, even a pundit, would have challenged a guest to explain such a fanatical contention. The left had always accused the right of being fascistically inclined, but BlueAnon was unfettered in this regard.

"I'm beginning to see what happened in Germany," the second most powerful member in the House, Jim Clyburn, warned. "Adolf

Hitler was elected chancellor of Germany. And he went about the business of discrediting institutions to the point that people bought into it," he told NBC News. "Nobody would have believed it now. But swastikas hung in churches throughout Germany. We had better be very careful."[11]

Congressman Hank Johnson compared the president to Hitler in a speech to the NAACP.[12] "He's sort of like Goebbels,"[13] Joe Biden said of Trump in 2020, later reusing the same comparison against Senator Ted Cruz in 2021.[14]

"Donald Trump increasingly compared to Adolf Hitler," explained a 2016 CBS News piece that pointed out that the president asked attendees at one of his rallies to raise their hands and pledge to vote for him as if it were a Nuremberg rally.[15] (Meanwhile, conservatives on social media also provided dozens of examples of Democrats engaged in the same behavior over the years.)

Practically every week during the Trump presidency, one could read a new think piece about the uncanny parallels between Trump (and his fans) and National Socialists. Even innocuous, traditional GOP efforts—tax cuts or pro-life efforts or deregulation or support for originalist justices—were cast as planks in the rise of German-style authoritarianism. Intellectuals, historians, public officials all began openly making the case that the Republican Party desired fascism. Perhaps even genocide.

It got so bad, a subgenre emerged that justified calling the president the most murderous of all time. "It's not wrong to compare Trump's America to the Holocaust. Here's why" was one useful explainer in the *Washington Post*. Another *Post* op-ed implored people not to "compare Donald Trump to Adolf Hitler." Why? "It belittles Hitler."[16] "Is it wrong to compare Trump to Hitler?" asked a *Philadelphia Inquirer* columnist as Trump was making noise about running again. The answer? "No."[17]

In 2023, former senator and now–TV pundit Claire McCaskill warned that Trump was even "more dangerous than Hitler," because the former president "has no philosophy he believes in" and "is not going for a grandiose scheme of international dominance."[18] One has to employ otherworldly pretzel logic to argue that the former president is more dangerous than Hitler *because* he is without any overriding philosophical disposition and thus is uninterested in warmongering. But no one said conspiracy theorists had to make sense.

The real key differences between Donald Trump and the German fascist, MSNBC contributor Bruce Bartlett explained, was that "Hitler served honorably in the military, Trump didn't; Hitler was faithful to his wife, Trump cheated on all his wives; Hitler wrote a book, Trump's were all ghostwritten."[19]

A long 2024 *Politico* piece took a deep dive into Trump's sense of humor, noting that critics "call it a sign of his autocratic tendencies." You see, as the writer Ruth Ben-Ghiat contends, Italian fascists like Benito Mussolini also "had the same twisted sense of humor." Everyone knows Hitler was a real prankster too.

"He wants to cancel the news, so they're done," Sara Haines, cohost of *The View* concluded in October 2023. No, Rachel Maddow, insisted, "He wants to put MSNBC on trial for treason so he can execute us."[20]

It's not just Trump. BlueAnon sees Nazis everywhere.

In "Long Day's Journey into CPAC," late-night TNT host Samantha Bee went on the hunt for white supremacists at the famous conservative conference.[21] One of her producers walked through the crowd and mocked people who had "Nazi hair," a reference to a hairstyle that is short on the sides and left much longer on top—which kind of looks like what a person in a New Wave band might sport.

It is exceedingly unlikely that any of the young people captured in that segment had anything to do with white supremacists. But, we learned, one of the young men, Kyle Coddington, had gotten the haircut not as a nod to 1930s fascists, but rather because he was getting chemotherapy treatments for stage 4 brain cancer.

Bee later apologized, but that didn't change the fact that she thought a bunch of young people hanging out at a right-of-center policy gathering would be sporting *Nazi haircuts in the first place.*

Speaking of CPAC, in 2021 a group of geniuses in the media figured out that the CPAC stage at the Hyatt Regency hotel in Orlando looked like a "Norse rune" used by Nazis during their rallies. A photo of the stage went viral on social media, with thousands of leftists accusing attendees of secretly constructing a stage to "reconstruct a mythic 'Aryan' past," as the Anti-Defamation League put it. "Nod or blunder? No CPAC 2021 apology for a stage shaped like a white supremacist symbol," *USA Today* reported.[22] Hyatt hotels, where the conference was being held, was compelled to release a statement noting that a stage resembling Nazi rune was "abhorrent."

Was it a "blunder"? I don't know, *maybe*? But abhorrent? I bet there are items in your home right now that resemble the shape of the othala rune. Would you apologize for owning them?

When the newly elected Trump administration began trying to implement a "zero tolerance" policy on illegal border crossings, the left screamed that it was snatching children like a depraved American Gestapo and throwing them into "cages."

"This is the United States of America. This is not Nazi Germany," Dianne Feinstein said. Soon-to-be presidential candidate Joe Biden explained that a "policy that separates young children from their parents isn't a deterrent, it's unconscionable."[23] Biden went on to describe the child-separation policy that was first implemented under the Obama administration as "abhorrent," and one that threatened "to make us a pariah in the world."

The entire media spent weeks contemplating the depth of our collective immorality. Joe Scarborough compared border agents to SS guards.[24] The *New York Times'* Charles Blow argued Donald Trump was a "baby snatcher."[25] "These are children!" he exclaimed.

When Alexandria Ocasio-Cortez, fashionably attired in a white outfit, attended a 2018 protest on a road outside a tent city shelter in Texas that was used to detain migrant children, she broke down in tears for a photo op. The pictures of the New York congresswoman circulated widely throughout the media. "The United States is running concentration camps on our southern border, and that is what they are," the socialist explained.[26]

Though some aspects of Trump's effort to get hold of the border crisis had been ham-fisted, zero people died in the fenced detention areas near the border. The policy was institutionalized before Trump had come into office. Only parents charged with entering the country illegally *and* who claimed asylum after being apprehended were detained. Adults who opted not to be deported after entering illegally were compelled to wait for adjudication of their cases. While they waited, the law prohibited children from being held in the same detention centers as adults, for their protection. This was implemented by a judge, not Trump. It was a tragic situation, but handing over children to strangers without knowing if they are really the parents would also be inhumane.

When all this angst was being whipped up by BlueAnon, there were around 2,000 children being detained by the Border Patrol. By the end of the first year of the Biden presidency, around 3,200 migrant children were being held in Border Patrol facilities—a record—with almost half being held past the three-day legal limit.[27] That number kept climbing during Biden's presidency, until the media stopped reporting on "cages" altogether.

Not one person in the establishment media, incidentally, compared Democrats to Nazis.

By the 2024 presidential campaign, Joe Biden's campaign stopped pussyfooting around and joined the fun, posting a graphic on the platform X, directly associating Donald Trump with Adolf Hitler. The tweet featured the former president and a sampling of his more boorish—though out-of-context—claims regarding illegal immigrants, communists, and political opponents on one side of the meme with some of Hitler's vaguely similar quotes on the other.[28]

You know who else took his political opponents' quotes out of context?

RISE OF THE SEMIFASCISTS

They're a threat to our very democracy.
—JOE BIDEN

BlueAnon's toxic brand of acrimony and mistrust has been amped up to such hysterical, paranoiac levels that it likely has irreparably altered the landscape of American life, not merely our politics.

In August 2022, Joe Biden took to the campaign trail in Maryland to help Democrats in the upcoming midterms, accusing Republican *voters* of not merely supporting Donald Trump, but of taking a dark turn toward "semifascism." It is rare, if not unprecedented, for presidents—who, just as a reminder, represent all American citizens—to attack constituents.

We soon learned that this was not one of Biden's elderly flubs. It was the game plan. The president soon elaborated on this extraordinary accusation during a prime-time speech—a time slot typically reserved for historic moments of unity or momentous news. "The MAGA Republicans don't just threaten our personal rights and economic security," the choleric Biden warned, standing in front of an ominous—dare I say, fascisty—crimson light that had been projected onto the front walls of Philadelphia's Independence Hall. "They're a threat to our very democracy. They refuse to accept the will of the people. They embrace—embrace—political violence. They don't believe in democracy," he went on.[29]

They had done no such thing. Or no more so than the left, and probably less. Trump, for all his aggressiveness and boisterousness, had not embraced violence. Certainly, the vast majority of GOPers were no more authoritarian than the most ardent self-styled left-wing defender of "democracy."

It can be convincingly argued that Trump's first term was healthier for the constitutional order than Biden's multipronged effort to reimagine American governance unilaterally through executive power. Yes, *some* right-wingers had become violent, just as *some* left-wingers had resorted to violence. The summer of 2020, lest we forget—as the media wishes we did—saw the most destructive rioting in American history.

The contention that Republicans represent a unique threat to the future of "democracy" dominates virtually every facet of Democrats' rhetoric and election efforts. The president, contradictorily—very much like real-world authoritarians—argues that the only way to preserve "democracy" is to dispense with not only Trump but indeed the entire opposition party. And in many ways, the system itself is now seen as the enemy. Any vote for Republicans, any Republican, was a vote for illiberalism. Which was objectively absurd.

Also, this brand of preemptive "denialism" was, as Biden noted in the very speech he was giving, "un-American." The midterms, the president went on, were "going to determine whether democracy will long endure," because "democracy is on the ballot for us all."

None of this was new. "We're in danger of losing our democracy. Most Americans are in denial," one of the *Washington Post*'s many dishonest hysterics, Max Boot, argued in the lead-up to the 2022 midterms. The only way to save the country, Boot explained, was to cleanse the nation of its Republican politicians. Otherwise, he cautioned, Trump would:

- Institute his own "authoritarian agenda" (which Trump had somehow forgotten to institute during his first term)

- Place his own lackies into federal positions (as every other president in history had done, mind you)

- "Shoot peaceful protesters and launch missiles at Mexico," among other appalling crimes against humanity.[30]

This is not normal political rhetoric. It's not an argument against the other side's policies. It's not even hyperbole. Trump wasn't even running yet. *Boot was writing about a midterm.* These are conspiratorial ravings that are no less unhinged than people on social media ranting about how the NFL rigged the 2024 Super Bowl so that the Chiefs would win and singer Taylor Swift, who was pals with the KC quarterback, would endorse Joe Biden.[31] Well, it's worse, actually. This was the *Washington Post*, not a rando account on Facebook. (And let's not forget that Swift, who once claimed that Donald Trump was engaged in "calculated dismantling" of the U.S. Postal Service to "blatantly cheat" the election, isn't exactly innocent in conspiracizing herself.[32])

It did not matter that most MAGA-centric candidates and voters often took completely traditional Republican stances on a variety of issues. Nor did it matter that some of those positions were once held by Joe Biden. The very presence of Trump made every GOP candidate, from every school board member to every senator, a threat to the American way of life. Chasing them out of public office was no longer a political imperative. It was a moral one.

When *BlueAnon feared* that Ron DeSantis, who opposed Trump in the 2024 Republican presidential primaries, might become a threat, the Florida governor was swiftly transformed into the most dangerous person in history. Worse than Trump, even.

BlueAnon spent the entirety of the COVID pandemic accusing DeSantis, who had rather quickly realized that policies shuttering the economy did nothing to stem the spread of the disease, of being a nihilist. "The GOP's Death Cult Comes for the Children"[33] and "Ron DeSantis and the Conservative Death Cult of Freedom"[34] were the kinds of headlines left-wing media regularly produced. Republicans weren't wrong. For some reason, they wanted their own constituents to die.

Whenever it was convenient, the *New York Times'* Paul Krugman wrote about the Republican "death cult" and accused DeSantis of effectively acting "as an ally of the coronavirus." The fact that some northeastern states he regularly praised had higher death tolls did not seem to bother him. MSNBC's Mika Brzezinski referred to one COVID breakout as "the DeSantis variant," in part because the Florida governor opposed mask mandates.[35]

Why conservatives would want to join a death cult was never explained.

After the pandemic had passed, California governor Gavin Newsom said DeSantis was "fundamentally authoritarian." "Ron DeSantis Would Kill Democracy Slowly and Methodically," warned Jonathan Chait.[36] "Believe It: A DeSantis Presidency Could Be Even Worse Than Trump" was the *New Republic*'s take.[37] MSNBC's partisan Michael Cohen stated that "DeSantis is a far more dangerous politician than Donald Trump."[38]

"I say this with conviction," former Republican and leading scaremonger David Jolly noted: "Ron DeSantis is far more dangerous than Donald Trump for a very specific reason." While the former president was "transactional," DeSantis wanted to "take us back 100 years and believes he can use the Constitution to do that."[39]

An evil genius, DeSantis had hatched a plan to use *the law of the land* to push through his totalitarian agenda.

For Biden, an unpopular president saddled with a bad economy, a border crisis, and a dangerously counterproductive foreign policy, there was little choice but to keep pretending his opposition were violent

Nazis. When the president kicked off the new year in 2024 with an event near the historic town of Valley Forge, Pennsylvania, he invoked the spirit of the founding and George Washington to contend that the reelection of Donald Trump heralded the end of the American experiment. "We're living in an era," the president explained, "where a determined minority is doing everything in its power to try to destroy our democracy for their own agenda."[40]

As the *Wall Street Journal* pointed out, the word *democracy* made forty appearances in his speech, slightly ahead of the word *Trump*.[41]

Biden demanded that his paranoid rendering of the country be adopted more vigorously by the press. The campaign met with reporters regularly, armed with spreadsheets detailing the alleged failings of their stories. A couple of weeks before his speech in Valley Forge, the president's campaign openly petitioned the supposedly free press to join BlueAnon to ramp up the scare tactics about the hypothetical Trumpian dictatorship.

"For the political press corp [*sic*]—especially our friends at the Gray Lady," the White House pleaded in a November 2023 letter to the media, "it's time to meet the moment and responsibly inform the electorate of what their lives might look like if the leading GOP candidate for president is allowed back in the WH."[42]

The media, naturally, obliged.

Within weeks of the email's release, a large number of pieces graphically detailing a looming autocracy appeared in major media. "Trump dictatorship is increasingly inevitable," Robert Kagan, an editor at large at the *Washington Post*, wrote in a six-thousand-word essay that depicted messy partisan battles of DC as the new Weimar Germany.[43]

It was nice of Kagan to not only conjure up comparisons with Hitler's ascent but to broaden his warning to include Napoleon's ruin of France and Caesar's crossing of the Rubicon. The meaning was clear: the end of the republic was near.

The "Gray Lady" also heeded the call, running a sprawling three-bylined piece itemizing many of the potential horrors of a second Trump term. Another presidency, the authors wrote, promised to be even "more radical" than the first.[44]

One of the major trepidations of the *Times* writers was the possibility that Trump might "use the Justice Department to wreak vengeance against his adversaries" and "get prosecutors to go after his enemies." These reporters apparently saw no irony in the fact that those sentences were being typed even as Democrats across the country were prosecuting Trump and his lawyers. Indeed, even as BlueAnon was ramping up the Trump-is-Hitler caravan, Democrats in Colorado and Maine were attempting to remove the leading GOP presidential candidate from state ballots for "engaging in insurrection." The former president was not found guilty of such a crime. He hadn't even been charged with it. Setting aside debates over the proper use of the Fourteenth Amendment, there was certainly nothing "democratic" about unilaterally throwing the leading Republican presidential candidate off ballots.

In January 2024, the *Atlantic,* the most reliable repository of highbrow Trump-era hysterics, published an entire issue devoted to the harrowing prospects of a potential second term, which one columnist noted would merely be validating the "violent ideologies of far-right extremists."[45] Again, granted he was a big talker, Trump's agenda and triangulations on social issues made him, by historical standards—especially on social and economic issues—a moderate Republican.

Our old friend Joe Scarborough didn't need to rise to the White House's challenge. He had never stopped fearmongering. "Morning Joe" dialed the histrionic volume to 11 throughout the Trump presidency. For him, no conspiracy was beneath repeating, no panic worth ignoring. Perhaps Scarborough, an early and obsequious booster of Trump,[46] was (understandably) upset that the future president insulted his (now-wife) Mika Brzezinski. Or maybe it was good for ratings. Whatever drove him, as Trump moved toward winning the GOP nomination, Morning Joe found another gear.

"He will do, he will get away with, he will imprison, he will execute whoever he's allowed to imprison, execute, drive from the country, just look at his past," ranted Scarborough.[47] Only a month earlier, his colleague Rachel Maddow had also theorized that Trump wanted to execute members of the media. I certainly do not claim to predict the future, but I do wonder why Trump never tried to censor anyone. Much less arrest a single journalist during his first term.

In the meantime, it was Trump allies like Steve Bannon and Peter Navarro who ended up in prison not long after these comments.

If Trump wins the 2024 presidential election, warned Miles Taylor —a former midlevel bureaucrat in the Trump White House who famously wrote a *New York Times* essay under the nom de plume "anonymous," he might "turn off the Internet."[48]

Now they were just repeating themselves. We were told in 2017, when Federal Communications Commission chairman Ajit Pai spearheaded the repeal of "net neutrality" rules, the Obama-era menu of internet regulations that classified the internet as a public utility like a telephone company, that the internet was as good as dead. The internet operated with little or no government oversight for decades, and it was about as democratic a system as possible. Now the norms and status quo from the invention of the online world to 2016 suddenly turned into a dark, fascistic enterprise.

"Ending net neutrality will destroy everything that makes the internet great"—*everything*, warned a 2017 op-ed on the NBC News site.[49] "It sounds like a nightmare," wrote Evan Greer, "but if a proposal unveiled by the Federal Communications Commission (FCC) this week is enacted, this hellscape of extra fees, slow-loading apps and censorship could be the future of the internet." A *GQ* story headlined "How the FCC's Killing of Net Neutrality Will Ruin the Internet Forever" described the dystopian future:

Think of everything that you've ever loved about the Internet. That website that gave you all of the Grand Theft Auto: Vice City cheat codes. YouTube videos of animals being friends. The illegal music you downloaded on Napster or Kazaa. The legal music you've streamed on Spotify. . . . The movies and TV shows you've binged on Netflix and Amazon and Hulu. The dating site that helped you find the person you're now married to. All of these things are thanks to net neutrality.

Across tech outlets, hysterical warnings about the end of the internet proliferated. Nancy Pelosi declared that democracy itself was at stake.[50]

The tenor of this hyperbole matched the tone of the cable networks' coverage of the issue. The *Washington Post* reported that the "FCC plan would give Internet providers power to choose the sites customers see and use." "The FCC Is Trying to Destroy the Internet."[51] "Killing Net Neutrality Is a Death Blow for Innovation."[52] "FCC Is Revving Up to Destroy the Internet as We Know It."[53] CNN's front page announced that it was "the end of the internet as we know it."

In February 2018, Senate Democrats tweeted this:

If

we

don't

save

net

neutrality,

you'll

get

the

internet

one

word

at

a

time.[54]

Polls found that an amazing 80 percent of Americans supported "net neutrality." My wholly unscientific contention is that perhaps 1 percent of them could have explained why. It's fine to disagree over policy. Why would anyone believe that the Republicans *wanted* to destroy the entire internet and innovation and hurt consumers?

None of these dire predictions came true, as was the case with most contrived left-wing panics. Americans still had unfettered access to their favorite websites. Companies were again free from draconian regulatory oversight and could innovate. Internet speeds had increased nearly 40 percent since net neutrality was abolished.[55] And they keep improving. The internet, for better or worse, is still with us. Stronger than ever. Then again . . .

BlueAnon
just
moved
to
the
next
hysteria.

Trump may well do terrible things in a second term; no one knows the future. But the executive abuses of his first term were well within the unfortunate norm. Nothing in his past tells me that a second Trump term would be marked by executing journalists or turning off the internet.

In truth, Trump, an opportunist, had few ideologically consistent positions. His positions on government spending and social issues were well in line with moderate Republicans of the past.

Besides, when the former president did have a chance to "wreak vengeance" against Hillary Clinton—a target-rich environment, no doubt—he did not pursue her or anyone else. The opposite. "I don't want to hurt the Clintons, I really don't," Trump said in 2017. "She went through a lot and suffered greatly in many different ways."[56]

The great irony of all the histrionics was that it was the Democrats who had spent years delegitimizing the Supreme Court and the rule of law, undermining legislative norms, cheering on unprecedented and blatant executive abuses. No modern president flouted separation of powers quite like Biden—though Barack Obama came close. The president used the power of the state to censor Americans, regularly ignored the Supreme Court, utilized lawfare to target political enemies both large (Trump's inner circle) and small (school board protesters), and relied on the power of agencies like the Occupational Safety and Health Administration (OSHA) to force a vaccine on the population by threatening to fine employers with unvaccinated workers over $13,000 per violation.[57]

Biden regularly ignored the Supreme Court, most notably on student loan "forgiveness." He used the power of bureaucracy to institute radical changes without the consent of the people.

Within a single week of becoming president, Biden signed more consequential executive actions than most presidents had in their entire terms. Even the *New York Times* gently chided Biden for his unprecedented early unilateral governance, which is a clue to how extraordinary the president's abuse was.[58] This "is no way to make law," the *Times* noted. "A polarized, narrowly divided Congress may offer Mr. Biden little choice but to employ executive actions or see his entire agenda held hostage. These directives, however, are a flawed substitute for legislation."

Early in the 2024 race, liberals, as they had done during the first Trump term, were already openly planning to undermine the outcome of the election through bureaucratic means. "A network of public interest groups and lawmakers, nervous about former President Trump's potential return to power, is quietly devising plans to foil any effort on his part to pressure the U.S. military to carry out his political agenda," reported the NBC News.[59]

This kind of plan could hardly be considered compatible with "democracy." Subverting civilian control over the military was a hallmark of authoritarian rule. Yet Democrats openly bragged about such efforts.

Say what you will about MAGA fans—they might be wrong, or they may be misinformed, or confused, or possibly hypocrites—but their philosophy wasn't fascistic, semi or quasi. Their outlook, despite the endless stories and claims of radicalism, and hysteria that went with it, was well within the norms of American political debate.

JIM CROW 2.0

Racism is part of Republicans' ideological
DNA. It's just that simple.
—PULITZER PRIZE WINNER LEONARD PITTS JR.[60]

Perhaps BlueAnon's most pernicious effort at undermining elections is the conspiracy theory of "voter suppression."

Millions of Democrats now believe that half the country is systemically barring black Americans from participating in democracy, stripping them of agency and rights, when, outside of some isolated incidents, no such effort exists in the United States.

The "voter suppression" myth is highly effective because it is always evolving and open-ended, and it encompasses practically any regulation that upholds voter integrity. If the GOP agreed to the Democrats' demands today to make elections "fair," tomorrow Republicans would be accused of undermining elections for failing to institute a whole set of new demands. Until Republicans promise to personally drive every minority voter to a polling station, they will be accused of suppressing the vote.

And because "voter suppression" is tethered to genuine historical misconduct fresh in the collective memory, it holds more salience and power than other similar efforts.

In a recent Kaiser Family Foundation survey of black voters, seven in ten said they were concerned about "voter suppression interfering with a fair and accurate election in their state." Yet when asked if they had ever personally experienced suppression efforts, only half said "they have experienced waiting in long lines at their polling place in the past, and one in five have experienced potential voter suppression such as having their registration or identification questioned."[61]

All of which is to say, BlueAnon's hyped-up fears of voter "suppression" have been normalized to such an extent that many African Americans who face commonplace inconveniences associated with voting, like standing on a line or having their identity checked, are now under the impression that they have fallen victim to systemic white oppression.

Election laws aren't perfect, of course, and in some jurisdictions, including liberal ones, polling places are understaffed or run by less-than-competent poll workers. That is nothing new. Partisans try to gerrymander favorable districts. That isn't new either. But, despite what Americans may believe, the state has no duty to come to anyone's home, knock on their door, and convince them to expend the minimal effort needed to participate in democracy. Yet anything less than door-to-door service is spun as "suppression" by BlueAnon.

Since running for president in 2020, Joe Biden has made imaginary suppression and "voting rights" central to his political message.

When Georgia's Election Integrity Act—both a tightening of election laws and, in many ways, a liberalization of them—was on the ballot in 2022, the president told a crowd in Atlanta right before Election Day that the "next few days, when these bills come to a vote, will mark a turning point in this nation's history. Will we choose democracy over autocracy, light over shadows, justice over injustice? I know where I stand. I will not yield. I will not flinch. I will defend your right to vote, our democracy against all enemies foreign and domestic. And the question is: Where will the institution of the United States Senate stand?"[62]

These were the mendacious ravings of a deranged demagogue.

Biden's warped argument is predicated on the claim that anyone who supports voter ID laws, or any time restrictions on mail-in ballots, or any consistent hours for early voting, or any bans on ballot harvesting, is no better than Bull Connor, the racist commissioner of public safety for Birmingham, Alabama, during the civil rights era.

Biden called the Georgia law, which passed overwhelmingly, "odious," "vicious," "unconscionable," a "subversion" and "suppression," the "twenty-first-century Jim Crow." He stirred up anger by falsely contending that voters stuck on lines could be denied a mere glass of water, though the restriction was aimed specifically at curtailing campaign handouts. These restrictions are hardly unique. Thirty-eight states, including Biden's home state of Delaware, prevent campaign workers from handing out water or food or any paraphernalia to voters within a certain distance of a polling place.

The president also suggested that anyone opposing the Democrats' federal voting rights bill that was then being debated in Congress—which would have overturned thousands of state laws—was not only a bigot but a seditious "domestic" enemy of the United States.

Biden's comparison of Jim Crow laws, which upheld racial segregation, to contemporary election integrity laws in Georgia was not just a cynical play on racial anxieties. It was a detestable historical analogy. Jim Crow was an often-violent suppression of minority rights while

GOP-led voting integrity laws entail some of the most liberal electoral regulations in the world.

It is, contra the perception created by BlueAnon, easier to cast a ballot in America today than ever. It is as easy to vote—even in states like Texas and Georgia, which are most often accused of "suppressing" the vote—as it is in any other free country in the world. These days, most voters need not leave the comforts of their home to cast a ballot. In every state in the union, citizens can request that the government send them a ballot in the mail. In most states, a person can get a ballot in a dozen or so languages. One can do so for weeks before an election. In some states, a ballot will be sent to your home even if you didn't ask for one. And the ballots that are sent are more user-friendly than ever. It is easier to vote than to send a FedEx package or sign up for a streaming service or buy a book on Amazon.

Yet the concocted suspicion surrounding "suppression" has freed BlueAnon to spread outlandish ideas with little blowback. Democrats, for example, will often claim that it is easier for a young African American to buy a firearm than to vote.[63] To purchase a gun, a person not only needs government identification, but they must also be over twenty-one and pass a criminal background check by the FBI. In states such as New York, Maryland, and California, handgun laws are so prohibitive, they require citizens to take a class or ask the local sheriff for permission to own a handgun.

In other words, if obtaining a ballot was half as difficult as obtaining a legal firearm, Democrats would be completely justified in calling it suppression. (What all this does tell us is that the ability of Americans to practice their Second Amendment rights is being suppressed, but that's a story for another book.)

One of the reasons BlueAnon is compelled to spin mythologies is that the specific policies Democrats oppose are quite popular. When pollsters use straightforward language, most Americans, including most African Americans, support voter ID laws.[64] Many of the recent requirements that Democrats refer to as authoritarian were instituted to shore up the emergence of lax COVID-era election rules. These "restrictions" were not only the norm a few years ago, but they are the norm in effectively every free country around the world.

Most Americans—most people in the free world, really—believe it is eminently reasonable to expect voters to identify themselves before participating in democracy. If Democrats believed the vote was sacred, so would they. Though it's possible, unfortunately, that some of those peddling "voter suppression" believe minorities are less capable of procuring ballots and identification than they are.

Voting conspiracies, of course, do not end with "suppression." For a couple of weeks before the election, leftists began chaining themselves to mailboxes across the nation as if they were holding out against the Roman legions atop Masada. Online, photos and videos that showed mailboxes being taken off the streets were circulated as evidence of voter suppression. Even PolitiFact said that the "conspiracy floodgates" were open.[65]

During the summer of 2020, Democrats began spreading pictures of locked mailboxes in places such as Burbank, California—apparently a hotbed of Trumpism—where local post offices closed them down to stem local criminality, not voting. It wasn't just some fringe partisans spreading the rumors. Representative Gerry Connolly of Virginia, chair of the committee overseeing the Postal Service, accused Postmaster General Louis DeJoy of ginning up a "modified organizational structure" reform to stop voters. "It's really a Trojan Horse," Connolly claimed. "Deliberate sabotage to disrupt mail service on the eve of the election—an election that hinges on mail-in ballots."

Carolyn Maloney of New York, who chairs the Government Oversight Committee, claimed that the "drastic changes to the Postal Service by an overtly partisan Postmaster General are another example of the President's attempts to prevent millions of Americans from having their votes counted."[66]

Then–House Speaker Nancy Pelosi even called back representatives for an emergency session to deal with the "crisis" of "operational changes" that were "slowing the mail and jeopardizing the integrity of the election." These turned out to be routine cost-cutting reforms, which Pelosi and others knew well, and had absolutely nothing to do with slowing delivery or shuttering mailboxes. It was another effort to corrode trust in 2020 and advocate the anarchic COVID-era voting regimes that Democrats now want to normalize in every state.

It's no wonder Democrats are primed to believe elections are stolen from them.

There is not a single documented instance of a person's mail being purposely diverted or slowed or pilfered by the post office to deny anyone the right to vote. It was a BlueAnon conspiracy theory, and online users spread it. The media covered it as if it were a real story. Politicians used the coverage to mainstream the conspiracy.

Rest assured, your conservative friend who believes chemtrails are seeding the sky is a lot less of a threat to democracy than the government officials who convince constituents that the Postal Service was stealing the presidential election.

Still, this imaginary corruption had become such a serious threat to democracy that only two weeks before the presidential vote in November 2020, MSNBC host Nicolle Wallace was asking leading Democrats if perhaps it made sense to call in foreign countries to monitor American elections.

"The threats to our elections in what, two and a half weeks, are so pervasive, and they're so dire, and they include violence—I mean do you think it's time to ask for friends and allies to come over and help us monitor our elections?" the host asked, adding, "We used to do that in other burgeoning and threatened democracies." Jim Himes, a

Democrat who sits on the House Intelligence Committee and knew well that none of what Wallace was claiming was remotely true, concurred, then compared Republican state governments to authoritarian regimes in Russia, China, North Korea, and Iran.[67]

Incidentally, international observers come to the United States every election cycle to *learn* about our system.

"Given the unprecedented circumstances leading up to Election Day and President Trump's efforts to undermine the election's integrity before it took place, many feared widespread violence on Tuesday," began a *Washington Post* postelection report.[68]

Somehow this distorted assessment of elections could be maintained even after a peaceful election was conducted. The threat of violence was so "pervasive," "dire," and unprecedented that there was not a single act of reported "violence" meant to stop the election, despite over 155 million Americans casting votes.

To better comprehend the bogus nature of left-wing hysterics over election "denialism" and "suppression," and the enduring double standards that dictate the debate, let's turn to the story of Stacey Abrams, one of the nation's leading peddlers of election conspiracy theories.

After losing the 2018 Georgia gubernatorial election, Abrams famously refused to concede to Republican Brian Kemp. She fully embraced every definition of "denialism" later adopted by Democrats to slam Republicans after 2020.

Did it hurt her career? No, it lifted her to national fame.

"We had this little election back in 2018 and despite the final tally and the inauguration and the situation we find ourselves in," Abrams said during a speech at the National Action Network convention, a group founded by famed antisemitic conspiracy theorist and presidential adviser Reverend Al Sharpton (more on him in Chapter 8) back in 1991, "I do have one very affirmative statement to make: we won."[69] In a speech at the Health Action Conference, the host noted that Abrams had lost "by less than 2 percent of 3.9 million votes," to which she replied, "We didn't lose. We just didn't get the governor's mansion."[70]

On at least thirty-three other occasions, Abrams has publicly denied that she lost the election.[71]

Rather than being ostracized, Abrams became a regular on cable news and late-night talk shows, spreading familiar fictions about elections. Oftentimes, Abrams was interviewed by the very same hosts who went on to righteously condemn GOP election denialism. Abrams made a cameo in the Season 4 finale of *Star Trek: Discovery*, playing *the president of earth*. Talk about wishcasting! I wonder if the "president of earth" gets to wear a tinfoil tiara.

When Abrams ran for governor again in 2022, Oprah Winfrey helped her fundraise, with scores of celebrities praising her. Few in the media ever confronted her about spreading misinformation and undermining the public's confidence in free and fair elections. At best, she was gingerly asked to elucidate her claims. CNN's Jake Tapper, who later made a big show of refusing to interview any Republican "who lies about American democracy in the 2020 election,"[72] not only regularly featured Abrams as a guest but also cohosted events where they both hawked their novels.[73]

Nearly every major Democrat in the nation supported Abrams's baseless claims. Hillary Clinton said that Abrams "would have won" Georgia's gubernatorial race "if she had a fair election." She went on to say that Abrams was "[d]eprived of the votes [she] otherwise would have gotten."[74] This story sounded conspicuously like the one Donald Trump told when losing the very same state.

President Biden maintained, without any evidence, that "voter suppression is the reason why Stacey Abrams isn't governor right now."[75] Cabinet member and former presidential candidate Pete Buttigieg said "racially motivated" suppression had tripped up Abrams, who "ought to be governor."[76]

Future 2024 presidential candidate Kamala Harris claimed that "without voter suppression, Stacey Abrams would be the governor of Georgia"—and added for good measure that Andrew Gillum, who lost his own gubernatorial race, would be "the governor of Florida."[77]

Obama attorney general Eric Holder ("I tend to think Stacey Abrams won that election"[78]), Cory Booker ("I think that Stacey Abrams's election is being stolen from her"[79]), Sherrod Brown ("if Stacey Abrams doesn't win in Georgia, they stole it"[80]), and Elizabeth Warren ("the evidence seems to suggest" the race was stolen from Abrams[81]) were happy to spread the myth that Abrams was cheated before and after the election.

By the way, Abrams lost the election by 54,723 votes. As of this writing the number of Georgians who were stopped from voting was zero.

The Abrams-led tale of suppression was so pervasive and successful in the age of Black Lives Matter that Democrats convinced major companies and institutions to take part. The 2021's Major League Baseball All-Star Game was taken away from Atlanta, and with it $100 million in revenues. This was the year the league planned to honor former Braves legend Hank Aaron. The game was moved to Denver.[82]

Before the MLB's decision, Abrams championed boycotts in a *USA Today* piece, referring to Georgia's bill as "Jim Crow in a suit"—though avoiding endorsing an outright boycott in Atlanta. She was later caught stealthily rewriting that editorial after publication—with the help of the newspaper—to avoid being blamed for driving revenue out of her state.[83]

USA Today wasn't alone. Sports news outlets like ESPN happily spread Abrams's propaganda, noting that the boycott was "in response to a new Georgia law that has civil rights groups concerned about its potential to restrict voting access for people of color."[84] Or in other words, in a show of solidarity with African Americans, a professional sports league stripped Atlanta, a city with a 51 percent black population (the largest black-majority metro area in America), of a major economically beneficial event and moved it to a ciy with a black population somewhere around 9 percent.

Way to go, Stacey. Show 'em how to be an antiracist.

Colorado's voting laws, incidentally, were in most ways about as stringent as Georgia's. Denver residents, like Atlanta residents, needed photo identification to register to vote. Like Colorado, Georgia allows voters without ID to use the last four digits of their Social Security number, a bank statement or utility bill, a paycheck, or any other government document with their name and address. All are perfectly reasonable ways to prove one's identity. Colorado also requires signature verification for mail-in ballots.

When Democrats again picked up the mantle of democracy's guardians after 2020, and Abrams decided to run for governor again, her contradictory positions became a bit too obvious. And so her tune changed. During her second campaign for governor in 2022—which, incidentally, she lost by an even bigger margin, despite Democrats winning an important Senate runoff in the state—Abrams told the fawning hosts of *The View* that "I have never denied that I lost. I don't live in the governor's mansion; I would have noticed."[85]

Well, Donald Trump did not live in the White House in 2022 either, yet no Democrat called him anything but an election denier.

Surprise. By the 2022 midterms, when the new Georgia law was already implemented, there were far more overall early votes cast than in any other midterm in the state's history. The record for absentee and mail-in votes was broken in Georgia. And well, basically, every record for voting was broken.

Buoyed by black voters in the Atlanta area, African American Raphael Warnock beat African American Herschel Walker in one of the most hotly contested Senate races in the nation.

That doesn't mean that the handy, unfalsifiable "voter suppression" claim, so instrumental in causing fear among voters around the country, was dropped. When asked about the historic turnout in the state, White House spokesperson Karine Jean-Pierre noted that "suppression" still existed, though she offered not a single instance of a voter being denied their right to cast a ballot. Senate Majority Leader Chuck Schumer told reporters, after praising election denier Stacey Abrams, "Despite the efforts of the Republican legislature to make it harder to vote, our people voted, people voted, Georgians voted. They said, 'We're not going to let these barriers stand in our way, even if we have to wait in line in the rain.'"[86]

Republicans were apparently empowered with the ability to make it rain—but only on Democrats.

WHITE SUPREMACISTS

I've covered extremism and violent ideologies around the world over my career. Have never come across a political force more nihilistic, dangerous & contemptible than today's Republicans. Nothing close.

—EDWARD LUCE[87]

I agree.

—GENERAL MICHAEL HAYDEN, FORMER CIA DIRECTOR[88]

In the spring of 2023, the president of the United States warned graduates at the historically black college of Howard University in Washington, DC, that "white supremacy" was the single "most dangerous terrorist threat" facing the nation.

"The harsh reality of racism has long torn us apart," Joe Biden declared, not for the first time. "It's a battle. It's never really over, but on the best days, enough of us have the guts and the hearts to stand up for the best in us, to choose love over hate."[89]

We don't know how many young African American graduates head out into the real world each year believing that white supremacists are threatening their lives or future. What we do know is that every major, "respectable" institution has been inundating them with alarmism for years:

"Homeland Security Dept. Affirms Threat of White Supremacy After Years of Prodding"—*New York Times*, October 1, 2019[90]

"The Grave Threats of White Supremacy and Far-Right Extremism"—*New York Times*, February 22, 2019[91]

"DHS draft document: White supremacists are greatest terror threat"—*Politico*, September 9, 2020[92]

"White supremacists remain deadliest US terror threat, Homeland Security report says"—CNN, October 4, 2020[93]

"White supremacist groups have carried out a majority of 'terrorist plots and attacks'"—*New York Times*, January 20, 2021[94]

"FBI chief warns violent 'domestic terrorism' growing in US"—Associated Press, March 2, 2021[95]

"U.S. report warns of threats from white supremacists, militias"—Reuters, March 17, 2021[96]

"Top law enforcement officials say the biggest domestic terror threat comes from white supremacists"—*New York Times*, June 15, 2021[97]

"FBI, DHS and social media firms like Meta, TikTok aren't adequately addressing threat of domestic extremists, Senate report says"—NBC News, November 16, 2022[98]

"Experts warn of increased risk of US terror attacks by rightwing 'lone wolf' actors"—*Guardian*, May 28, 2023[99]

"White Supremacy Is a Threat Because Republicans Use It"—
New York, May 19, 2023[100]

"Far-right violence a growing threat and law enforcement's top
domestic terrorism concern"—PBS, September 5, 2023[101]

"Exclusive: Donald Trump Followers Targeted by FBI as 2024
Election Nears"—*Newsweek*, October 4, 2023[102]

And on and on it goes.

"The federal government believes that the threat of violence and major civil disturbances around the 2024 U.S. presidential election is so
great that it has quietly created a new category of extremists that it seeks
to track and counter: Donald Trump's army of MAGA followers," the
Newsweek story reported, a year before the 2024 presidential elections.[103]

Even as leftist, antisemitic, pro-Hamas rioters were vandalizing
buildings and threatening Jews across the country, BlueAnon was
warning that the threat of "anti-government or anti-authority violent
extremism" of the right was "persistent, evolving, and deadly."

What Biden and BlueAnon would not want graduates at Howard or anywhere else to know was that the threat of *any* domestic terror event in
America—Islamic, white supremacist, black supremacist—was minuscule. It happens, but it is rare.

The Center for Strategic and International Studies found that the
average number of annual deaths caused by all American-based terrorists from the years 2014 and 2021 was thirty-one—or approximately
the same number of Americans who are killed by lightning every year.[104]

Though murder rates rose in major cities around the country during
COVID, there was no corresponding rise in right-wing political crimes,
or any political crimes, according to the widely cited Global Terrorism
Database (GTD).[105]

In 2022, the last year of FBI reporting as of this writing, there were twenty-one homicides linked to white supremacists in the United States. Even those crimes were rarely cut-and-dried cases that meet the definition of terrorism.

Add to this the fact that the classification of "domestic terrorism" is muddy at best, and often arbitrary and self-serving. An act of terrorism is meant to utilize violence and threats of violence to instill fear in the populace, and to intimidate them into embracing the political, religious, or ideological goals. It's a great stretch to consider most of the incidents that government refers to as terrorism to meet that standard in any traditional sense.

For example, though we still do not know the motivations of the Las Vegas shooter who in 2017 murdered fifty-nine people, the GTD categorized him as an "anti-government extremist."[106] Was the GTD privy to information that we were not? Of the thirty-two incidents of right-wing terrorism that same year, twelve featured perpetrators who were merely "suspected" of being on the right (mostly because they had white skin). Almost all the incidents were the work of single persons unaffiliated with any groups. Sometimes numerous incidents were committed by one terrorist, like a person setting fires to churches in the Midwest, a person calling in bomb threats in California, or the person with a pellet gun shooting Muslims in New York.

In other episodes, we are asked to treat patently insane people as if they had coherent political agendas. In one incident in San Juan, Puerto Rico—apparently a hotbed of Trumpist white supremacy—an incendiary device was thrown into a gay nightclub. As of this writing, no one has been arrested and the motive is still unknown. The GTD simply assumes it is terrorism. In 2020, "pro-Trump" terror acts included an assailant setting fire to "hay bales emblazoned with a pro-Biden message at Holiday Brook Farm along North Street in Dalton, Massachusetts, United States."

In one recent Department of Homeland Security investigation into domestic terrorism, we learned that "28 attacks in the United States [were] committed by WSEs [Violent *White Supremacist* Extremists], which collectively resulted in 51 fatalities" from 2000 to mid-2016.[107] The document, like many similar offerings, gave no citations or law enforcement documents to prove its contentions. My industrious colleague at *The Federalist*, John Davidson, however, dug into some of the cases and found that many, if not most, were perpetrated by white men with opaque ideological views—some of them obviously mentally ill.[108]

When New Jersey's Democratic governor Philip Murphy's administration published a widely covered report on the national scourge of "domestic terrorism," it took a very similar tack.[109] In one incident, an alleged member of the Aryan Nations shot a police officer, who was also white, after an argument about a traffic stop. In other incidents, a black man was burned by a white roommate at a home for the mentally impaired, and a white mentally unbalanced homeless man attacked a black man while yelling racial insults. When a thirty-three-year-old woman, along with five other skinheads, attacked a black man in Pennsylvania, the attack was counted as six separate incidents.[110] These are all tragic and ugly crimes that deserve to be condemned, but are they really part of a white supremacist terror network?

If the GTD was this meticulous about incidents perpetrated by anticapitalists throwing rocks through the windows or "pro-Palestinian" activists vandalizing Jewish places of worship, the number of left-wing terror incidents would dramatically spike.

Sometimes, it should be said, it is clear the paranoia over impending violence is just used as a pretext to quash speech.

In 2021, Attorney General Merrick Garland wrote a directive to the FBI and U.S. attorneys' offices directing both agencies to investigate parents who were protesting school boards over the teaching of critical race theory and mask mandates. The National School Boards Association (NSBA) penned a hysterical letter to the administration requesting federal assistance after threats against teachers, likening the actions of parents to "domestic terrorism."

Though the entire kerfuffle was predicated on some nasty emails from parents to board members, you would have thought a civil war had broken out in Virginia. "What it's like to be on the front lines of the school board culture war" was one NPR explainer on the matter.[111] These stories painted a picture of hordes of angry, irrational parents threatening innocent administrators and teachers. This was framing taken up by the entirety of BlueAnon. Soon the debate incorporated all the typical hobbyhorses.

"It's really important to remember why we are talking about school boards at all: because it's about white supremacy, and that's on the rise in the Republican Party," said CNN's then-senior legal analyst, Jeffrey Toobin, bundling a collection of BlueAnon obsessions. "The reason school boards are controversial is that some school boards have dared to teach that, you know, civil rights and African American rights have not been so great in this country over the centuries, like when we had slavery and when we had Jim Crow. And that has so outraged the Republican Party—telling the truth about race in America—that they feel the way to win elections and to win the governorship in Virginia is to demonize these school boards for daring to tell the truth about race in America. And that's really the core of what's going on here."[112]

None of this was even remotely true.

The protests had nothing to do with stopping schools from teaching about Jim Crow, or civil rights, or about African American history. They largely centered on COVID restrictions, sexually explicit books, books that celebrated gender dysphoria, and the trendy act of teaching children that the founding of the United States was undertaken to preserve slavery—a lie.

Now, you can disagree with the protesting parents. But there were few if any instances of anger spilling into illegality. Certainly not enough to call in the feds. There were already laws in place against "terroristic threats." Nor was this some kind of right-wing orgy of anger. The most passionate protests occurred in heavily Democratic Northern Virginia.

It is the God-given right of every parent to dress down a school board member. Now parents were worried that they would get a visit from the feds. This apprehension is created to chill speech.

We soon learned that the NSBA letter was a setup. Email correspondence later obtained by the nonpartisan Parents Defending Education found that the White House officials coordinated with the NSBA, urging it to detail "specific threats" of "domestic terror" so the federal government would have the pretext to investigate.[113]

In one version of the letter, the "threats" leveled by protesting parents asked the administration to call out the National Guard and military police to be deployed to certain school districts.

There was not a single act of violence against teachers in Virginia due to these protests. Even the *New York Times* acknowledged that "Garland did not detail any specific threats of violence or offer reasons for the increase in harassment and threats."[114] The only reason to get involved was to chill speech and intimidate parents. The NSBA apologized for writing the letter. The Biden administration, on the other hand, refused to dissolve the "task force" investigating parents. It simply moved on to the next conspiracy.

As we've seen, the paranoiac rhetoric aimed at Donald Trump and his supporters is beyond normal political hyperbole. And if you keep telling people that their political opponents are Nazis at some point they're going to start believing you. In July of 2024, Donald Trump was shot in the ear in an attempted assassination during a campaign rally. This came a few years after U.S. House Majority Whip Steve Scalise was shot in Alexandria by a progressive named James Hodgkinson, who tried to eliminate the entire GOP House conference in a Congressional baseball game. There was also the attempted assassination of Justice Brett Kavanaugh—not to mention Antifa, pro-Hamas, and BLM riots, which were stoked by conspiracies and lies mentioned in this book.

Most people were probably impressed by the picture of Trump, face streaked with blood, pumped fist in front of a American flag. But the morning after Trump was nearly murdered by an assassin's bullet in Butler, Pennsylvania, the top political adviser to Democratic Party mega-donor Reid Hoffman sent an email to journalists wondering why "NOT ONE NEWSPAPER OR OPINION LEADER IN AMERICA IS WILLING TO OPENLY CONSIDER THE POSSIBILITY THAT TRUMP AND PUTIN STAGED THIS ON PURPOSE."[115]

Dmitri Mehlhorn implored reporters to consider the "possibility—which feels horrific and alien and absurd in America but is quite common globally— . . . that this 'shooting' was encouraged and maybe even staged so Trump could get the photos and benefit from the backlash."

Mehlhorn wasn't alone. A Morning Consult poll found that a third of Democrats believed the assassination might have been staged, and the bullet fired by Thomas Crooks, which missed killing the former president by millimeters, was never intended to murder him.[116] Indeed, it was horrific to see social media explode with claims the attempt was "staged" and a "false flag." These garnered tens of millions of likes, retweets, and views from leftists. Plenty of people who should know better participated. Mehlhorn's boss, the founder of LinkedIn, isn't some unhinged commenter on Reddit; he is worth $2.5 billion. He pledged $100 million to fund efforts to oppose President Trump in 2020 and was on the same path in 2024.[117]

Perhaps Mehlhorn felt comfortable posing conspiratorial questions to reporters because, as we have seen, they have been quite receptive in the past. Mehlhorn, for example, padded his plea to journalists with a conspiratorial mainstay—theorizing that the assassination staging was a "classic Russian tactic" and urging them to consider "how often Putin and his allies run this play." (Mehlhorn apologized for his remarks after they were made public.)

As noted earlier in this book, the Russian collusion conspiracy theory is the most successful and consequential in American history, conceived by a major political party and spread by establishment media. In 2024, Nancy Pelosi was still on MSNBC claiming that Putin probably "had" something "financial" on Trump.

But the left's unhinged paranoia about Trump has been widespread and normalized. In an implicit admission of the environment the hyper-hyperbole had created, MSNBC did not air "Morning Joe" the morning after the assassination, instead going with breaking news coverage of the attempted assassination of the former president. CNN reported that executives were nervous about what would be said on a show that had been spreading ridiculous conspiracy theories for years.[118] It was a tacit admission that the station was employing BlueAnon devotees.

HANDS UP, DON'T SHOOT

Our country should be more fearful of white
men across the country because they are actually
causing most of the deaths within this country.
—ILHAN OMAR[119]

In the summer of 2014, Darren Wilson, a white police officer in Ferguson, Missouri, shot and killed an eighteen-year-old black man named Michael Brown. Because of long-simmering tensions between local law enforcement and citizens, who alleged that cops had regularly exhibited brutish and racist behavior, the shooting sparked angry protests.

Though Wilson claimed to have acted in self-defense after Brown attacked him, rumors began circulating among the protesters that cops had executed the young man, who was merely walking down the street minding his own business, even after he raised his hands to surrender and mouthed the words "Don't shoot." The phrase and the gesture were quickly taken up by locals as a representation of police brutality against African Americans.

"Hands Up, Don't Shoot" is a visceral and powerful protest slogan. It has a resonance that's difficult to ignore. It encapsulates the evil of police brutality, and the hold that the powerful have over the powerless. And it would become a national symbol of the alleged systemic police racism that was sweeping the nation. Media personalities, Democratic politicians, and left-wing leaders all took up the phrase. At places like CNN, alleged journalists like Margaret Hoover, Sally Kohn, Sunny Hostin, and Mel Robbins put their hands up on live television in a show of solidarity with the cause.

The only problem was that the "hands up, don't shoot" moment never happened. It was merely another example of BlueAnon ginning up politically advantageous conspiracies to fuel anger and exacerbate divisions.

Even if one believed Wilson should not have used lethal force in the shooting of Brown, there had never been any evidence that the officer acted with any racial animus. Again, it was merely assumed because of his skin color. More importantly, the contention that Wilson shot Brown after the latter raised his hands to submit, much less used the words "don't shoot," wasn't based on any established evidence. Quite the contrary.

When video emerged of Brown stealing cigars from a local convenience store, proving he was not merely an innocent man minding his own business, a lawyer for the family argued that the same cops who had "assassinated him" were now "trying to assassinate his character." Al Sharpton, adviser to the Brown family, convinced left-wingers that the cops were waging a "smear campaign."

According to an investigation by Barack Obama's Justice Department, however, Wilson's account was corroborated by forensic and witness testimony. Consequently, he was cleared of any civil rights violations. The feds' report found that Brown reached into Wilson's police vehicle and grabbed him by the neck, and then lunged toward the officer before he was shot. I'm sorry, it doesn't matter what color you are, attacking a cop will never end well.

The Justice Department found that although a few individuals asserted Brown held up his hands, their accounts were "inconsistent with the physical and forensic evidence." Others, the Justice Department stated, had altered their stories to be "materially inconsistent with that witness's own prior statements with no explanation, credible [or] otherwise, as to why those accounts changed over time."

Nevertheless, to this day, the "hands up, don't shoot" gesture is a mainstay at protests over police brutality. On the fifth anniversary of the shooting in 2019, Democratic presidential candidates Elizabeth Warren and Kamala Harris falsely claimed that Brown was "murdered" by police. Every candidate running for the nomination at the time— Tim Ryan, Cory Booker, Beto O'Rourke, Kirsten Gillibrand, Bernie Sanders, and Bill de Blasio—sent out remembrances either strongly intimating or outright stating falsehoods regarding the case.

During the Black Lives Matter protests, Brown's name was featured prominently in speeches and signs and embedded in the argument that black men are needlessly massacred by racist police. When, in 2022, X owner Elon Musk tweeted that the mantra was "made up," CNN's Don Lemon "fact-checked" his statement, noting that "some said" Brown was trying to surrender when killed by Wilson. "So remember, 'Hands up, don't shoot' after Ferguson became a nationwide protest symbol for police mistreatment of minorities," Lemon explained. "It was about more than the shooting of Michael Brown. It was about the pattern of police shootings and brutality in this country."[120]

A poetic truth.

There is no arguing with the fact that bigots still exist. The claim that black men are being systemically "hunted" by white cops or that there is a "pattern" of this behavior is a myth to fuel anger in black communities.

Many of the most famous cases of police brutality against black Americans have no proven racial component—other than the left's unfalsifiable contention that white people are inherently disposed to hurting other people or ethnicities.

When white Wisconsin police officer Rusten Sheskey shot twenty-nine-year-old black man Jacob Blake in the summer of 2020, it immediately blew up into another instance of racial injustice. The American Civil Liberties Union posted "Justice for Jacob Blake" pages, the media framed the incident in a long line of murders against unarmed black men, and pundits wondered if the nation could ever shed systemic racism. Then-candidate Joe Biden promised to launch an investigation into the shooting if he became president, and then-senator Kamala Harris demanded that people be "held accountable."[121] Riots broke out in cities like Kenosha, Wisconsin.

As it turned out, Sheskey had responded to a 911 call from the mother of Blake's children. Blake himself had an arrest warrant out for numerous charges, including third-degree sexual assault. When police attempted to arrest Blake, he went to his car and grabbed a knife.[122] (Blake claimed he had dropped his knife and was just picking it back up.) After an investigation by the Biden Justice Department, no charges were filed against Sheskey.

It has gotten so bad that even cases where it is indisputable that the shooting was necessary are now framed as racially motivated. After a twenty-six-year-old man named Dexter Reed was tragically killed after being stopped by cops for a seat belt violation in Chicago in April 2024, the *entire* media ran stories about the same themes. "Deadly Chicago traffic stop where police fired 96 shots raises serious questions about use of force," the Associated Press headline read. CNN, the *Washington Post*, and the *New York Times* all ran a picture of Reed in his high school graduation cap and gown.[123] A person would typically have to read deep into the story to learn that Reed had pulled a gun and fired on officers first.

Never let facts get in the way of a good narrative.

• • • • •

Even the most infamous incident of police abuse, the killing of George Floyd, has never been convincingly tied to racism. When Floyd died under the knee of Minneapolis police officer Derek Chauvin, it ignited protests (and riots) across the nation. We were told racial reckoning had arrived. Minnesota governor Tim Walz decried the presence of "fundamental, institutional racism."[124] Barack Obama said racist acts had become "tragically, painfully, maddeningly 'normal.'"[125]

Nearly everyone in the political world said something along those lines. Corporations donated billions to Black Lives Matter and other "antiracist" movements. Virtually every leader and politician felt compelled to say something about the scourge of systemic violence against black men. Yet there has never been any evidence presented, not by anyone in the media nor by anyone at Chauvin's trial, that he was a racist or that his actions were motivated by bigotry. It was merely assumed.

The results were the culmination of decades of marginal racism compounded by a mythology about cops. In 2020, the Skeptic Research Center found that nearly half of liberals surveyed estimated that approximately 1,000 to 10,000 unarmed black men were killed every year by cops. Twenty percent of conservatives agreed with this estimate.[126] Over 80 percent of liberals believed that 100 unarmed black men are killed every year by cops. Another 66 percent of moderates and 54 percent of conservatives did as well.[127]

According to a database compiled by Mapping Police Violence, the actual number of black men killed by the police that year was 27—almost all of them in incidents where police officers were cleared of wrongdoing.

In truth, police officers fatally shoot about 1,000 civilians per year, the vast majority inarguably dangerous. As the Manhattan Institute has found, unarmed victims in fatal police shootings comprise under

0.5 percent of the total. Of the 375 million contacts that police officers have with civilians each year, few result in any violence. Black Americans account for about 23 percent of them, though the percentage of interactions between black civilians and cops is far higher.[128]

Again, it is inarguable that there are bigoted and abusive cops out there. There are cases of bad behavior every year. But we are far away from the racist dystopia that BlueAnon keeps assuring us is real.

Still, there is little that can't be chalked up to racism these days.

After a railroad accident in Ohio, Secretary of Transportation Pete Buttigieg told Al Sharpton that there was a crisis "when it comes to roadway fatalities in America. We lose about 40,000 people every year. It's a level that's comparable to gun violence. And we see a lot of racial disparities—black and brown, tribal citizens, and rural residents are much more likely to lose their lives whether it is in a car or as a pedestrian being hit by the car." Not only trains and cars target minorities, Buttigieg pointed out, but roads were "designed and built" to create racial disparities.[129]

Two dozen Democrats immediately signed a letter to call for reform of "racist traffic enforcement" on the nation's roadways.[130]

When race guru and progressive favorite Ibram X. Kendi saw a picture of Justice Amy Coney Barrett's adopted Haitian children, he did not see a loving family, but rather noted that some "White colonizers 'adopted' Black children. They 'civilized' these 'savage' children in the 'superior' ways of White people, while using them as props in their lifelong pictures of denial, while cutting the biological parents of these children out of the picture of humanity."[131]

When Black Lives Matter was at its height, a rope was found hanging in the garage stall of black NASCAR driver Bubba Wallace. It was a national story. There was much consternation among sports media and Americans alike. Someone, it was clear, left a noose in the Wallaces' garage. The FBI even opened an investigation. It found that the rope was a garage door pull that had been in that same spot since 2019.

When you have been pushed to see everything through the prism of race and identity, you can get pretty paranoid.

CONSERVATIVES FOR SLAVERY

At a time when there are those who seek to ban books and bury history, I'll be clear: darkness and denialism can hide much, but they erase nothing. We should learn everything: the good, bad, and truth of who we are. That's what great nations do, and we are a great nation.

—JOE BIDEN[132]

In a 2023 speech to black sorority Delta Sigma Theta, soon-to-be 2024 presidential candidate Kamala Harris told an audience that Republicans were teaching students that American slaves had benefited from bondage.

"Just yesterday in the state of Florida," the vice president explained, speaking about a new Florida history curriculum, "they decided middle school students will be taught that enslaved people benefited from slavery. They insult us in an attempt to gaslight us, and we will not stand for it." To this day, the vice president continues to make this claim.[133]

This fabrication—that conservatives believed slavery provided a net good for black Americans—quickly ossified as truth in leftist circles, as these kinds of lurid contentions often do. Josh Marshall, the editor of Talking Points Memo, a breeding ground for biased reporters who end up in cushy mainstream media jobs, noted they were "recasting slavery as a two-century vocational program."[134] The *Washington Post*'s Philip Bump said the GOP thought slavery was "a line item for their résumés."[135] Whoopi Goldberg took it a bit further and accused

Florida governor Ron DeSantis of trying to *bring back slavery*: "It's our American history because you need to know so we don't repeat it, and here you come, DeSantis, trying to repeat it! . . . You're a disgrace!"[136]

The falsehood, born of a single line in Florida's 2023 social studies course, was a statement of an objective fact. Some slaves had "developed skills which, in some instances, could be applied for their personal benefit."[137] Yet anyone who spent ten minutes perusing the Florida curriculum would immediately see that Harris's claim was ridiculous.

When *National Review* writer Charlie Cooke read the lesson plan, he noted 191 instances in which slavery was mentioned and discussed in highly negative terms. Because of course it was.

Remarks covered the horrible "living conditions of slaves in British North American colonies, the Caribbean, Central America and South America, including infant mortality rates"; "the harsh conditions and their consequences," of "undernourishment, climate conditions, infant and child mortality rates of the enslaved vs. the free"; "the harsh conditions in the Caribbean plantations (i.e., poor nutrition, rigorous labor, disease)"; the "overwhelming death rates"; "the ramifications of prejudice, racism and stereotyping on individual freedoms"; and "the struggles faced by African American women in the 19th century as it relates to issues of suffrage, business and access to education"; and so on.[138]

Does that sound like a curriculum arguing that slavery was a beneficial institution?[139]

Likewise, William B. Allen, a former chairman of the U.S. Commission on Civil Rights and cowriter of the Florida curriculum, pointed out that Frederick Douglass and Booker T. Washington had acquired skills "under adverse circumstances, or who came with skills that enabled them to not only survive adverse circumstances, but also to go on to further accomplishments."[140]

There was wide agreement on this point. So wide, it turned out, that the Advanced Placement (AP) African American studies curriculum released by the College Board—the one that Harris and other Democrats praised—agreed. It too argued that slaves learned "specialized trades" during bondage and parlayed "these skills to provide for themselves and others" once free.[141]

In the AP syllabus on "Slavery, Labor, and American Law," the lesson tells kids that slaves learned to become "painters, carpenters, tailors, musicians, and healers" and subsequently "used these skills to provide for themselves and others."[142] Mentioning objective historical facts does nothing to diminish the odiousness of the slavery trade.

The Florida slavery lie was unleashed in conjunction with a batch of stories meant to create the impression that the American right was trying to erase the history of slavery, and even defend it.

"'Slavery Was Wrong' and 5 Other Things Some Educators Won't Teach Anymore"[143] was one *Washington Post* piece (it turned out that a progressive administrator was either confused or purposely misread the law). *Education Week* ran a piece headlined "Here's the Long List of Topics Republicans Want Banned from the Classroom,"[144] in which we learn that "legislation is aimed at stifling conversation about racism and oppression."

"State GOP Lawmakers Try to Limit Teaching About Race, Racism," read a more tempered Associated Press headline.[145] In the story, we learn that Oklahoma teachers would be prohibited from teaching that certain people are "inherently racist or oppressive, whether consciously or unconsciously." Which is to say that they would be prohibited from teaching the wholly unscientific, racist ideological view that you are born a bigot.

Other bills that BlueAnon complained about would also seek to rectify historical myths. One Virginia bill would have prevented teachers from saying that "market-based economics is inherently racist," while several Mississippi bills would ban teaching that "the concepts of capitalism, free markets, or working for a private party in exchange for wages are racist and sexist."[146]

Market capitalism is not inherently racist, but the opposite. It is a system that makes no racial or gender or ethnic distinctions. There is no reason that parents functioning in a democracy should allow a government school to indoctrinate children with ideological twaddle. But BlueAnon cast these Republican bills as examples of white racism, rather than a reaction to decade-long aggressive indoctrination efforts of the left in K–12 teaching.

When Democrats claim that Republican legislatures stop teaching slavery or racism, they mean that they stop the teaching of critical race theory and the pseudohistory of the "1619 Project," a book and curriculum written by Nikole Hannah-Jones, which now-infamously claimed that during the American Revolution, "one of the primary reasons the colonists decided to declare their independence from Britain was because they wanted to protect the institution of slavery."[147]

Hannah-Jones, who is not a historian, wrote this book despite being warned by the historians who reviewed the original essay that the core contention was unsupportable by facts. It is an author's prerogative to write whatever she likes, but it is not the prerogative of taxpayer-funded schools to teach fantasies to children.

Why would Democrats believe that conservatives did not want to teach their kids about slavery? One can only assume because they are racists pining for the good old days of human bondage. And millions of leftists now walk around believing that Republican parents did not want their kids to believe that racism was bad.

It is true that in an effort to reclaim educational systems from anti-American, historically unsound, leftist curriculums, Red States began passing laws to ban public schools from teaching critical race theory (CRT) and fake history and collective guilt that puts the color of one's skin at the center of American life—or, in other words, racialist ideas that contend that white Americans are inherently, genetically, and temperamentally racist.

Not only did they not ban the history of slavery and racism, but most of the places that had been accused of failing to teach kids about these topics actually *mandated* they be taught. In Texas, one of the states that removed CRT from its lesson plans, a law mandated that students learn "the history of white supremacy, including but not limited to the institution of slavery, the eugenics movement, and the Ku Klux Klan, and the ways in which it is morally wrong."

But this makes no difference to the left, because facts and context don't matter to conspiracy theorists.

CULTURE OF PARANOIA

When a person can be married in the morning and thrown out of a restaurant for being gay in the afternoon, something is fundamentally wrong with this country. And that still exists.
—JOE BIDEN

Below are a smattering of headlines that appeared on March 8, 2022:

Florida Just Passed the "Don't Say Gay" Bill—*Time*[1]

Florida Lawmakers Pass "Don't Say Gay"—ABC News[2]

Florida House Passes "Don't Say Gay" Bill—NBC News[3]

Florida House Passes Controversial "Don't Say Gay" Bill—CBS News[4]

"Don't Say Gay" Bill Passes in the Florida House—NPR[5]

The only problem with all of them was that "Don't Say Gay" is not real. It does not exist. It never did. There is no such law. There is no such diktat. There is no such effort.

In the winter of 2022, the Florida Senate passed the Parental Rights in Education Act, barring state educators from offering "classroom instruction" on sexual orientation, gender identity, or sex-related issues in classrooms to prepubescent kids in kindergarten through third grade.[6] One could certainly disagree with the intent of the policy if they chose, but it was neither particularly radical nor stunning. The law did not make it illegal to say gay or use the word *gay* or talk about being gay. The media's nickname for the bill was an intentionally deceptive moniker concocted to create suspicion and mislead national voters about the law and about their worldview.

Why did BlueAnon target Florida? Because, at the time, Ron DeSantis was a popular governor, was a GOP presidential prospect. And so BlueAnon worked to convince millions of Americans that anyone who spoke about being gay in Florida could be fired. As of this writing, not a single person has been fired in Florida for merely uttering the word *gay* or talking about being gay or being gay. And it is exceedingly unlikely that anyone ever will be.

What the law does is prohibit public school educators from teaching young kids about sexuality against the will of parents. But within a short time, the claim that it was illegal to utter the word *gay* in Florida schools was firmly embedded in political debate as a fact. Every major Democratic Party leader in the nation casually dropped the claim as fact in interviews and speeches. Protesters regularly held up signs protesting this imaginary restriction.

On *The View*, the top daytime program in the country, cohost Ana Navarro bragged about leaning out the window of her car yelling "We say gay!" whenever she was near Florida's Republican governor Ron DeSantis or his supporters—acting as if she were a refusenik in the Soviet Union. The credulous audience cheered her on.[7]

While BlueAnon depicted Florida as a Gileadian enclave where gay Americans were living in the shadows, voters saw it differently.

When plainly asked about the provisions in the bill, they were all quite popular. *Politico*/Morning Consult somewhat accurately described the law in a poll and found that a majority of Florida Democrats supported it.[8] When Public Opinion Strategies used the language featured in the bill itself to poll Floridians, it found strong support across all party lines and all subsets (including 55–29 percent support among *Democrats*, 58–26 percent among independents, and 67–24 percent among parents).[9]

Leaving the responsibility of explaining gender dysphoria to the parents of first graders was still a popular position among Americans. At the very least, the bill was no more controversial than any other partisan issue. As it stands, any Florida parents interested in teaching their six-year-olds that they are imbued with a metaphysical power to dismiss the objective realities of biology are free to do so. Parents whose values don't comport with that worldview, however, are now on equal footing.

But the contemporary left's inability or refusal to debate issues compels them to create an alternative reality, a conspiracy theory to inspire fear and outrage. Thus "Don't Say Gay."

Though exceptionally little of substance changed in the lives of the average Floridians—if anything, the parental rights bill was a proactive measure—for the first time in history, the Human Rights Campaign, the largest gay "rights" organization in the country, declared a "'State of Emergency' for LGBTQ+ Americans travelling or moving in Florida."[10] The group was joined by other left-wing organizations—the once-respected NAACP, the League of United Latin American Citizens, the Florida Immigrant Coalition, and Equality Florida—all cautioning gay Americans about traveling or relocating to the Sunshine State. Why? Because it could be "dangerous."

Which was, of course, completely irrational.

The legacy media did its best to track down a few dozen gay Floridians who professed they were moving from the state to create an impression that a mass exodus was underway. "LGBTQ+ people are leaving Florida. They blame the Legislature," the *Tampa Bay Times* reported.[11] "Florida anti-LGBTQ laws prompt some families to flee state," the *Washington Post* reported.[12] "LGBT+ people are fleeing Florida in 'mass migration' over 'Don't Say Gay' law."[13] "As conservative states target trans rights, a Florida teen flees for a better life,"[14] said NPR.

As you can tell, "fleeing"—as in running away from a place or situation of danger—was the key word. It was another imaginary exodus.

There was no genuine evidence that a significant number of gay Floridians had moved. From July 2021 to July 2022, during the "Don't Say Gay" debate and passage of the bill, more than 400,000 people moved to Florida, an increase of over 180,000 from the previous year.[15] Surely many gay people were among the newcomers. There was no evidence that there was a net loss of gay citizens. There are numerous vibrant gay neighborhoods across Florida.

Also, Florida remained the number one tourist destination in the country in 2022 and 2023.[16] In the summer of 2023, in fact, we learned from NBC News that "tens of thousands of LGBTQ+ people flock to Florida for Gay Days festival," which was weird, considering not only that the state was dangerous for gay Americans, but you couldn't even "say gay."[17]

Other scary laws alleged torch-carrying homophobic mobs are targeting Americans with include "bathroom bans" (sex-appropriate bathrooms in public schools); "sports participation bans" (bans on allowing biological men to compete with women); "anti-drag bans" (the banning of sexualized drag frag shows in front of children—most often in publicly funded libraries); "pronoun refusal laws" (barring teachers from calling kids by the wrong biological pronoun—usually against the wishes, or unbeknownst to parents); and "LGBT erasure laws," which as best I can tell mean to "dismiss or downplay" the significance of gay Americans—"Queer history."

Ever since social conservatives and others started pushing back against the growing trend of children "identifying" as something other than their "assigned" biological sex—a debate that often revolved around biological boys playing in girls' sports or sharing locker rooms and bathrooms with the opposite sex—BlueAnon has convinced trans people they are in constant mortal danger.

On 2023's "Transgender Day of Remembrance"—grossly named to elicit memories of the Holocaust—White House press secretary Karine Jean-Pierre noted that twenty-six transgender Americans were killed in 2022. "Year after year, we see that these victims are disproportionately black women and women of color."

Every one of these deaths is a tragedy, but the majority of these twenty-six incidents that year—compiled by Human Rights Campaign's list—had nothing to do with hate or transgenderism. One incident was a murder-suicide.[18] Some were related to drug crimes and prostitution. In some instances, it was mental illness. In one case a security guard killed a transgender person who was defending himself after being violently attacked.[19]

In 2020, there was a record-high 266 hate crimes aimed at transgender people and 44 murders. As the journalist Dennis Kneale noted, that works out "to a murder rate for trans people of just 2.66 people per 100,000 transgender people. The murder rate in the general population is almost three times as high—6.52 people per 100,000."[20]

Gay and trans Americans are as safe as any other group. If only they were safe from disinformation.

Yet, Joe Biden would go as far as arguing that troubled teenagers "need" mastectomies, facial surgery, and genital removal to feel "loved."[21] Biden is, of course, right that Americans should be free from threats of violence. That includes kids who are now subjected to abuse at the hands of people who have adopted this trendy quackery.

BOOK BANS

Did you ever think we'd be talking about banning
books in America? Banning history? I'm serious.
—JOE BIDEN[22]

As was often the case, Joe Biden was not being serious. He was being absurd. Books are banned in America in the same way a person can't say the word *gay* in Florida.

Just as every item on the "banned" book display table at your local Barnes & Noble is already a massive (sometimes generational) bestseller, BlueAnon's "banned" book claim is a racket. It allows leftists to feign indignation over the alleged censoriousness of Republicans who don't want their kids reading racist identitarian pseudohistories, and who think books written for children depicting oral sex, rape, violence, and gender dysphoria don't belong in schools and libraries.

Book ban is merely a BlueAnon euphemism for the curating of a library in a way that upsets left-wing activists. Yet major media now regularly assert, as indisputable fact, that "book bans" are in place. Millions of left-wing Americans almost certainly believe that conservatives are the modern-day equivalent of book burners. The hysterical allegation is now also embedded in the Democrats' daily rhetoric.

PEN America's Index of School Book Bans claims there are nearly 1,500 "instances of book banning in schools, affecting 874 different titles" during the first half of the 2023 school year. The organization stresses that locals are "banning" books "typically" written by "female, black, gay, and transgender authors."[23] Yes, many of the books on the list feature sexually explicit scenes—and many have minority and gay characters, because progressives have decided to teach kids to measure themselves by their immutable physical characteristics, sexual choices, and "gender expression," rather than achievements and deeds. That doesn't make the books good reading for kids.

For another thing, "book bans," though fake, are also rare. When the writer Micah Mattix crunched the numbers, he found that of the 117,341 libraries in the U.S., 76,807 were elementary and secondary school libraries. Those libraries saw 1,269 unique challenges in 2022. Some books were challenged multiple times. In other words, less than 1 percent of children's libraries in the United States saw even a single challenge to any book.[24]

More importantly, not one book on PEN's list is very difficult to obtain. Parents don't even need to leave their homes to buy them. They can order any of the titles in mere minutes and have them delivered to their front door in days or less.

There are no "banned books." There are, however, cultural imperialists, ideologues, cowardly politicians, and creepy activists trying to force books about sexuality onto children against the will of moms and dads.

"Plot twist: Activists Skirt Book Bans with Guerrilla Giveaways and Pop-Up Libraries" was a recent fun NPR piece exploring the ways leftists are "fighting back" against "book bans."[25] In the piece, the reader learns that with "a record number of book bans" on the horizon, "some activists are finding creative ways to make banned books available to young readers anyway."

What they mean by "creative ways" is: "activists" are *buying* the books at local stores, where an endless supply exists—because no book is banned by the state—and then handing them to other people's children against the wishes of parents.

That's not so much "creative" as it is exceptionally inappropriate. NPR makes it sound as if these activists were risking their lives trading samizdat only one step ahead of the Soviet secret police. Any dope with a car, a bus pass, a bicycle, legs, or an internet connection can hand some impressionable kid soft-core porn.

Rest assured, if conservative activists set up "pop-up" libraries around the corner from schools in progressive districts and handed out *Adventures of Huckleberry Finn* and books celebrating the Second Amendment or the superiority of traditional families, NPR would not applaud the circumvention of "bans."

This imaginary problem got so bad that the Biden administration even appointed an "anti–book ban coordinator" as part of new LGBTQ protections. The existence of such "bans," contended White House domestic policy adviser Neera Tanden, "erodes our democracy" and "removes vital resources for student learning, and can contribute to stigma and isolation."[26]

Okay, let's take one of the most famous "banned books," *Lawn Boy*. It describes ten-year-old boys performing oral sex on each other. "'What if I told you I touched another guy's d-ck?' I said. . . . 'I was ten years old, but it's true. I put Doug Goble's d-ck in my mouth. . . .'" and so on. The *School Library Journal* praised *Lawn Boy* as an exploration of "race, sexual identity, and the crushing weight of American capitalism."[27]

Is this really a *vital* resource for kids? Or is it okay to not include that book in a school library?

It doesn't have to be *Lawn Boy*, though. It could be the graphic "novel" *Gender Queer*, banned by the Cherry Creek School District in Colorado, according to PEN. It features passages like "I got off once while driving just by rubbing the front of my jeans and imagining getting a blow job."[28] Other "banned books," like *It Feels So Good to Be Yourself*, are meant to normalize trendy pseudoscientific jargon and ideas among kindergartners and first graders, filling their heads with terms like *nonbinary*, *gender-fluid*, and *gender-expansive*.

I don't know what *gender expansive* means, but it's hard to imagine anything as expansive as the left's acceptance of new sexual mores.

If reactionary parents won't teach kids these progressive concepts, someone else has got to. And that's bad enough. Democrats understandably have little interest in explaining to voters why middle schoolers need to have access to the vulgar, graphic sexual scenes of incest and child rape featured in Sapphire's "banned" novel *Push*, for example. They would rather peddle a conspiracy about "banned" books.

One of the central ideas behind the development of public schools was that they would break down ethnic, social, and class barriers and build shared patriotic virtues and civic understanding. Instead, they are often used to trap kids and then indoctrinate them with leftist cultural attitudes. Those who resist are branded fascists.

Surely not every book removed from libraries is pornography or badly written or useless. Perhaps *Push* tells the story of an abused girl using appropriately realistic yet horrifying words. Even so, the topic of brutal sexual violence isn't morally or educationally tantamount to a math lesson. Simply because parents, not teachers or Joe Biden, decide when, how, or if their kids read about it does not make them societal "book banners."

Why do conservatives need to "ban" books? It's pretty simple. The left-wing unions who run virtually every major school district in the nation already dictate curriculums. It is no conspiracy that parents can only initiate change by voting for officials who will implement standards that administrators and teachers refuse. That's the point of elections. The unstated fact is that the contemporary left doesn't believe that parents have any say in which state-run school their children attend, or what they are taught in them.

Who's the authoritarian, again?

PANIC MONGERS

We cannot stand up for hate. We cannot stand next to hate.
—*JEOPARDY!* CONTESTANT

On the night of April 27, 2021, social media erupted in a panic after a nondescript white middle-aged *Jeopardy!* contestant named Kelly

Donohue, winner of $80,601, flashed a gesture using three fingers of his right hand.

To most unsuspecting viewers, the signal probably seemed innocuous—if it went noticed at all—but to thousands of newly minted white supremacist chasers, including notable "resistance" figures with millions of followers on social media, it was obvious that Donohue was signaling his racist buddies across the country.

By the next day, the gesture had become national news. "'Jeopardy!' Winner Accused of Flashing White Power Symbol," the *New York Post* reported.[29] "Jeopardy Should Probably Speak Up About Contestant's Controversial Gesture," Vice suggested.[30] "'Jeopardy!' Slammed for Winner's Alleged White Power Hand Gesture," noted the *Hollywood Reporter*.[31] And so on.

A histrionic letter signed by nearly *six hundred* former *Jeopardy!* contestants said, "We cannot stand onstage with something that looks like hate."[32] The signees demanded to know why *Jeopardy!* producers even allowed such a reprehensible hand signal to be aired in the first place. "Based on the evidence we've seen being bandied about elsewhere, there is a real possibility he was giving either a white power or a Three Percenter hand gesture," a former contestant told thousands of members of a popular *Jeopardy!* Facebook group. "We can't know his intent," they went on; "we're not here to provide safe harbor for white supremacists."

Now, in all honesty, though I consider myself somewhat savvy on domestic political issues, I had never recalled running across the term *Three Percenter* until writing this book—and I suspect most of you haven't until reading it. Was it a splinter faction of the QAnon movement? Was it a racist paramilitary organization? What did the term mean?

My guess is that somewhere in the neighborhood of .00003 percent of Americans subscribe to this confusing ideological position. Yet apparently the group is well-known to BlueAnonists, who have the equivalent of PhDs in right-wing extremist studies. The folks at the Southern Poverty Law Center (SPLC), the nation's leading scare-mongers on fringe movements, helpfully define Three Percenterism as a subracist ideological disposition "that falls within the larger anti-government militia movement."[33] The Three Percenters maintain that only 3 percent of American colonists fought against the British during the American Revolution, "a claim that has never been proven," the folks at SPLC helpfully note.[34]

In any event, all the hand-wringing was for naught. There was no evidence that Donohue, who worked at a bank in Winthrop, Massa-chusetts, was any kind of white supremacist or racist or even a right-winger, for that matter. In two statements, the "horrified" Donohue profusely apologized for any misunderstanding. Though a white man himself, he abhorred white supremacy, as one does. After his first vic-tory, Donohue waved one finger to his family and friends. After the second one, two. And the next night, three fingers. The signal had as much to do with white supremacy as the rest of the panic over white supremacy—which is to say, nothing.

Yet the contemporary left believes not only that white supremacism is widespread enough to be on the brink of a takeover, but also that its adherents are secretly signaling each other on national television. In one YouGov poll, 76 percent of Democrats believed "white suprem-acy" is a "a very serious problem" in the country.[35]

To most of us, the "okay" hand gesture is a way of indicating that "all is well." Since the anxiety-stricken environment of the Trump age, it has become a chilling sign of the restive forces of revolution. The Anti-Defamation League, a left-wing advocacy group masquerading as a civil rights organization, features the okay sign on its "Hate on Dis-play" database. The group explains that in some corners of the inter-net the index-finger-to-thumb sign has become associated with white supremacy and the far right.

Oren Segal, director of the ADL's Center on Extremism, said "it can now carry a nefarious message." If Brett Kavanaugh is a stealth white-power candidate for the Supreme Court, why would someone on his side go out of her way to advertise that fact on national television?

There is no rest for weary groups chasing down the latest racist hand signals. In 2019, Army cadets and Navy midshipmen flashed something resembling an okay hand symbol during the pregame of a nationally broadcasted ESPN college football game. The cadets were immediately vilified by numerous pundits. "White power symbols. From Army cadets. Knowing they are on live television," Bleacher Report's Mike Freeman said. "These guys should be kicked out immediately."[36]

Rather than surrender to the mob and summarily eject cadets from school for flashing a hand signal, both the United States Military Academy at West Point and the United States Naval Academy launched investigations into the incident and reached the conclusion that the young men were playing a "sophomoric" contest known as "the circle game," which had zero to do with race or politics.[37]

The incident was reminiscent of one that involved a Harvard Law School graduate and mother of three named Zina Bash, who had volunteered to help Supreme Court nominee Kavanaugh with his confirmation hearings in 2018. At one point during the proceedings, Bash, who was sitting behind the nominee, put her two fingers together into a shape that might be seen as a reverse of the okay sign.

Social media blew up. Major leftist "resistance" accounts with hundreds of thousands of followers came to the immediate conclusion that a white supremacist joined Kavanaugh's team and was sending messages to the cabal. The well-known author and activist Amy Siskind noted that the gesture, even if it was coming from a subordinate white supremacist rather than the nominee himself, disqualified Kavanaugh—who had an exemplary record as a judge and had never, as far as anyone knew, uttered a racist word in his life—from the Supreme Court.[38]

It should be noted that the okay sign as a white-power signal—the fingers secretly representing a *W* for *White* and a *P* for *Power*—began as a hoax. In 2015, an obscure Vine video maker (Vine was a TikTok precursor, for those who, like myself, have trouble keeping up with social media trends) made a similar gesture and captioned it "White guys be like." Soon after, white supremacists, or more likely trolls, began occasionally making the hand sign to upset liberals.

The next year, 4chan users (another group of trolling racists) started a hoax—"Operation O-KKK"—to spread the sign around the internet and claim it as a symbol of white supremacy. The anonymous 4channer who started the trend added a graphic demonstrating how the gesture could spell out the letters *WP* for *white power*. "Leftists have dug so deep down in their lunacy, we must force [them] to dig more," a poster wrote. "Until the rest of society ain't going anywhere near that shit."[39]

Mission accomplished.

DOG WHISTLES

Listen closely and you'll hear these phrases everywhere.
—MOLLY JONG-FAST[40]

If you're on the left these days, nearly everything you hear the political opposition say carries some deeper, darker, bigoted significance.

During the COVID era, conservatives began using *woke* as a catchall pejorative to describe progressive cultural pieties and attitudes regarding "social justice," sexuality, race, and economics. The word was appropriated from young leftists, who in the mid-2010s had begun using #Staywoke hashtags on social media to project their enlightened worldview.

Suddenly, using the same word became a secret racist siren call.

In *Time* magazine's "Why 'Woke' Is a Convenient Republican Dog Whistle," two professors argue that because a larger proportion of black Americans identify with the term *woke* than other people groups, the only logical conclusion is that those trying to turn the phrase into a slur are engaging in racist dog-whistling. Though the roots of *woke* may well lie in the black community, it had long gone mainstream and become the domain of the young white urban progressives, and then conservatives.

Still further, the authors compared use of the word *woke* to the kind of ugly rhetoric used by segregationists. The professors argued that while conservatives have moved away "from the language of Strom Thurmond and George Wallace, who overtly rallied their supporters against threats to the racial hierarchy, Republican candidates in the post–Civil Rights era stoke fear and anger over this threat via coded language."[41]

But it doesn't end there.

In a *Washington Post* magazine piece, columnist Damon Young took it even further: "Woke is now a dog whistle for Black. What's Next?"[42] What was next was an array of phrases and commonplace words used by Americans every day, many of them useful and factual terms. Among them: "at-risk," "underserved," "fatherless," "[m]arginalized," "low-income," "Chicago," "Democratic strongholds," "thug," "terror," "illegals," "socialists," "unAmerican," "transient" "affirmative action," "diversity," "ungrateful," "intimidating," "aggressive," "lazy," "Marxists," "inner-city," "urban," and "renters."

Boy, there are lots of words to avoid. It's almost as if merely speaking itself is a racist endeavor.

Other phrases deemed by various left-wing commentators have included "law and order," "international banks," "New York values" (a phrase Ted Cruz used to attack Donald Trump, who is from New York City, when running against him in the 2016 primary),[43] "crack pipe," "let parents decide," and (surprise!) "socialism."[44]

In the paranoiac mind of the contemporary left, pointing out that Chicago is a poorly run city (to put it mildly) is an act of racial aggression. Had it never occurred to them that associating all those words with racism simply showed that they were the ones obsessed with race?

There is rarely a political event today where the left won't sniff out some unseemly underlying racial dimension. When former president Trump pointed out that ISIS leader Abu Bakr al-Baghdadi "died like a dog" after his assassination, a professor emeritus at the University of California noted that calling someone a dog was more than a throw-away insult. "My scholarship," she stated, "focuses on representations of race and animals in literature and popular culture. In my view, Trump's comments echo a troubled history of using dogs as weapons against people of color, as well as pejorative depictions of people of color as animals."[45]

Though Abu Bakr al-Baghdadi was a "man of color" in the modern leftist's definition, he was also, more importantly, a genocidal mass murderer who engendered sexual slavery, mass organized rape, torture, and genocide.

Using the phrase "like a dog," a *Washington Post* reporter explained, was nothing new. Trump has a long history of using canine insults to "dehumanize enemies."[46] When Trump fired former reality show contestant Omarosa Manigault-Newman from his administration, the *Post* reported, "The president's calling a woman a dog—and not just any woman, but the highest-ranking African American who has served on his White House staff—drew stern condemnations," wrote Philip Rucker.

Now, Trump's use of the word *dog* is certainly uncouth—as his speech can often be—but his crudeness isn't aimed at any one type of person. Trump has used the "dog" slur to attack James Comey, Steve Bannon, Mitt Romney, Marco Rubio, David Gregory, and Erick Erickson, all white men. Yet this did not deter the press from pretending that Trump's knee-jerk rudeness was a sophisticated, surreptitious, racist speech pattern meant for the ears of all his bigoted confederates.

The left's obsession with identity politics allows them to treat standard political rhetoric as something odious. For example, when Marco Rubio attacks progressive prosecutors who were funded by Democratic superfunder George Soros, it ignites accusations of antisemitism.[47]

"This is how anti-Semitism takes root and spreads," Randi Weingarten, head of the powerful American Federation of Teachers, warned.[48] "What is a 'Soros' backed prosecutor? Soros is a Hungarian Jew who survived the Holocaust," the *Washington Post*'s reliably unscrupulous Max Boot wrote. "Every time Republicans say 'Soros' you should hear 'the Jews.'"[49] "The right's fixation with Mr. Soros has waxed and waned for years," but Trump-era politics has "given new life to what critics have long contended is a fixation tinged with antisemitic bigotry," added the *New York Times* in an editorial that failed to provide a single tangible example of mainstream Republicans tingeing their rhetoric with anti-Jewish subtext.[50]

When Republican presidential candidate Ron DeSantis decried the work of an African American "Soros-backed Manhattan prosecutor," MSNBC anchor Joy Reid accused him of spreading the idea "that black folks in positions of power are controlled by some Jewish overseer who is pulling the strings."

President Joe Biden's special envoy to monitor and combat antisemitism, Deborah Lipstadt, tweeted that "it is entirely disingenuous to deny that many ad hominem attacks on [Soros] rely on classic antisemitic tropes and rhetoric."[51]

But they are not baseless. The claims were tethered to an indisputable fact that had nothing to do with faith or ethnicity. Both DeSantis and Rubio, whether you agree with their position on prosecutors or not, are stating an incontestable truth. The "Hungarian billionaire" who has never showed any interest in Judaism and funds anti-Israel groups has spent a decade funding local anti-incarceration efforts with tens of millions of dollars.

We know this because a 2016 *Politico* piece detailed how Soros was engaged in a "quiet overhaul of the U.S. justice system."[52] Soros, "Democratic mega-donor," the story informs us, "has directed his wealth into an under-the-radar 2016 campaign to advance one of the progressive movement's core goals—reshaping the American justice system."

Indeed, detractors could also have read about the effort *from the man himself* in a *Wall Street Journal* editorial headlined "Why I Support Reform Prosecutors," where he explains his plans in detail.[53]

But forget all of that for a moment. The more pertinent question is why two Florida politicians with long records of championing Israel and the Jewish people would be sending antisemitic dog whistles in the first place. Florida is home to the third-largest Jewish population in the country. Republicans—like Democrats, who have aimed their ire toward Jewish Republican donor Sheldon Adelson—go after big funders all the time because it's politically useful. If your political instincts are racked with groundless anxiety, you tend not to think rationally.

None of this is to say that fringe types never connect George Soros to a worldwide Jewish conspiracy. Seemingly the only time "antisemitism"—or the Holocaust, for that matter—is useful to progressives is when they can appropriate it to slander their opponents. Cynical, politically motivated accusations of antisemitism are odious because they diminish the seriousness of the real thing.

We also shouldn't forget that most of Rubio's and DeSantis's detractors have never uttered a harsh word about the vile antisemites of "The Squad," many of whom peddle modern-day blood libels and cheer on terrorists (much more on this later). Or, for that matter, even Weingarten, who *led* the fight to deny Jewish communities access not only to public schools but to their private schools during COVID.[54] When confronted on this issue, Weingarten said, "American Jews are now part of the ownership class. What I hear when I hear that question is that those who are in the ownership class now want to take that ladder of opportunity away from those who do not have it."[55]

Images of Jews hoarding wealth and denying others similar success is one of the vilest and oldest tropes in the world.

This isn't a book detailing double standards, but can you imagine the media's reaction if a powerful Republican had groused about the Jewish "ownership class"? Weingarten is regurgitating an enduring antisemitic canard: Jews hoard power to deny others success. There is not a single person who's had even fleeting acquaintance with American Jewish communities who could possibly believe that Jews are trying to take away "the ladder of opportunity." For the modern leftists who judge people by their ethnicity and faith, it is perfectly normal to see everything through the prism of identity. They can fall on either side of the paranoiac pendulum depending on the circumstance.

It must be exhausting to keep an eye out for these ciphers. When former Alaska governor Sarah Palin retweeted a story that was headlined "Trump Gives Speech to the People of Poland, Says 14 Words That Leave Americans Stunned," BlueAnon experts quickly detected something malicious afoot. According to Business Insider and numerous other leftists, using the phrase "14 words" was a secret message to white supremacists because, apparently, some white supremacists have a saying that's fourteen words long.[56]

On Joy Reid's show on MSNBC, the always-raving Steve Schmidt remarked that Trump's contention that he needed "six months to a year" to reform the federal government was a "racist code whistle to every white supremacist in the country because it's how long it took Adolf Hitler to take Weimar Germany to a complete and total dictatorship."[57] (Note to self: avoid planning in six-month increments.)

When the Trump administration's surgeon general Jerome Adams (who is black) implored minority communities to "avoid alcohol, tobacco, and drugs" as a way of protecting against COVID—adding, "Do this, if not for yourself, then for your abuela. Do it for your granddaddy, do it for your Big Mama, do it for your pop-pop"—Representative Maxine Waters noted that it was Trump's "new vessel by which to spew his racist dog whistles" and "racist tropes."[58]

Time published a piece titled "'A War of Words.' Why Describing the George Floyd Protests as 'Riots' Is So Loaded." It quotes someone who says the term is full of "racial undertones." The author wants people to instead use terms that make the riots sound justified, writing, "Compared to riot, a word like uprising or rebellion does more to suggest a struggle for justice, a warranted response to oppression, an attempt to demand change outside a system that has failed to yield it."[59]

But of course, the truthers on the left have no hidden suggestions or implications in the language they use.

HOAXVILLE

We are with you, Jussie.

—JOE BIDEN

Donald Trump had barely won the 2016 election when a rash of imaginary attacks on minorities broke out. Democrats had long promised white supremacist violence would descend upon the land if the Republicans prevailed. One might have gotten the impression that Brownshirts were freely roaming the streets of liberal towns across the nation. "My guess," wrote columnist Matthew Yglesias two weeks before election day, "is that in a Trump administration angry mobs will beat and murder Jews and people of color with impunity."[60]

On election night in 2016, a gay man named Chris Ball claimed to have been beaten by Trump supporters in the white supremacist, MAGA enclave of Santa Monica, California. It was quickly a national story, a portent of things to come. Police, however, could find no evidence that the attacked had ever occurred.[61]

The next day, a grainy picture of the Ku Klux Klan marching to intimidate minorities in Meban, North Carolina, went viral on social media. This was a ruse. The picture was of a conservative group standing on interstate overpasses waving American and Gadsden flags.[62]

That same day, a Bowling Green State University student name Eleesha Long claimed she was attacked by a group of stone-throwing white men wearing "Trump" T-shirts. Again, the story was widely disseminated and covered. She hadn't been near the alleged location of the attack.[63]

That same week, "civil rights" activist Shaun King, who has millions of followers on social media, sent out an image purportedly of two students at Southern Illinois University wearing blackface in front of a Confederate flag celebrating the Trump victory. Turns out the picture was of a torn Confederate flag and a young woman had on a Boscia face mask. (Yes, I had to look it up too.) Nonetheless, the university released a statement about offensive images being shared on social media in the wake of Trump's election.[64]

"'Heil Trump,' Swastika, Gay Slur Spray Painted on Indiana Church," reported CBS News a few days after the election. It was one of many national outlets to cover this ugly incident.[65] It turned out the church's organist had done it.[66] Why? According to numerous reporters, it was to warn the public about the dangers of a Trump presidency.

The day after the election, a female student at the University of Louisiana reported that her hijab was ripped off her head and her wallet stolen by two white men, quite conveniently also wearing Trump hats. Police soon found out that she had fabricated the story.[67]

In New York, another young woman named Yasmin Seweid allegedly had a run-in with a group of men she heard talking about Trump. "They were surrounding me from behind and they were like, 'Oh look, it's an f***ing terrorist,'" she claimed. "I didn't answer. They pulled my strap of the bag and it ripped, and that's when I turned around and I was really polite and I was like, 'Can you please leave me alone?' and everyone was looking, no one said a thing, everyone just looked away." Seweid explained that no one stopped the men, not even when they tried to tear off her hijab.[68]

Though the story made national news, it turned out she had made the entire thing up.

Which gives us a moment to ponder the anti-Islamic violence that we are constantly being warned about by BlueAnon. Since 9/11, we've been waiting for this impending violent backlash against Muslims. Yet even after terrorist acts perpetrated by homegrown Islamists, it still hasn't happened. Despite the presence of idiotic, violent people—a plague on all cultures and ethnicities, regrettably—Americans have shown far more tolerance in the ways that matter most. That goes for both sides of the political divide.

When we consider the depth and sprawl of our diversity, it's clear we are unique to history. Look at any place in the world. When some groups, faiths, or ethnicities converge, there is almost always strife and violence. On any average year, around 20 percent of hate crimes are of a religious bias. Among those, 50 percent are typically antisemitic and 20 percent are anti-Muslim. (Also, around 18 percent are committed against one of the Christian faiths, which the FBI divides into multiple categories.)[69]

But you would never know this from the coverage. BlueAnon works to convince us that America is uniquely racist.

Yet, no matter how many hoaxes of this manner were perpetrated, Democrats continued to be dupes. And why not? These accusations all comport with the left's ugly view of the American right as a gang of roving violent thugs.

In January 2019, *Empire* actor Jussie Smollett told police that he had been attacked by two Trump fans in the ultraliberal Streetsville neighborhood of Chicago. After he got a sandwich at 2 a.m., Smollett told cops, two white men poured an unknown chemical substance on him while yelling racial and homophobic slurs. This is "MAGA country!" they allegedly said as they wrapped a rope around his neck.[70]

Virtually the entire left and media amplified this *highly* unlikely story without an ounce of skepticism. Even as conservatives began punching holes in it, Cory Booker urged Congress to pass a federal anti-lynching bill, even though, of course, lynching was 100 percent illegal already.[71]

Joe Biden implored Americans to "stand up and demand that we no longer give this hate safe harbor; that homophobia and racism have no place on our streets or in our hearts."[72]

Future 2024 presidential hopeful Kamala Harris called it a "modern-day lynching" and assured her followers that Smollett was "one of the kindest, most gentle human beings" she knew. "No one," the senator said, "should have to fear for their life because of their sexuality or color of their skin. We must confront this hate."[73]

Leftist reporter April Ryan asked Donald Trump—the center of this hate—about the attack. The president said, "I think that's horrible. It doesn't get worse, as far as I'm concerned."[74]

It does. In a few months we learned that Smollett had hired a pair of Nigerian brothers who worked as extras on *Empire* and staged the attack. In the end, the actor was ordered to pay a $25,000 fine plus more than $120,000 in restitution to the city for wasting their time, and to serve a 150-day jail sentence.

Neither Biden nor Harris nor any of the loads of left-wingers who spread this preposterous story ever apologized or even bothered to remove their comments from social media. As far as I can tell, none were asked by media to explain why they readily believed such a preposterous story.

There were many more hoaxes and the same process unfurled for each of them. The initial lie was widely disseminated, and then the correction was hardly seen. In each case, whether it turned out to be true or not—and the vast majority did not—the picture of a rising, violent right wing was put together.

Of course, even if a handful of people acted out in criminal and hateful ways, it would not be an indictment of any party or the nation. Yet the contemporary media plays a significant role in perpetuating the delusional belief that modern conservatism stimulates sociopathic mobs of predatory bigots.

No matter how many of these hoaxes were debunked, Democrats would keep falling for them (or pretending to). Blowing them up. Pointing to them as examples of America's deeply engrained racism. One of the most infamous press failures of the past few years offers us important insight into how journalists and activists work together to galvanize racial anxiety.

On January 18, 2019, a Friday, a video of a group of teenage boys from Covington Catholic High School in Kentucky went viral. At first glance, it appeared the boys were mocking, bullying, and harassing an elderly Native American Vietnam War veteran named Nathan Phillips near the Lincoln Memorial in Washington, DC.

In one infamous screenshot, a teen named Nicholas Sandmann, donning a red MAGA baseball cap and a smirk, his face within inches of Phillips's, allegedly ridiculed the man while his friends egged him on. This painted a vivid picture of the dangerous and reprehensible state of American political life. The incident was the ultimate expression of white privilege. Not only had the contemporary social conservative been captured by hateful ideas but *even their children* engaged in this vile behavior.

"Covington school kids intimidated Native Americans. Who taught them that?" asked one columnist.[75] The *New York Times* later contended that the moment was an "explosive convergence of race, religion and ideological beliefs."[76] At the time, practically every major news organization covered the event from the perspective of those who alleged the boys had terrorized peaceful demonstrators. They all implied that it was even worse than it seemed.

The *Washington Post* interviewed Phillips, who explained that he'd come to the aid of a group of black counterprotesters at the event being harassed by the boys. "I heard them say, 'Build that wall, build that wall,'" Phillips claimed. "We always took care of our elders, took care of our children. We always provided for them, you know? We taught them right from wrong. I wish I could see that energy of the young men to, you know, put that energy to make this country really great. Helping those that are hungry."

Virtually every news organization picked up Phillips's self-aggrandizing narrative. "A series of viral videos is sparking outrage across the political spectrum," reported ABC News.[77] Kentucky secretary of state Alison Lundergan Grimes called the viral videos "horrific." "This Veteran put his life on the line for our country. The students' display of blatant hate, disrespect, and intolerance is a signal of how common decency has decayed under this administration," wrote Representative Deb Haaland (D-NM), who often speaks on Native American issues.[78] "The contrast between the calm dignity and quiet strength of Mr. Phillips and the behavior of the #MAGA brats who have absorbed the spirit of Trumpism—this spectacle is a lesson which all Americans can learn," former Republican Bill Kristol tweeted.[79]

Thousands of social media accounts, some with hundreds of thousands or millions of followers, joined the mob. Then–CNN talking head Reza Aslan tweeted that Sandmann had a "punchable" face.[80] Comedian Patton Oswalt saw "bland, frightened, forgettable kids who'll grow up to be bland, frightened, forgotten adult wastes."[81] Jesuit media personality James Martin wrote that the kids' "actions are not Catholic, not Christian, and not acceptable. Would that these students fully understood the dignity of all human life—including this man's."[82]

There were widespread calls to release the names of the students and even for the District of Columbia to prosecute them. Many of the high schoolers received death threats in the coming days, and Covington Catholic High School was shuttered for safety reasons.[83]

Even the cowed diocese of Covington issued a statement condemning "the actions of the Covington Catholic High School students towards Nathan Phillips specifically, and Native Americans in general. . . . We extend our deepest apologies to Mr. Phillips. This behavior is opposed to the Church's teachings on the dignity and respect of the human person. The matter is being investigated and we will take appropriate action, up to and including expulsion."[84]

Journalists soon dug deeper, not to confirm or contextualize what was in the videos being spread by the digital mob, but rather to expose the decrepit Red State culture that produced such vile children. This was key to creating a picture of a fallen society.

"SEE IT: Covington Catholic High Students in Blackface at Past Basketball Game," blared a headline from the New York *Daily News*.[85] Pictures from a 2012 basketball game, in which fans put on various colors of face paint, were framed to make students look like they donned blackface to mock opposing black players whereas in fact none of it had to do with race.

Rather than find out what happened, NBC News ran an interview with a "gay high school valedictorian" *from another school* who noted that Covington was "notorious for being a not-well-disciplined school."[86]

They had it coming was the message, because of the cultural problems of white social conservatism. "It was only a matter of time that something this school community did would blow up to this degree, and I think they need to be held accountable," said Christian Bales, who attended nearby Holy Cross High School.[87]

Others dug up old pictures of Covington basketball players and fans holding their thumb and index fingers together, with the other three fingers up in the air—the okay sign—which was the standard celebration after scoring a three-pointer. "Covington's finest throwing up the new nazi sign," wrote Kathy Griffin. Actor Jim Carrey tweeted a work of art that depicted the Covington kids as "baby snakes."[88]

Not only was the ugly incident afforded tremendous coverage—far larger than the massive yearly anti-abortion March for Life was ever given—but it was fodder for seemingly endless and overwrought analysis about the state of America. The event plunged us into another national conversation on race, on Trumpism, and on the problems of right-wing discourse.

The problem, again, was that all of it was wrong.

Because the incident occurred during a mass protest, there was plenty of video to prove it—though no major news organization waited to see what truly happened before tarnishing the reputations of the high school students. A MAGA-hat-wearing teenager would never be given the benefit of the doubt.

The boys, who had broken off from their group to find their buses, did not threaten anyone. They did run into counterprotesters from both the Indigenous Peoples Movement and Black Israelites (a long-time group of racists and antisemites). Videos show that Phillips, who had a long history of activist stunts,[89] initiated the confrontation. There was no evidence that the boys chanted "build a wall"—which, incidentally, would have been their right. No, the group of Black Israelites were the ones who harassed the boys, calling them "crackers" and "incest babies."[90]

According to the students, the African American student among the small group was told that the white people would "harvest his organs." That kind of language would not be out of character for the racist, extremist group.[91]

Phillips, who claimed that the teens swarmed around him and made him feel threatened, had misled the press.[92] News outlets such as the *Washington Post*, CNN, and the *New York Times* all referred to Phillips as a Vietnam veteran—adding a bit of patriotic color to the fabricated story—but that turned out to be untrue as well.[93] In a later correction, the *Times* claimed that the information had come to them from the Indigenous Peoples Movement. The *Post* noted that the leader of the Lakota People's Law Project said that group erroneously represented Phillips as a Vietnam vet.

One of the big stories here was the lack of journalistic integrity that was endemic. Sandmann ended up suing several media organizations for smearing him. The *Washington Post*, CNN, and NBC all settled. The many elected Democrats who slandered the boys were lucky to be protected by legislative immunity.

The first thing to remember here is that had there not been dispositive evidence, the press and activists would have gotten away with it. The second is that the purpose of blowing up an isolated incident to begin with was to emphasize minor incidents and keep feeding the fiction that the nation has taken a wicked, violent turn. After all, even if a few high school kids from Kentucky behaved poorly at an event attended by a million people, it would have said almost nothing about protesters or the school, much less the nation.

The actions of a few hundred rioters would, however, give BlueAnon the pretext they needed to pretend the country was in a state of civil war.

THE JEWS!

*The conspiracy theory of the Jew as the hypnotic
conspirator, the duplicitous manipulator, the sinister
puppeteer is one with ancient roots and a bloody history.*
—BARI WEISS

A few years back, an assemblywoman from Brooklyn named Diane Richardson took the podium during a council meeting about local zoning ordinances, then went on a near-hourlong rant, accusing Jews of conspiring to gentrify her district.

At one point, Richardson referred to one of her legislative colleagues as "the Jewish senator from southern Brooklyn." Later, when a board member was grousing about people ringing her doorbell during the night, the assemblywoman helpfully interjected to say it "must be Jewish people."[1]

Now, this is not some far-flung hamlet in flyover country, mind you, but a New York City borough that is home to approximately 2.7 million people, including hundreds of thousands of Jews. This is Brooklyn, where in 2022, All-Star Nets point guard Kyrie Irving invited his millions of followers (via Twitter and Instagram) to watch a documentary called *Hebrews to Negroes.*[2]

Now, this is not some film one just happens upon when browsing Netflix. The movie is based on the ideas of a Black Hebrew Israelite sect. It purports to prove that blacks are true Jews, and that Jews had been engaged in a centuries-long "cover-up" (that includes the Holocaust) to "conceal their nature and protect their status and power."[3] When asked about a case regarding a group of Black Hebrew Israelites in her Senate confirmation hearing, future Supreme Court justice Ketanji Brown Jackson called them a "small community, a cultural community of people who believe in vegan lifestyles" and "healthy living."[4] This was the equivalent of a conservative judicial candidate referring to a white supremacist group as "a cultural community centered on body art."

Vegans? Yes. Also, most factions of the Black Hebrew Israelites preach the vilest antisemitism and racism you could imagine. White people—especially Jews—they maintain, are Satan's tools. And the Black Hebrew Israelite's messiah (who was supposed to appear in 2000 but is running a bit late) will one day seek vengeance on everyone but blacks.

That said, Irving had yet to accuse the Jews of making it rain.

Not long before Richardson's rant, a DC Council member named Trayon White Sr., a Democrat who represents the Eighth Ward of the capital of the free world, Washington DC, posted a video offering some of his thoughts on how "the Rothschilds"—an eighteenth-century Jewish banking family that has been wrapped up in nearly every major conspiracy theory since—were controlling the climate and making it snow in Washington to try to squeeze money out of the oppressed.[5]

Now, White certainly wasn't the first to talk about Jews controlling the weather. Around the same time, future GOP congresswoman Marjorie Taylor Green was penning a rambling Facebook post on weather machines and the California wildfires.[6] But left-wingers who spread antisemitic myths are often framed as innocuous oddballs by the press, rather than people who reflect a deeper and prevalent intolerance within their movements.

Blaming shady Jewish cabals for the maladies befalling communities is nothing new. For groups that have experienced historical discrimination, this kind of trepidation is prevalent for obvious reasons. Because of the minefield associated with any topic intertwining politics and race, it is rarely spoken about, but antisemitic conspiracy theories are rampant in one of the left's core constituencies: the African American community.

Despite Jewish allyship in the civil rights movement of the 1960s and the proximity of the two peoples in American urban areas—or perhaps because of it—portions of the black community have long indulged in conspiracies about Jewish people. A recent paper by Eitan Hersh of Tufts University and Laura Royden of Harvard University found that young African Americans exhibited even higher rates of antisemitic views than young white men who identify as alt-right.[7]

Study after study shows that black Americans are far more likely to believe conspiracy theories about Jews. Eunice G. Pollack, a professor of history and Jewish studies, has thoroughly outlined the racialized forms of antisemitism and anti-Zionism that have been popularized by African Americans from the era of Malcolm X to the Black Lives Matter movement.

In a 1970 study, 73 percent of young African Americans ranked high on the index of antisemitism. In 1978, a survey of black leaders found that 81 percent of them agreed that "Jews chose money over people." In 1981, another study showed that 42 percent of blacks, as opposed to 20 percent of white Americans, agreed that "Jews have too much power in the United States." In a 2005 study, 36 percent of African Americans held "strong antisemitic beliefs"—four times the percentage of whites.[8] Little has changed. And there is no societal pressure to tamper down this kind of thinking. In fact, many on the left who engage in it are rewarded.

• • • • •

Take Reverend Al Sharpton, one of the most notorious American conspiracy theorists of the past forty years. He now works for the left's top
cable news station, MSNBC, offering his wisdom, basking in the admi-
ration of liberal pundits and the deference of Democratic politicians.

Sharpton began his career in the 1970s advocating for poor black
families but rose to national prominence in the late 1980s on the
strength of engaging in hoaxes and peddling conspiracy theories. His
lies about white people whipped up anger in New York's black community and often caused deadly damage.

In 1991, the reverend used the death of a seven-year-old black boy
named Gavin Cato, who had died in an accident caused by a Jewish
driver (who was following a procession led by an unmarked police
car), to help incite a three-day race riot in Crown Heights. Sharpton,
Joe Klein wrote at the time, "placed Gavin Cato in a heavenly pantheon of the victims of white-racist violence," even though the driver
had no racist intent and was never charged with a crime.[9] Sharpton laid
the groundwork by warning of the Jewish "nexus" between "Tel Aviv"
and "South Africa" and the "diamond merchants" of Crown Heights at
Gavin's funeral (at the time, South Africa was an "apartheid regime,"
which has now become the preferred smear of many progressives).[10]
The mob found a man with a yarmulke named Yankel Rosenbaum, a
twenty-nine-year-old Orthodox Jew visiting from Australia, who had
the bad fortune of turning down the wrong street at the wrong time.
Rosenbaum was dragged from his car to the shouts of "Kill the Jews!"
by throngs of angry protesters and stabbed to death.[11]

For years, Sharpton also hosted a radio show on New York airwaves
that stoked racial division.[12] In one infamous incident, his show helped
transform an ordinary dispute over rent between a Jewish landlord and
a black tenant at Freddy's Fashion Mart Harlem into a deadly event.[13]
Sharpton had cheered on the venomous protests in front of the store

to the point that the crowd soon began to resemble an angry mob. At one point a man with a gun asked all the black patrons to leave, and then killed everyone else. The "white interloper" who Sharpton predicted was going to take over did not.[14]

Sharpton, of course, had famously thrown the entire city into turmoil in 1987 when he exploited a hoax centered on a black teen girl named Tawana Brawley, who claimed to have been raped, kidnapped, covered with feces, and left wrapped in a plastic bag by a "cult" of white men in Dutchess County, New York. Sharpton accused prosecutor Steven Pagones of abduction and rape of a teenager—"On 33 separate occasions," according to the Associated Press—destroying the man's career, destroying a teenager's life, and exacerbating racial tensions in the city.[15] Sharpton blamed a secret cabal led by the Irish Republican Army for the rape. In truth, Brawley had made up the story, likely to cover up for missing her curfew, covering herself in dog feces.[16]

None of this stopped his career trajectory. In fact, it helped him. During the Obama administration, Sharpton emerged as *the* go-to civil rights guru for the White House, according to numerous publications. "If anything," a piece in *Politico* noted, "the Ferguson crisis [the shooting of Michael Brown, which the federal government ruled was not prompted by racial animus] has underscored Sharpton's role as the national black leader Obama leans on most, a remarkable personal and political transformation for a man once regarded with suspicion and disdain by many in his own party."[17]

There was little suspicion and disdain of Sharpton outside of Jewish Democrats. Despite this history, most Democrats running for president *still* visit Sharpton at his Harlem office and kiss the ring. This kind of meeting was tantamount to the GOP asking David Duke for his endorsement. Yet, in 2020, Kamala Harris, Bernie Sanders, Pete Buttigieg, and others all took the chance for a photo op with Sharpton to solidify black support.

President Joe Biden has met Sharpton on numerous occasions, referring to him as a "leading" civil rights champion and friend. Sharpton, in fact, was the first person in the "press" that Biden told he was going to run for president. It was not an accident.

Sharpton has spent years playing on suspicions entrenched within the black community. Throughout the 1980s and '90s, for example, conspiracies about crack cocaine and AIDS were prevalent among African Americans.

In 1996, the San Jose *Mercury News* famously published a series of stories about the CIA and its role in bringing crack into American urban neighborhoods. Soon the series was picked up by the *Raleigh News & Observer*, *Denver Post*, *Pittsburgh Post-Gazette*, and numerous other major newspapers around the nation. The series became a sensation on African American radio stations and newspapers, as well.

"In the African American community, the allegations have hit a nerve, highlighting an inclination, born of bitter history and captured in polls, to accept as fact unsubstantiated reports or rumors about conspiracies targeting blacks," wrote the *Washington Post* in 1996.[18] Members of the Congressional Black Caucus and others demanded an investigation.

Follow-up stories by the *Post* and the *New York Times*, however, found nothing to substantiate the claims. Even Jerry Ceppos, then editor of the *Mercury News*, admits that the reporter, Gary Webb, threaded together a few strands of truth to create a big conspiracy theory—which is, of course, how it's always done. "Certainly talk radio in a lot of cities has made the leap. We've tried to correct it wherever we could," Ceppos explained.

Even Webb was later compelled to agree that he had no hard evidence that anyone in the CIA had ever participated in crack-trafficking. It didn't matter. The idea that the CIA was behind the crack epidemic would never be shaken. Even in 2023, Netflix was still running documentaries like *Crack: Cocaine, Corruption & Conspiracy*, which gave these debunked speculations a serious hearing.

Similarly, a large number of African Americans were convinced that AIDS originated in a government lab, developed by scientists as a means of hurting and destroying their communities. Nearly half of African Americans surveyed in 2005 believed that HIV was man-made. Over 50 percent believed that the government held back information about a cure.[19]

The contemporary progressive left has adopted a similarly toxic view of Jews.

The original Black Lives Matter, ostensibly an American civil rights movement, took time in their original platform to contend that the Jewish state was "complicit in the genocide taking place against the Palestinian people" and called Israel an "apartheid state."[20] To claim that the only democracy in the Middle East, which grants more liberal rights to its Muslim citizens than any Arab nation, is an "apartheid regime" is, on an intellectual level, grossly disingenuous or incredibly ignorant. It is reserved for one people and it is peddled regularly by the progressive left.

But what did Israel have to do with civil rights for black Americans, anyway?

Absolutely nothing. Why bring up Israel and not Bangladesh, China, Russia, Angola, or dozens of other real authoritarian nations? You know why. Yet more than six hundred left-wing Jewish organizations supported Black Lives Matter.[21] If someone dared point out the nuttery of BLM leaders during its heyday of 2020–21, they would be immediately branded racist. After the Hamas massacre of Jews in October 2023, the Chicago chapter of the group, which had more than sixty thousand followers, posted a picture of a person paragliding—how some Hamas killers entered Israel—with a Palestinian flag attached to its parachute and the words *I stand with Palestine.*

Take a dive into American leftist literature and you always end up learning something insane about Israel.

In 2018, Jewish Voice for Peace, a progressive front masquerading as a religious organization, published a report called "Deadly Exchange," in which the group claimed that American police forces were taught racial discrimination and oppressive tactics by the Israelis. Also, after the murder of forty-six-year-old George Floyd by Minneapolis cop Derek Chauvin, progressives began widely circulating a conspiracy theory that Israelis trained cops to engage in human rights violence.[22]

"With Whom Are Many U.S. Police Departments Training? With a Chronic Human Rights Violator—Israel," read an Amnesty International piece. A petition by academics and students in the University of California system also invoked the police exchanges while claiming that the chokehold "used to murder George Floyd" was "perfected" by Israeli forces.[23]

"The Israeli military trains US police in racist and repressive policing tactics, which systematically targets Black and Brown bodies. The recent murders of George Floyd, Breonna Taylor, and Ahmaud Arbery are examples of racialized, systematized violence," tweeted one Black Lives Matter–affiliated group.

Arbery, of course, was murdered by a retired sheriff, with his son and neighbor, neither of them police officers. None of them had anything remotely to do with "Israeli training." Taylor was killed in a botched drug raid and Floyd by a cop who knelt on his neck—a move he did not learn from the Israeli military.

Though American police, mostly senior law enforcement officials, have gone on trips to meet with Israeli experts to, as the ADL explained, learn about "extremist and terrorist violence, mass casualty attacks and community resilience," no tactical training was given.

This wasn't an isolated incident. Many progressive activist groups, who normally championed minority rights and labor issues completely unrelated to Israel, got in on the action. Recall as well that the Women's

March, not only a popular mainstream left-wing protest group of the Trump era but one of the largest organized political demonstrations in American history, was run by a number of Jew-haters. Many of the cofounders spread vile revisionist histories about Jews. Among them were prominent voices like Tamika Mallory and Linda Sarsour.

In the aftermath of the October 7 massacre, Sarsour described Jews who put up posters of kidnapped children as "provocateurs" who were "everywhere." "They are on your college campus, they are outside the supermarket," she told a crowd of pro-Hamas protesters.[24]

It was unsurprising. Both Mallory and Sarsour were supporters of the antisemitic Nation of Islam. At the height of the Women's March's success, Mallory attended a speech given by Louis Farrakhan, posed with the minister for a selfie, and wrote "GOAT"—the greatest of all time. Mallory, who by this time was a beneficiary of mass adulation from mainstream publications,[25] told the *New York Times* that "white Jews" were among those who "uphold white supremacy." One of the Jewish cofounders of the Women's March, Vanessa Wruble, left the group because she claimed that Mallory and another cofounder, Carmen Perez regularly condoned antisemitism, spreading historical conspiracies about Jews running the American chattel slave trade—a fiction first spread by black nationalists in the 1960s. (Mallory and Perez unconvincingly denied the claims.)[26]

Even after all this history was aired, many Democrats still defended the group. When Valerie Jarrett, a former senior adviser to President Barack Obama, was asked by cohost Meghan McCain on *The View* about Mallory's affection for Farrakhan, she replied, "You work with people all the time with whom you disagree. Goodness knows I met with the Koch brothers when we were working on criminal justice or Rupert Murdoch when we were working on immigration reform."[27]

Jarrett's contention that Murdoch, the owner of Fox News, or the Koch brothers, libertarians who fund an array of issues well within the norms of American debate, were morally equivalent to a person who described Hitler as "a very great man" tells us not only about the allowance they make for hate but about the paranoia they harbor about their political opposition.[28]

Mallory's hero Louis Farrakhan was not merely some eccentric political voice; he was the leader of the largest racial supremacist group in the United States. Farrakhan has prodigiously spread some of the most vile and recognizable conspiracies about Jewish people, conspiracies that are now popularized within the progressive activist movement.

The Islamic preacher had a wider political reach than *any* racist group in the United States, right or left. So wide, in fact, that when then-senator Barack Obama—who was mentored by another racist, Jeremiah Wright, and was friends with former Palestine Liberation Organization spokesperson and "historian" Rashid Khalidi—was running for the Senate, he met and posed for a picture with Farrakhan. This snapshot was suppressed by the media until years after his presidency.[29] It was no surprise that Obama was antagonistic toward the Jewish state. What was once seen as fringe behavior on the left would soon be normalized.

One of these theories alleged that Jewish people were responsible for the American slave trade. Farrakhan once told a crowd that Jews who "owned a lot of plantations" were responsible for undermining black emancipation after the Civil War. Farrakhan has long argued that "lying, murderous Zionist Jews" were behind 9/11 and contends that Jews conspired to control the government, the economy, black communities, and basically every organization worth running. "When they talk about Farrakhan," the minister said in 2018, "they call me a hater, you know how they do—call me an anti-Semite. Stop it, I'm anti-termite!" The Nation of Islam hosted lectures accusing Jewish doctors in Chicago of infecting Black babies with AIDS as part of a genocidal plot against African Americans, among other imaginary atrocities.[30]

• • • • •

Farrakhan's messaging resonated with the Women's March and BLM, and other factions of the progressive left. But it was not merely activist groups that worked with and helped the man. Numerous congressional Democrats appeared at events with the man who obsessed over "the Satanic Jew."

Among them:

- California representative Maxine Waters, who as of this writing is the ranking member of the House Financial Services Committee, serving in her seventeenth term in Congress, and a regular guest on cable news shows.[31]

- Barbara Lee, the onetime chair of the Congressional Black Caucus and lately California primary candidate for the Senate. Biden honored Lee as representative of the United States at the 78th Session of the General Assembly of the United Nations.

- Illinois representative Danny Davis, who once said of Farrakhan, "I personally know him, I've been to his home, done meetings, participated in events with him," and called him an "outstanding human being."[32]

- Indiana representative Andre Carson, only the second Muslim elected to Congress. When confronted, Carson said he would not rule out further meetings with the preacher.[33]

- New York representative Gregory Meeks, who chaired the House Committee on Foreign Affairs from 2021 to 2023 and still sits on the committee as ranking member.[34]

- Former Minnesota representative Keith Ellison, the first Muslim ever elected to Congress, and former deputy chair of the Democratic National Committee. A Farrakhan acolyte in his younger years, Ellison attended a private dinner with

Iranian regime "president" and holocaust denier Hassan Rouhani, Farrakhan, and Democratic congressmen Carson and Meeks in 2018.[35]

There is no comparable example of this kind of behavior among modern Republicans. Only in the imagination of BlueAnon.

And these politicians weren't even the worst offenders.

IT'S ALL ABOUT THE BENJAMINS, BABY!

The notion that this is a massacre of
Jews is a fabricated narrative.
—WOMAN SPEAKING AT AN OAKLAND CITY
COUNCIL MEETING IN NOVEMBER 2023

In November 2023, a month after the Hamas attack on southern Israel that murdered 1,300 people (including more than thirty American citizens)—the worst slaughter of Jews since the Holocaust—the Oakland City Council debated a "cease-fire" resolution between Hamas and Israel.

"I want Jewish children to live as much as I want Palestinian children to live," council member Carroll Fife, author of the resolution, explained.[36]

The Bay Area might have been more than seven thousand miles from either Gaza City or Tel Aviv, but hundreds of locals lined up to have their say about Middle East policy during a five-hour public forum. "There have not been beheadings of babies and rapings," one unnamed woman assured the council, despite overwhelming video and physical evidence of Hamas's atrocities against civilians. "Israel," she went on, "murdered their own people on October 7."

Those who condemn Hamas were nothing but "old White supremacists" spreading "genocidal propaganda," another man stated. And on and on it went, with numerous participants accusing Israel of the mass murder not only of Palestinians, but also of its own people.[37]

It was by that point unsurprising to witness conspiratorial, anti-Jewish accusations being leveled by leftists. This was happening around the nation and in the media.

So much so that after the October 7 attacks on Israel, Jonathan Greenblatt of the Anti-Defamation League—a Democratic partisan group that has spent years highlighting every dog whistle (real and imagined) while ignoring or actively diminishing the rise of antisemitism on the left—felt compelled to ask producers at MSNBC, the leading left-wing cable network, "Who is writing the scripts? Hamas?"[38]

Maybe. One of the hosts on the network at the time, Mehdi Hasan, had started his career working for the Qatar state-funded theocratic network Al Jazeera. The host had once called non-Muslims no better than "cattle" and now regularly spreads contemporary blood libels about the Jewish state by making a series of unfounded claims of "genocide" based on casualty numbers provided by the terror group Hamas.[39]

According to a December 2023 *Economist*/YouGov poll, nearly twice as many Democrats and Biden supporters believed "The Holocaust is a myth" as did Republicans and Trump supporters. Five times as many urbanites as rural dwellers.[40] As did one in five Americans under thirty. This obsession with Jews, a hallmark of all ideological extremes, has been embedded in the hard left's activist agenda for decades. When identity politics and class warfare propel your movement, as it does modern progressivism, it's almost inevitable that the Jews, who have tended to successfully navigate meritocracies, will become targets.

The Hamas massacre of October 7 opened the floodgates for conspiracy-theorizing antisemites to engage in widespread protests, threats, violence, and rioting aimed at Jews and Jewish institutions. Israel was the pretext. A few years ago, a Pew Research Center poll found that 79 percent of Republicans say they sympathize more with Israel than with the Palestinians, compared with just 27 percent of Democrats.[41] That was alarming enough. By 2023, a Harvard poll found that 36 percent of "liberals" of all ages *agreed* that the Hamas attack was "justified," compared to 15 percent of "conservatives."[42] The number among young people was even worse.

On college campuses, on social media platforms, in the streets of major American cities, on major U.S. news programs, and in the halls of Congress, a leftist outburst of pro-Hamas, anti-Jewish sentiment erupted. Here is a small sampling of headlines:

Indianapolis Woman Arrested for Plowing Car into Building She Thought Was a Jewish School[43]

Jewish Cemetery in Cleveland Vandalized with Swastika Graffiti[44]

Pro-Hamas Mob Attacks Jews Outside Museum of Tolerance in LA[45]

"Holocaust 2.0" Graffitied on the University of Maryland[46]

Jewish Man Killed after Being Struck by Pro-Palestinian Protester in Los Angeles[47]

Jewish Student's Dorm Room Set on Fire at Drexel University[48]

Pro-Palestinian Student Group Violently Mobs Jewish Students, Screaming "Go Back to Poland"[49]

UMass Student Arrested for Punching Jewish Student at Hillel Vigil[50]

There would be scores more. But you'll notice two similarities among all the above stories: (1) the attacks were all aimed at Jews, not "Zionists," and (2), not one of the incidents took place in a conservative area.

• • • • •

College campuses in particular have become bastions of left-wing antisemitic quackery, a culmination of decades of progressive activism and ideological indoctrination. Quack progressive theories regarding "intersectionality" and "decolonization" are intrinsically bound up in tropes about puppet masters, racialist notions of power—and no people represented privilege in the mind of the hard leftist quite like the "Zionist." In the minds of many progressives, the Jewish state represented a pristine colonialism and "white" degradation of "brown" people.

Take the University of California, Berkeley, one of many universities teeming with Jew-baiting race hustlers and pseudointellectuals. In 2022, eleven student groups at the California school set up zones excluding any pro-Israel speakers (wink, wink) on campus.[51] Kenneth Marcus, chairman of the Brandeis Center for Human Rights Under Law, correctly coined them "Jew-free zones."[52] It is so bad that in a *Wall Street Journal* piece, Steven Davidoff Solomon, a law professor at Berkeley, implored firms *not to hire* his own students because they have become a clique who "advocate hate and practice discrimination."[53]

The more prestigious the school, the more dangerous it seemed for Jews.

On the day of the Hamas attack, before the dead could be counted or Israelis had a chance to retaliate, a coalition of more than thirty Harvard student groups posted an open letter bundling a bunch of conspiracy theories about the Jewish state to contend that its citizens were "entirely responsible" for the violence that ended up killing over a thousand of them.

"For the last two decades, millions of Palestinians in Gaza have been forced to live in an open-air prison," the letter claimed, though the people of Gaza were given autonomy in 2005 and could have set up a free political system if they desired. "Israeli officials promise to 'open the gates of hell,'" the letter went on, "and the massacres in Gaza have already commenced." This too was a devious lie based on the comment of a single Israeli official, Ghassan Alian, who had said that *Hamas* had "opened the gates of hell" when it murdered, sexually tortured, and kidnapped over 1,200 civilians.[54]

"The apartheid regime is the only one to blame," the students claimed, though Arabs in Israel had not only equal rights but more liberties than Arabs anywhere in the Middle East. And the fact that the Jewish state was always singled out as an evil entity, despite the slew of theocratic regimes and genocidal states in the region, was telling.

At the University of Pennsylvania, antisemitic messages projected onto buildings around campus, including Penn Commons, Huntsman Hall, and Irvine Auditorium, adulating the "martyrs" of Hamas.[55] At Yale and the Massachusetts Institute of Technology, students protested while airing ancient grievances against Jews. Many even ripped down posters of kidnapped Israelis—some of them Americans. When asked why, some claimed that no one was killed or kidnapped. Others compared the Jewish state to Nazis who engaged in genocide.

These college students' views on international Jewry mirror the broader hard left's outlook. The biggest difference in the BlueAnon age, however, was that elected officials were leading the charge. Some of them were the most infamous anti-Jewish conspiracists in the country.

In 2018, Ilhan Omar and Rashida Tlaib became the first two Muslim women elected to Congress. Minnesota's Ilhan, who replaced Keith Ellison, is a Somali refugee. She came to Congress with a celebrity aura and an uplifting story. Yet, curiously unmentioned in all the flattering postelection media coverage is the inconvenient truth that she harbored some . . . exotic thoughts about the Jewish people.

Omar, you see, was prone to spreading *Protocols of the Elders of Zion*-style conspiracies on Twitter, claiming on Twitter, "Israel has hypnotized the world, may Allah awaken the people and help them see the evil doings of Israel."[56]

The age-old antisemitic trope aside, I must say: as a Jew, it would be so great to have the supernatural ability to hypnotize the world.

The writer David Steinberg identified 105 news stories written in the immediate aftermath of Omar's victory, and not one of the celebratory odes to identity politics mentions anything about her propensity toward Jew-baiting derangement.[57]

Omar's tweet was just the start. Before long, the congresswoman, who as a Minnesota state legislator voted against a bill to deny life insurance payments to any person convicted of aiding or committing terror acts,[58] was soon comparing Israel *and* the United States *to Islamic terrorist groups like Hamas and the Taliban.*[59] She diminishes the 9/11 attacks—"Some people did something"—and continuously and wildly exaggerates the presence of "Islamophobia" in America.

Even after Omar's antisemitism was uncovered, House Speaker Nancy Pelosi appeared with the congresswoman on the cover of *Rolling Stone*'s "women shaping the future" issue.[60] Pelosi also elevated Omar to the Foreign Affairs Committee, where she continued to share her fanatical "ideas." When evidence of Omar's conspiratorial antisemitic outlook began to pile up, the leader of the Democrats justified her rhetoric, claiming that the congresswoman "has a different experience in the use of words" and "doesn't understand that some of them are fraught with meaning."[61]

When twelve Jewish *Democrats* gently chided the congresswoman for her rhetoric, Omar's spokesperson, Jeremy Slevin, claimed that "the far right is ginning up" Islamophobic "hate." Whenever called out, Omar hid behind her faith, one time contending that criticism was "rooted in bigotry toward a belief about what Muslims are stereotyped to believe."[62]

It wasn't until Omar alleged that Jewish "political influence in this country" was pushing "allegiance to a foreign country" that there was any significant left-wing backlash—and then, again, almost exclusively from Jewish Democrats.[63] Omar claimed that support for Israel was bought by the pro-Israel group AIPAC's shadowy work—and then retweeted a person pointing out that she might as well call all Jews "hook-nosed."[64]

The claim that Jews purchase loyalty is another enduring trope, one of the bedrocks of Jewish antagonism. There is, of course, a significant difference between disagreeing with AIPAC's positions supporting Israel and contending that anyone who supports the Jewish state is bribed by AIPAC to do so—implying that people support Israel not for good-faith reasons, but because, as Omar tweeted, "it's all about the Benjamins."

Her claim was both ideologically and *objectively* untrue. Most politicians who gravitate to AIPAC do so because they are pro-Israel or want their constituents to believe they are. It is no different than a host of other issues and organizations. AIPAC is funded by Americans, not foreigners. In this case, the fiscal benefit is at best tiny. AIPAC is one of the most milquetoast bipartisan outfits in DC and doesn't directly give politicians *any* money.[65] Even with its supernatural ability to hypnotize Americans, AIPAC spends only about $3.5 million on lobbying for Israeli policies in a good year, which rarely breaks the top fifty lobbyist efforts in the nation.[66]

The antisemitic paranoiac will often imbue AIPAC with magical powers of control. When a large group of Democrats voted for a bipartisan bill to ban Chinese-owned social media platform TikTok, Pam Keith, an ex-representative from Florida's 18th Congressional District, tweeted, "Wow! I am f*****g SHOCKED that Dems are voting to ban Tik Tok. This is AIPAC at work."[67]

The underlying contention, however, is that only those bought by Jewish money could possibly be brought to support "evil." Yet even after this outburst, most Democrats refused to denounce Omar. Instead they drafted a resolution condemning an array of ancient anti-Jewish cases, including the 1894 prosecution of *Alfred Dreyfus and the 1915 lynching of Leo Frank*, though still not specifically mentioning the Minnesotan in question.

Democrats, as a matter of fact, refused to even condemn antisemitism specifically, watering down the resolution with a platitudinous laundry list of all censurable hatreds. "We all have a responsibility to speak out against anti-Semitism, Islamophobia, homophobia, transphobia, racism, and all forms of hatred and bigotry, especially as we see a spike in hate crimes in America," explained then-senator Kamala Harris.[68]

Every time Omar was called out for her bigotry and conspiracy theories, she followed the strategy many other progressives employ: accuse critics of being racist and then claim there is nothing wrong with being "critical" of Israel.

In November 2023, Israel began retaliating against Hamas and uprooting the terror organization, which had entrenched itself within the civilian population of Gaza. Omar became a leading propagator of misinformation and conspiracy theories, often sharing imaginary death toll numbers provided by Hamas. At one point Omar reposted a photo of dead children, labeling it "Child Genocide in Palestine." The shot was of an attack on Syrian children by "President" Bashar Assad's troops in August 2013.[69]

This kind of ugly fabrication was the specialty of Omar's friend Rashida Tlaib, a daughter of Palestinian immigrants whose platform in 2018 promised to cut aid to the only democratic nation in the Middle East because it did not "fit the values of our country." Tlaib, who put a (wishcasting) sticker that read "Palestine" over Israel proper on a map in her office, became a leading apologist for Hamas and an anti-Jewish crank, regularly accusing supporters of Israel of harboring dual loyalties—essentially, an accusation of sedition. In one tweet, the congresswoman who has made championing "Palestine" her central cause, accused Israel supporters in Congress of forgetting "what country they represent."[70]

Anyone who disagreed, she contended, was targeting Muslims. At one "Progressive Town Hall" in Washington, DC, Tlaib theorized that her "Jewish colleagues" were targeting her and Omar because they "are Muslim."[71]

Tlaib regularly unsheathed antisemitic tropes about people "behind the curtain" who exploit "regular Americans" for "their profit."[72] Though it went unreported at the time of her campaign, we learned that in the 2000s Tlaib wrote for *The Final Call*, a blog founded by Louis Farrakhan, and other similarly conspiratorial publications.[73] Tlaib regularly spread conspiracies about Israel engaging in "ethnic cleansing" and "genocide," a new spin on an ancient blood libel.

There are two things to note: One, Israel's laws make absolutely no distinctions based on a person's race. Every person in Israel can participate in the democratic process, and all have equal standing under the law. Muslims in Israel have more liberal rights than Muslims anywhere in the Arab world do. Two, Israel—which provides water and electricity to Gaza—has the firepower to decimate the entire strip within minutes if it wanted to. Instead it often puts its own soldiers in danger to avoid civilian casualties.

Tlaib, though, *was* a fan of Hamas's genocidal chant "From the river to the sea, Palestine will be free"—meaning no Jews from the Jordan River to the Mediterranean Sea. She later risibly argued that the misunderstood chant was actually referring to "freedom, human rights, and peaceful coexistence."[74]

In one particularly egregious instance of disinformation, Tlaib tweeted that "Israel just bombed the Baptist Hospital killing 500 Palestinians."[75] To be fair to her, though, the *New York Times*, longtime antagonist of the Jewish state, ran the story without any substantiation. Since the newspaper hadn't done any investigation and merely passed on Hamas's claims, it was left without any confirmation or pictures. So the editors simply put a picture of another bombed-out building (not a hospital) on its front page, strongly insinuating that Israel was responsible for the tragedy. That, by the way, is the sort of blatant fake news you see on conspiracy theory websites.

Unlike the fake news stories on many of those sites, however, this tale was laundered in a professional package, incited worldwide condemnation and recrimination, and sparked antisemitic backlash from many on the left. But it wasn't true. Israel does not target hospitals with missiles, even if terrorists often hide underneath them. The damage was inflicted by a misfired rocket launched by Islamic Jihad, another genocidal terror group operating in Gaza. And hundreds of people did not die. There was an explosion in a parking lot.

As of this writing, Tlaib's tweet is still up.

Omar and Tlaib were both members of the Squad, which, at the time, also included Alexandria Ocasio-Cortez, Ayanna Pressley, Jamaal Bowman, Cori Bush, Greg Casar, Summer Lee, and other progressive conspiracy theorists. All of them began spreading justifications for the attack and then lying about the Israeli reaction. Ocasio-Cortez, like many others on the progressive left, supported the "boycott, divestment, and sanctions" (BDS) movement, an effort to economically destroy the Jewish state—and everyone in it, whether they support "settlements" or not. (Not even the Palestinian Authority, incidentally, which relies on Israeli capitalism to survive, supports BDS. American progressives are moving to a position more extreme than Fatah's.)

More than four hundred congressional staffers signed a pro-Hamas statement for Israel to cease destroying Hamas and hundreds of congressional staffers put on masks and rallied in front of Congress.[76] The chances that any were Republican are slim. The chances that the Squad's staff attended are high.

When a politician singles out Jewish allies as "evil" but ignores every brutal theocratic regime in the world, you don't have to do much digging to understand the reason. "Anti-Zionism" is the predominant justification for violence, murder, and hatred against Jews in Europe and the Middle East. Though relatively modern, it is girded by ancient tropes about Jewish power and influence. From ancient Rome to Middle Age blood libels, from Nazism to Marxism to Islamist fundamentalism, similar tropes are a feature of all authoritarian ideologies. Many of these anti-Zionist conspiracies were cooked up in the Soviet Union during the Cold War and then quickly popularized among Western intellectual leftists.[77]

Yet it seems they have never been more popular than today.

APOCALYPSE NOW-ISH

Humans May Be Fueling Global Warming
by Breathing: New Study
—NEW YORK POST, 2023[1]

New Study Says Global Warming Could Kill
83M People by the End of the Century
—THE HILL

A few years back, I ran across a heartbreaking story of a Nebraska boy who may or may not have been killed by something called *Naegleria fowleri*, a shape-shifting amoeba, after swimming in a lake near his home. The chilling piece noted that "the climate crisis is fueling the spread of a brain-eating amoeba" in the United States, because *Naegleria fowleri* grows in warm fresh water, "making it well-suited to proliferate as temperatures rise in the US."[2]

Since the article was a bit short on specifics—and since I was alarmed—I googled "*Naegleria fowleri*" and found a number of other pieces about the deadly amoeba, almost all of them published around the same time and almost all offering similar highly alarming, nebulous warnings.

It was almost as if a public relations firm knew that the phrase "brain-eating amoebas" would shock most Americans and instructed a bunch of reporters to repeat it. None of the articles offered scientific substantiation for either the claim that climate change was "fueling cases" of *Naegleria fowleri* or even that it was "sweeping the globe" or "rapidly spreading," as one paper claimed. It was bunk.

Most Americans, understandably, have jobs and families and lives and can't afford to spend hours investigating every alarmist story that crosses their path. I can. And, after some digging, I found out that in the decade preceding the article, there was a total of 31 reported cases of the brain-eating amoeba attacks in the entire United States. There have been, perhaps—no one seems to be sure—around 150 such cases since 1962.[3]

In colder states, there are barely any cases, with Minnesota (and its 14,380 official lakes) leading the way with two in the past sixty years. In our southern states, where there is already warmer water, *Naegleria fowleri* is also extremely rare. To put it in perspective, for every *N. fowleri* death, tens of thousands of people have perished falling out of trees, off ladders, and slipping in bathtubs.

But perhaps those deaths will soon be blamed on global warming as well.

Panic-mongering about the climate apocalypse might hark back to ancient times, but the Mayans have nothing on BlueAnon. These days it is challenging to find *any* societal dilemma that isn't being exacerbated, caused, or spread by climate change. And I mean *any*:

"Is Climate Change Making Us Sick?"[4] (Yes.)

"Is Climate Change Making Us Angrier?"[5] (Yes.)

"Is climate change making us shrink?"[6] (Yes.)

"Is Climate Change Making Us More Vulnerable To Infectious Diseases?"[7] (Yes.)

"Could climate affect our eyes?"[8] (Yes.)

"Is climate change making us crazy?"[9] (Definitely yes.)

Climate change is transforming us into fat, irascible, bellicose, hate-mongering, unhealthy slobs. Not that it matters, because we're all going to be dead soon enough.

White House national climate adviser Gina McCarthy says that climate is now a "health emergency," and she is not kidding.[10]

Heart disease? Yes, it "may be explained by extreme weather conditions," says ABC News.[11]

What about asthma? Yes. The Asthma and Allergy Foundation of America contends that climate change is the leading cause of new cases.[12]

Fungi? "It's Time to Fear the Fungi," warns *Wired* magazine. "Humans have long been protected from fungal infections, thanks to our nice, warm blood. Climate change could ruin that."[13]

Have you been drinking a bit too much? Don't worry, it's not your fault. "The Climate Crisis Is Driving People to Substance Abuse," *Wired* also warned.[14] "A new study from Columbia University researchers found that during higher temperatures, hospitals see a larger number of drug- and alcohol-related admissions, leading to worries that as climate change warms the planet, it could also exacerbate the consequences of substance abuse and alcoholism," *Forbes* cautions.[15]

"Climate change may trigger increase in headaches, migraines," CBS News tells us.[16]

What about diabetes? "We calculated that a 1-degree Celsius rise in environmental temperature could account for more than 100,000 new diabetes cases per year in the USA alone," an expert on the disease told CNN.[17]

"ALS, Dementia and Strokes Worsened by Climate Change, Researchers Find," read another headline in *Forbes*. "As we witness the effects of a warming planet on human health, it is imperative that neurologists anticipate how neurologic disease may change," *The Hill* noted.[18]

Does climate change cause war? You bet it does. Weather has left mankind more exposed "to human trafficking, slavery, and most commonly, sex work," Reuters recently reported.[19] Climate change, in fact, has also been a major contributor to conflicts in the historically docile and peaceful Middle East—even in the rise of Islamic fundamentalism.

"How Climate Change Helped Strengthen the Taliban" is the headline on deep dive from CBS News, which explained that Afghanistan ranks sixth for nations most impacted by climate change, and this created more radicalism.[20] There is no word on how the Taliban got into power in 1996, before the effects of climate change had purportedly hit, or why similar warlords had been functioning in that area for centuries before fossil fuels were a thing. Just know that for every half degree of warming, CBS explains, we're expected to see a 10 or 20 percent increase in conflicts—which, let's face it, sounds like pseudoscientific gibberish.

Conflict also happens "at the individual levels," *New York* magazine editor David Wallace-Wells assured a credulous MSNBC *Morning Joe* panel, "so we'll see rises in murder rates and rape, domestic assault. It spikes the rates at which people are admitted to mental hospitals."[21] If that's not sensational enough for you, Wallace-Wells also wrote a piece titled "The Uninhabitable Earth: Famine, economic collapse, a sun that cooks us: What climate change could wreak—sooner than you think."[22]

He's not joking though. The Intergovernmental Panel on Climate Change (IPCC) says that climate change will be responsible for 180,000 more rapes by 2099.[23] In fact, the same study promises the United States will experience an additional:

22,000 murders

1.2 million aggravated assaults

2.3 million simple assaults

260,000 robberies

1.3 million burglaries

2.2 million cases of larceny

580,000 cases of vehicle theft[24]

Those are *highly* specific predictions. Indeed, they are also both un-provable and impossible to disprove, like most climate scaremongering.

By the way, are you hungry? Blame Exxon.

"Extreme weather is a driver of world hunger," the Biden adminis-tration warns.[25] *Foreign Policy* magazine concurs, stating that climate change "is a leading cause of hunger."

Also, incredibly enough, climate change is to blame for the rise in obesity. There is nothing global warming can't do. Virtually every ma-jor news outlet in the United States has, at one time or another, con-nected climate change and hotter temperatures with childhood obesity rates. The journal *Temperature*—which, you might not be surprised to learn, tends to confirm its priors—argues that "climate change, specif-ically warmer temperatures is making our children more inactive and more obese" because it's too hot to play outside. (Wouldn't this also mean that more kids in formerly cold areas are going outside?)

The White House has given the issue a twist, noting that global warming's threats "disproportionately affect poor and minority com-munities."[26] The Biden administration's National Strategy on Gender Equity also says that climate change is a cause of gender-based vio-lence and "disproportionate risks to the health, safety, and economic security of women and girls."[27]

All of this reminds me of the old joke about left-wing media cover-age of disasters: "World to End, Women and Minorities Hardest Hit."

A 2022 study found that an increase in hate speech on social media could be directly tied to higher temperatures. A flood of headlines confirm it. "Extreme Weather Can Lead to More Online Hate Speech" and "Climate Change Is Making People Angrier Online" and "Hotter Days Bring Out Hotter Tempers," and so on.

Another report tells us that workplace harassment and discrimination at the U.S. Postal Service rises when the temperature tops 90 degrees.[28]

Not even future children can be safe from the vicissitudes of the weather. A piece in the *New York Times* explained that babies in the womb can be negatively impacted by climate change, citing a study published in the *Journal of Child Psychology and Psychiatry*, which found higher rates of psychological issues among kids who lived through a hurricane while inside the womb. "The study's authors found that boys who were exposed to Sandy in the womb had elevated risks for attention-deficit/disruptive behavioral disorders," while girls had elevated risks for anxiety disorders, depressive disorders and phobias."[29]

But let's also not forget the obvious killer: the heat.

"Extreme heat kills more people in the United States than any other weather hazard," read the snazzy front-page *Washington Post* interactive feature in the summer of 2023. The piece ominously warned that 62 million Americans might be "exposed" to dangerous levels of heat that year. So the editors created a handy map to let you find out if you too were "at risk." Most of the Americans who were in danger's way—which includes anyone exposed to heat over 90 degrees—unsurprisingly lived in the southernmost spots in the country. And it was, after all, the summer. If 90 degrees is hazardous to your health, and you don't want to buy an air conditioner, perhaps Arizona isn't for you.

You'll never be disappointed when you look under the hood and investigate how BlueAnon comes up with its chilling predictions. In 2021 the journal *Nature Climate Change* published a paper, widely covered by the media, that claimed that between 1991 and 2018, more than one-third of all deaths associated with heat exposure were linked to global warming.[30] The researchers came to this number by relying on predictions made by scientists who were obstinately wrong for decades and then guesstimated what the weather would have been like without global warming. Then researchers added the number of people who they speculated were going to die without global warming and calculated the difference.

So, fiction.

Since I had always been under the impression that cold weather killed more people than hot, I did a little more digging. In a piece published only a few months earlier in the very same *Washington Post*, we learn that another recent peer-reviewed study in *BMJ* found that "cold weather is associated with nearly 20 times more deaths than hot weather."[31] Sure, cold is far more dangerous, but "climate change is complicated," explained the author.

Absolutely. The incontestable fact, always unmentioned in these reports, is that fewer people are dying from the heat *and* cold than ever, thanks to the advances of modern society (which of course, we have because of fossil fuels). But that's not any more compelling to a climate-crazy BlueAnon believer than a red light is to a drunk driver (whose intoxication, of course, was caused by climate change).

ECOANXIETY

You have stolen my dreams and my
childhood with your empty words.
—GRETA THUNBERG[32]

Are you depressed? You can chalk that up to climate change too. "Extreme Temperatures Are Hurting Our Mental Health," says

Bloomberg News.[33] Researchers for the American Psychological Association contend that mental health impacts come both immediately following extreme weather events tied to climate change, and gradually as temperatures and sea levels rise over the course of years and decades. "Trauma, post-traumatic stress disorder, and depression" all rank among the ailments linked to climate change.[34]

"There is a mental health crisis around the world, I think that one of the main reasons for that is that young people look at the fact that we are not yet solving the climate crisis," one of the world's leading climate alarmists, Al Gore, recently noted.[35] No, there is a mental health crisis around the world because the likes of Gore have created mass panic, pathologically scarring young people, whose lives are undermined by a political obsession.

In 2021, the medical journal *The Lancet* polled 10,000 people between the ages of 16 and 25 from around the world, including 1,000 from the United States. Nearly 60 percent of participants were "extremely worried" about climate change. Over half were "sad, anxious, angry, powerless, helpless, and guilty" because of climate change. Over 45 percent said that these feelings negatively affected how they function in everyday life, while 75 percent responded that they think the future is frightening because of climate change impacts.[36]

In most polls, somewhere around 30 percent of voters contend that it's "at least somewhat likely" that the earth will become uninhabitable, humanity wiped out, over the next ten to fifteen years. Half of voters under age thirty-five believe it is likely we are on the *edge of extinction*—54 percent of Americans, according to Pew, view climate change as a major threat, 78 percent of them Democrats.[37]

"Ecoanxiety," according to the American Psychological Association, is "the chronic fear of environmental cataclysm that comes from observing the seemingly irrevocable impact of climate change and the associated concern for one's future and that of next generations." Many young people struggle to deal with the imaginary apocalypse. And some young people are often used in propagandistic efforts.

Time famously named Greta Thunberg—then an uneducated sixteen-year-old—Person of the Year in 2019.[38] There was "something about her raw honesty around a message of blunt-force fear [that] turned this girl from invisible to global," CNN explained in a *news* report.[39]

It should be noted that "blunt-force fear" is the accurate way to describe the concerted misinformation that Thunberg has likely been subjected to since nursery school. In a just world, Thunberg would show up at the United Nations every year and profess her gratitude to the Western capitalistic world for bequeathing her this remarkable inheritance. Instead she, like millions of indoctrinated young Americans, acts as if she lives in a uniquely broken world on the precipice of disaster.

We've failed her, and millions of others, by raising a generation of panic-stricken hysterics.

"The climate apocalypse is coming. To prepare for it, we need to admit that we can't prevent it," renowned novelist Jonathan Franzen recently wrote in *New York* in a piece accompanied by art that showed a mother pushing her child on a swing surrounded by giant flames.[40]

This is the kind of panic Americans are confronted with daily.

Nearly every public school district in the United States promotes panic-stricken environmental alarmism in their auditoriums and classrooms. Kids are given excused absences to participate in politically motivated "climate" marches so they can gripe about the very thing that makes their lives so safe and prosperous. Guilt, grief, and angst over the future of the planet has become a major fear for young people. Climate alarmism permeates culture. Movies for kids are replete with climate change as the subtext. Most nature documentaries mention the creeping evil of climate change. Walk into any Barnes & Noble and you will find the children-section shelves stocked with tomes that spread panic about the weather.

One can start early with *Climate Change for Babies* and work their way to *When the Storm Comes* or *Our World Out of Balance: Understanding Climate Change and What We Can Do* and dozens of books teaching kids to become insufferable activists. Marxist author Naomi Klein's *How to Change Everything: The Young Human's Guide to Protecting the Planet and Each Other* or *Old Enough to Save the Planet* or *Cranky Uncle vs. Climate Change: How to Understand and Respond to Climate Science Deniers* are all instruction manuals that teach kids to drop their critical thinking abilities and join a worldwide panic.

Here's what a parent won't find in the bookstore or local library: a kids' book celebrating the fact that by almost every quantifiable measure, we live in a healthier, safer, and cleaner environment than humankind has ever enjoyed. Or any book celebrating the fact that humans have always adapted to organic and anthropogenic changes in the environment.

Then again, maybe those kids reading those books are lucky to be alive at all. According to a poll conducted by Ipsos, nearly a quarter of Americans between the ages of eighteen and forty-five say that climate change has made them rethink having kids.[41] In one NPR piece—"Should We Be Having Kids in the Age of Climate Change?"[42]—a couple ponders "the ethics of procreation and its impact on the climate" before starting a family, and a group of women in a prosperous New Hampshire town swap stories about how the "the climate crisis is a reproductive crisis."

The U.S. fertility rate is now well below the replacement level of about two births per woman, incidentally. That is a far bigger threat to the future than climate change.

All of this is the fault of ideologues who obsess over every weather event as if it were Armageddon, ignoring the massive moral upside of carbon-fueled modernity. It's the fault of the politicians, too cowardly to tell voters that their utopian vision of a world run on solar panels and windmills is a dangerous fairy tale. It's the fault of BlueAnon that constantly ignores overwhelming evidence that, on balance, climate change isn't undermining human flourishing.

ENDGAMES

We will soon be asking: is it perfectly OK to eat the
bodies of your dead because we're all so hungry?
—PAUL EHRLICH, 2014[43]

If we must pick a starting point for the environmental apocalypticism that has consumed the modern left, it would be the rise of the doomsday prophet Paul R. Ehrlich.

In the 1970s, Ehrlich created the template for modern end-of-day alarmism by adding the imprimatur of scientific authenticity to his dire—but relentlessly incorrect—predictions. "The battle to feed all of humanity is over," begins his most famous book, *The Population Bomb*, published in 1968. "In the 1970s hundreds of millions of people will starve to death in spite of any crash programs embarked upon now."[44]

Ehrlich appeared on Johnny Carson's *Tonight Show*[45] and many other popular talk shows during the 1970s, predicting that oceans would be without life by 1979 and the United States would see its population plummet to 23 million by 1999 due to pesticides. "The death rate will increase until at least 100–200 million people per year will be starving to death during the next ten years," he famously told *Mademoiselle* magazine in 1970.[46]

Like other climate alarmists, each time Ehrlich was proven wrong—which is basically every time—he upped the ante to compensate. In 2009, for example, Ehrlich said that "perhaps the most serious flaw" in *The Population Bomb* was that it was "much too optimistic" about the future.

In January 2023, around fifty-five years after Ehrlich's first predictions, *60 Minutes* featured the antihumanist nutjob so he could warn that the earth was quickly headed for a "sixth extinction." Which was odd, considering Ehrlich predicted numerous other extinctions over the past sixty years.

Of course, *60 Minutes* did not invite a single guest on to push back against Ehrlich's debunked theories. The media is teeming with environmental doomsayers and Malthusians who need to believe the world is in constant peril due to the excesses of capitalism, fears over "overpopulation" are regularly cited by journalists—who often live in the densest, yet also the wealthiest places—despite the world cutting extreme poverty in half over the past thirty years.[47]

Ehrlich, it should be noted, was hardly alone. Two years after the release of *The Population Bomb*, noted Harvard biologist George Wald, foreshadowing a wave of environmental panic, estimated that "civilization will end within 15 or 30 years unless immediate action is taken against problems facing mankind."[48]

In 1972, Maurice Strong, the United Nations' first executive director of the environment, warned that earth had only "ten years to stop the catastrophe."[49]

In 1977, Obama's future science "tsar" John Holdren coauthored a book with Ehrlich predicting that global warming could lead to the deaths of a billion people by the year 2020. To stem this inevitable catastrophe, the authors toyed with the idea of adding "sterilant to drinking water or staple foods" and argued that other "population-control laws, even including laws requiring compulsory abortion, could be sustained under the existing Constitution."[50] As we'll see, the more you normalize panic-stricken predictions, the more you normalize authoritarian solutions.

In 1982, Mostafa K. Tolba, executive director of the United Nations environmental program, cautioned that if something wasn't done in the *next* decade the world would face "an environmental catastrophe which will witness devastation as complete, as irreversible, as any nuclear holocaust."[51] Tolba amended this prediction in 1989, cautioning that if humans didn't act by 1999, "global disaster, nations wiped off the face of the earth, crop failures."[52] They are *always* compelled to amend their predictions.

By 2005, you'd think the left would have dropped the alarmism. But instead they adopted it as their de facto mode of operating. Climate scientists, activists, and politicians from around the world met to discuss how to deal with the coming apocalypse. The world had as little as ten years before it reached "the point of no return on global warming." Over the next decade, humans would soon be grappling with "widespread agricultural failure," "major droughts," "increased disease," "the death of forests," and the "switching-off of the North Atlantic Gulf Stream," among many other dreadful calamities.[53]

It didn't happen.

In 2006, Al Gore famously informed millions of Americans via his Oscar-winning documentary, *An Inconvenient Truth*, that sea levels would rise by twenty feet "in the near future."[54] The producers even offered chilling videos of major cities like Miami and New York underwater.

Gore was only off by around twenty feet. Anyway, his pseudoscientific movie has been largely forgotten, but South Beach, alas, is still with us.[55]

The next year, in 2007, Rajendra Pachauri, head of the UN climate panel, said, "If there is no action before 2012, that's too late."

Year after year after year, the end is always near.

In 2018, UN General Assembly president Maria Espinosa told twenty-two thousand delegates attending the 24th Conference of the Parties to the United Nations Framework Convention that "mankind" was "in danger of disappearing" if climate change is allowed to progress at its current pace.[56]

That same year, the Natural Resources Defense Council, which represents three million members, declared that the scientific consensus was that we have twenty years before there is no turning back for earth.[57]

NPR reported in 2021 that "Earth has 11 years to cut emissions to avoid dire climate scenarios, a report says."[58]

"We can't afford to stay where we are," Barack Obama told the United Nations Climate Change Conference in Glasgow, Scotland, in 2021. "The world has to step up, and it has to step up now. When it comes to climate, time really is running out."

"The world is going to end in twelve years if we don't address climate change," warned the popular progressive congresswoman Alexandria Ocasio-Cortez. *Smithsonian* magazine concurred. "The World Was Just Issued 12-Year Ultimatum on Climate Change," read a cover story in the government-backed magazine.[59]

Not eleven, or thirteen. Twelve years.

In a 2023 IPCC climate change report, scientists said the world is *likely to pass a dangerous temperature threshold within the next twenty years.*[60]

All this, even though John Kerry, Joe Biden's climate czar, argued in 2021 that the earth had nine years to avert the worst consequences of climate crisis: "There's no faking it on this one."

There was a lot of faking.

By the time Paul Ehrlich was appearing on *60 Minutes*, hundreds of millions *fewer* people were suffering from hunger than when *The Population Bomb* was released, despite there being around three billion more people inhabiting the earth.

Ehrlich's progeny are other media-favored hysterics by other antihumanists such as Gore or Thunberg—not to mention thousands of other Little Ehrlichs nudging you to eat insects, gluing themselves to paintings, and demanding you surrender the most basic conveniences and necessities of modernity.

Right now we are on the cusp of eradicating diseases like polio,

Guinea worm, Carrion's disease, lymphatic filariasis, measles, ovine rinderpest, pork tapeworm, rubella, syphilis, and many others. There has been great advancement in eliminating all mosquito-borne diseases. We are close to a cure for AIDS. Researchers are inching closer to a vaccine that may cut Alzheimer's disease cases in half.[61] Cancer survival rates have soared.[62] And that's not even mentioning the very long list of ailments science has cured or severely diminished over the past fifty years.

Deaths due to climate events have plummeted. Extreme global poverty has plummeted.[63] State-based conflicts have plummeted.[64] Air pollution has plummeted.[65] Deaths from air pollution have plummeted.[66] When the state of the earth is improving in almost every quantifiable way, alarmists are compelled to rely on prophecies that have not only been notoriously wrong but never account for the resilient human capacity to adapt.

Over the decades, there has been a spike in the use of genetically modified crops, as well as advances in heat-resistant crops, which has led to booming yields in agriculture. According to the UN, there were 200 million fewer hungry people in 2015 than there were in 1990.[67]

But no matter how many ailments science cures, no matter how many times science makes our lives more comfortable, the alarmism continues scaring us. Time is *always* running out. The end is just over the horizon.

EVERY STORM, A KILLER OPPORTUNITY

And, folks, look, the of survival our—our planet is on the ballot. And that sounds like hyperbole, but it genuinely is.
—JOE BIDEN, 2022[68]

Because none of the left's apocalyptic prophesies ever come to fruition, it's become necessary for politicians to ratchet up the alarmism by treating every hurricane, tornado, and flood as if one of the Seven Seals in the book of Revelation were being opened.

When Iowa was hit by rainstorms in 2019, then–presidential candidates Beto O'Rourke and Elizabeth Warren descended on the state to warn the residents that these floods will be more frequent and severe because of climate change.[69] Only a few years earlier, Massachusetts senator Warren was warning that drought was going to devour us.[70]

When a rare tornado warning hit the Washington, DC, area, Ocasio-Cortez suggested the "climate crisis" was at fault. "Different parts of the country deal with different climate issues," she explained, warning of extreme tornadoes.[71] "But ALL of these threats will be increasing in intensity as climate crisis grows and we fail to act appropriately."[72]

When a single, freak snowstorm hit Texas in 2021, the Biden administration spent its time pushing draconian policy interventions by claiming such events would be the new norm. "How the Texas Winter Storm Disaster Will Shape Joe Biden's Climate Agenda," read a *Time* magazine piece. But the Texas storm was no different than the rare Great Southeastern snowstorm of 1973.[73] It happens. And there's nothing we can do about it.

When Katrina, a Category 3 hurricane, hit New Orleans in August 2005 it inflicted tremendous damage on the ill-prepared city. Afterward, we were warned that it was a prelude to endless other storms and ecological disasters. Alarmists like Mike Tidwell were featured on major news programs discussing his book *The Ravaging Tide: Strange Weather, Future Katrinas, and the Coming Death of America's Coastal Cities.* "I think the biggest lesson from Katrina a year later is that those same ingredients, you know, a city below sea level hit by a major hurricane, will be replicated by global warming all along our Atlantic and Gulf coastlines," he told CBS News.[74]

And who can forget Al Gore, with his grade school "science" charts, cartoonish satellite images (water, the color of fire!), and didactic tone, emotionally manipulating audiences with images of destruction and suffering. The problem was, *An Inconvenient Truth* suggested—among numerous other dire predictions that would never come to pass—not only that climate change had caused Katrina, but that it portended the dawn of an age of shocking and intense hurricanes.

As it turns out, Florida didn't get hit with another hurricane until 2016. Louisiana didn't see a major one until 2020.[75] Of course, magazines like *Scientific American* explained that "Global Warming Causes Fewer Tropical Cyclones," so you can never really win.[76]

At some point hurricanes did hit land, and the hysterics were back. When surveying the damage after Hurricane Ida hit in 2021, Joe Biden told a crowd that the scene was a reckoning for the "climate crisis" and was "code red" for the world.[77] But hurricanes weren't touching land at higher frequencies[78] nor with more intensity.[79] According to the U.S. Natural Hazard Statistics, 2022 saw below the thirty-year average in deaths not only from tornadoes but also from heat, flooding, and lightning.[80]

Certainly, they aren't any more dangerous.

In 2022, Hurricane Ian, a serious Category 5, barreled toward Florida. It was the strongest hurricane to make landfall in Florida since Michael in 2018. "Hurricane Ian gets nasty quickly, turbocharged by warm water," warned the Associated Press, observing what has been true since the very first hurricane was formed.[81] More "climate havoc," the *New York Times* wrote, as Ian threatened to hit the same exact places the storms have always hit.[82]

Even when scientists approached the storm in a judicious manner, the media simply wouldn't have it. "What effect does climate change have on this phenomenon?" CNN's Don Lemon asked Jamie Rhome, the acting director of the National Oceanic and Atmospheric Administration's National Hurricane Center about Hurricane Ian. "Because it seems these storms are intensifying."[83]

"I don't think you can link climate change to any one event. On the whole, on the cumulative, climate change may be making storms worse. But to link it to any one event, I would caution against it," answers Rhome.

"Okay, listen, I grew up there. And these storms are intensifying," responds Lemon.

He grew up there. Is that the vaunted "science" we've been hearing so much about?

Joy Behar, cohost of *The View*, noted that Florida governor Ron DeSantis had refused to embrace alarmism, and "now, his state is getting hit with one of the worst hurricanes that we will ever see!" This is a quite common attack, but it makes little sense. Even if we accepted every forecast about anthropogenic global warming and embraced the Democrats' net-zero plan and banned gas-powered engines and fossil fuels by 2050 or 2030 or whenever, the temperature wouldn't be any different in 2022.

But that doesn't even matter because the entire claim is fiction.

Overall, the frequency of hurricanes has slightly declined since 1900. From 1851 to 1860, 19 hurricanes made landfall in the United States.[84] From 2011 to 2020, 19 hurricanes made landfall in the United States. The average per decade between 1860 and 2011 is about 18. In the decade of 1941–50, 10 major hurricanes hit the United States.[85]

The underlying claim is also untrue. Since Behar's birth in 1942, Florida has seen 48 hurricanes make landfall. Three of them have been Category 5 (the worst intensity), nine of them have been Category 4, and 11 of them Category 3.[86]

Granted, Behar was not around for 1900's Great Galveston hurricane, which hit eight years before Model Ts began emitting carbon into the air; it likely killed somewhere around 10,000 people in Texas.[87] The 1926 Great Miami hurricane killed 372, causing an estimated, inflation-adjusted $164 billion in damages.[88] Only around 150,000 people lived in all of Dade County back in those days. Financial damages are going to be far higher because far more people live in these areas. The Great

Labor Day Hurricane of 1935 was tied with 2019's Hurricane Dorian for strongest maximum sustained landfall winds (185 mph).[89]

Overall, weather accounts for somewhere around 0.07 percent of worldwide deaths, and 0.01 percent in the United States.[90] We're safer, even though far more people live in areas with extreme heat and freezing cold and in the paths of both hurricanes and tornadoes. By claiming we are in an unprecedented "crisis," we distort not only a proper understanding of our technological abilities, but our moral outlook as well.

There are good reasons for the hysterics that have persuaded millions that the end of the world might be right around the corner. Panic-mongering surrounding climate change manifests in dramatic and immediate calls for change. We are constantly told that the only way to save the very life of the planet is to embrace authoritarian policy ideas that would, at the very least, inhibit the economy in ways that have never been seen in American history.

To put the radical political goals in perspective, let's spend a moment recalling the most popular plan of the environmental left, the "Green New Deal."

The name itself speaks to pathological fears that propel the political left. When the Green New Deal was released, *every* Democratic Party presidential hopeful at the time—including Cory Booker, Kamala Harris, Elizabeth Warren, Kirsten Gillibrand, Julián Castro, and Beto O'Rourke—endorsed or expressed support for the plan.[91] All of them knew, of course, that it wasn't feasible to pass as it was initially written down. The nation would have collapsed. But the contemporary left, captured by the irrational dread surrounding climate change, was expected at the very least to offer aspirational support for the toppling of modernity and the destruction of massive amounts of wealth and technology.

The media was expected to cover the proposal with a reverential tone, admiring its boldness. And so they did.

It is not hyperbole to contend that the plan, written by socialist Alexandria Ocasio-Cortez, is by every measure the most illiberal proposal ever presented to the American people by an elected official. Not merely because it would necessitate a dismantling of the Constitution, but also because the societal costs are unfathomable.

The plan, which was to be implemented over the course of ten years, calls for the elimination of all fossil fuel energy production, which is still the most basic necessity of American industry and life, and includes not only all oil but also natural gas, one of the cheapest sources of energy. Natural gas is one of the reasons the United States has been able to lead the world in carbon-emissions reduction over the past few years.

More specifically, the Green New Deal called for the replacement of "combustion-engine vehicles"—trucks, airplanes, boats, and 99 percent of cars. It calls for the retrofitting of "every building in America" with "state of the art energy efficiency."[92] I repeat, "every building in America." That includes every home, factory, office, and apartment building, which will all need their entire working heating and cooling systems ripped out and replaced. Replaced with what? We do not know. And because one of the key pillars of contemporary environmentalism is to institute a collectivist economy, it also promises every American a government-guaranteed job with a "family-sustaining wage, family and medical leave, vacations, and a pension"; a free education for every American as long as they choose to attend college; a salubrious diet; "safe, affordable, adequate housing" for every American; and money and "economic security" for all who are "unable or unwilling" to work.

Let's just say the estimated cost of such a plan is probably somewhere near $10 kajillion.

It is worth stressing that climate hysteria has prepared people for other forms of authoritarian control. A *Nature* journal piece from 2021 argued that COVID lockdowns had primed Americans for more restrictions on liberty "that were unthinkable only one year before." We would be, the piece notes, "more prepared to accept tracking and limitations" to "achieve a safer climate."[93]

At the time, Eric Holthaus, a popular online climate change activist, argued that the economic restrictions of the coronavirus lockdowns were "roughly the same pace that the IPCC says we need to sustain every year until 2030 to be on pace to limit global warming to 1.5C and hit the Paris climate goals."

"We're doing it. It's possible!" he added.[94]

Because climate change is an existential threat to humanity, increasing numbers of leftists argue that Biden should unilaterally declare an emergency to save the planet.

Holthaus is correct that implementing a plan like the Green New Deal would hold approximately the same gruesome economic consequences as the coronavirus crisis—except, of course, they would last basically forever. The point of modern environmentalism is the destruction of wealth and inhibition of progress. This process is what Holthaus and many others euphemistically call "degrowth." Which is to say, that merely to *keep pace* with the IPCC recommendations on carbon emissions, Americans would be compelled to shut down virtually the entire economy. Tens of millions of people would lose their jobs and hundreds of millions of people would stop traveling and purchasing the things they had relied upon for decades.

Americans use over 20 million barrels of petroleum products every day—now more abundant and easier to extract than ever before. So, unless some completely new technology emerges, it will take a fascistic technocracy to eliminate our reliance on fossil fuels.

I don't use *fascistic* lightly here. Tyranny, among other factors, springs from societal panic. And the only way to mitigate or stop the threat of climate disaster, according to the modern left, is to empower the state to dictate every decision made by industry and individuals that relates to carbon emissions—which, to be clear, entails regulating every single aspect of the entire economy.[95]

IN THIS HOUSE WE BELIEVE SCIENCE IS REAL

Republicans' Anti-Science, Pro-Sickness
Agenda Is Making the Pandemic Worse
—DEMOCRATIC NATIONAL COMMITTEE

Do the positions of the stars determine our future?

Does life begin whenever we decide?

Can a person change their gender whenever they feel like it?

Because many on the left believe so.

There is a false perception that liberals are more inclined to "trust science" than conservatives, when it is more accurate to say that leftists reject science in different, often more consequential ways.

And one of the reasons polls have seen a growth in the conservative "distrust" of science is that the left has expanded the meaning of the word to include a downpour of pseudoscientific and social scientific concepts that are at worst dubious and at best debatable. That includes climate change alarmism.

Most of the recent "anti-science" accusations also hinge on the right wing's reticence about COVID vaccinations.

It's true that once the pandemic broke out, there was a scramble to find effective therapeutic solutions, or better yet a vaccine to stave off the spread of the disease. But the rapid pace in which a vaccine was finally made, the perceived lack of oversight, and the government's role in compelling citizens to take the new medicine, whether they wanted to or not, all had many conservatives questioning the efficacy and safety of vaccines.

But BlueAnon's memory is short.

During the 2020 election, Democrats were the ones who first fueled antivaccine conspiracies—the kind they would decry as dangerous misinformation only months later. They did it to deny Donald Trump credit for the White House's Operation Warp Speed. It is almost certain that, had Trump won in 2020, liberals would have been far bigger vaccine skeptics.

On numerous occasions during the campaign, vice presidential candidate Kamala Harris said that COVID vaccines in development would probably be unsafe. She claimed the public health experts who vouched for a vaccine were suspect, because they "will be muzzled, they will be suppressed, they will be sidelined, because [Trump] is looking at an election coming up in less than sixty days, and he's grasping for whatever he can get to pretend that he has been a leader on this issue, when he has not."

This alarmism wasn't based on any evidence.

Joe Biden was no better, suggesting that the vaccines might not be "real" or "safe,"[96] and arguing that they were "not likely to go through all the tests."[97] Harris and Biden weren't alone in propagating uncertainty. The pandemic's most incompetent governor, New York's Andrew Cuomo, then a hero on the left for his authoritarian approach to stopping the spread of a virus, both fueled and predicted the skepticism that would later be normalized.

"You're going to say to the American people now, 'Here's a vaccine, it was new, it was done quickly, but trust this federal administration and their health administration that it's safe? And we're not one hundred percent sure of the consequences.' I think it's going to be a very skeptical American public about taking the vaccine, and they should be."[98]

That was October 2020.

Using this logic, no vaccine developed during any Republican presidency would ever be reliable. Of course, it had to be done quickly. Americans were tired of being locked in their homes watching their businesses be destroyed by government lockdowns. Neither Harris nor Biden nor Cuomo ever offered evidence that Moncef Slaoui, the apolitical researcher who spearheaded numerous vaccine innovations while at GlaxoSmithKline, was being pressured by the administration or anyone else to deliver an untested vaccine before Election Day. Slaoui was forced to explain that vaccine production had "nothing to do with the election," stating that "the approach is 100 percent based on facts and data and nothing else." And no evidence has ever been unearthed to suggest otherwise.

At the time, most of the media treated this kind of skepticism as completely normal and a healthy inquiry into a new vaccine. Biden and Harris knew well that Trump wasn't cooking up a vaccine in the basement of Mar-a-Lago, his resort and residence in Palm Beach, Florida. And they knew that vaccines were showing promising results. Still, they cynically cast doubt on the efficacy of potentially lifesaving drugs to preemptively discredit the Trump administration before the election. It was a conspiracy theory.

Harris was given numerous opportunities to walk back or temper her claims that the process could be so easily corrupted. She doubled down, promising, "If Donald Trump tells us to take it, I'm not taking it."

In the end, Harris *did* take Trump's vaccine—the same vaccine the former president instructed his followers to take and the same vaccine that was coerced by the *Biden-Harris* administration on Americans.

Not only that, but the Biden administration then spent months trying to take credit for the work of Big Pharma and the Trump administration. The moment he became president, Biden began lying about the origins of the vaccine, taking credit for launching the program: "when I first started the vaccination program and we got all that vaccine, enough for everyone, we were vaccinating three million people a day, we were getting very close before things began to slow down."

Democrats were eager to point out that Trump had himself flirted with the claim that vaccine and autism was linked. "From Skeptic to

Cheerleader," the *New York Times* declared.[99] What they often forgot was that Barack Obama, among many others on the left, had similarly engaged in skepticism. "We've seen just a skyrocketing autism rate," Obama told a crowd in April 2008. "Some people are suspicious that it's connected to the vaccines. The science is right now inconclusive, but we have to research it."

It wasn't inconclusive. It was researched. Exhaustively. The vaccine-autism conspiracy originates from a single, since-retracted 1998 article published in *The Lancet*, in which a disgraced pediatrician named Andrew Wakefield invented evidence linking the measles, mumps, and rubella (MMR) vaccine to autism. By 2008, when Obama was asking the question, scientists had a decade of research and had overwhelmingly rejected the relationship between vaccinations and autism. Every peer-reviewed study conducted since 1998 (of which there were dozens) found no link.

Obama knew what he was doing. Before COVID, vaccine skepticism was nothing new on the left. The resistance to immunization was driven by conspiracies about capitalism and pharma companies, as well as a hippie impulse to reject anything that isn't "natural."

Some of the most vociferous skeptics, like Robert F. Kennedy Jr., now a hero to COVID skeptics, were on the progressive left. A 2015 *Pediatrics* study found that significant clusters of vaccine deniers lived in heavily left-wing areas like "northern San Francisco and southern Marin County."[100] For years Oregon was the leading state of vaccine opt-out for kids.[101] Portland didn't allow fluoride in the water until 2012.[102]

There has always been a contingent on the left of superorganic, "crunchy" vaccine skeptics. Additionally, large segments of the African American population—often due, in some part, to historical wrongs, including the Tuskegee Syphilis Study—were also prone to believing conspiracy theories about vaccines. When the media wrote about the high levels of COVID vaccine suspicion within black communities, they would do so by explaining why it existed. "Why Black Americans Distrust the New COVID-19 Vaccines" or "In Tuskegee, Painful History Shadows Efforts to Vaccinate African Americans" and so on. Fair enough. But polls taken during the pandemic usually found more distrust among black Americans, predominately Democrats, than any other group in the country.[103]

As we've seen, modern environmentalism perpetuates myths about the inorganic world and the evils of modernity.

Take genetically modified crops, a process that, in one form or another, humans have been engaged in for around ten thousand years. Conspiracies about the dangers of genetically modified organisms (GMOs) probably hurt society (the poor in particular) more than any scientific denialism on the right.

Over two thousand studies have confirmed that GMOs are safe.[104] Around the world, almost every respected scientific organization that has looked at GMOs has found that they are as safe as any other food.[105] They are beneficial, though, for productivity, in the environmental impact, and in the ability of the world's poor to enjoy healthier, high-caloric diets for a lot less money. GMOs save lives.

Yet progressives are constantly entertaining or passing legislation that blunts progress on this front or needlessly compels companies to label GMO products, which insinuates there are dangers attached to eating them. As far as we know, there are none. There is far more scientific unanimity on the question of GMOs than on any of the questions about climate alarmism. Yet one is seen as antiscience and the other is seen as healthy anticorporate skepticism. According to Pew, however, Republicans are evenly divided on whether genetically modified foods are unsafe, while Democrats believe they are unsafe by a 26-point margin.[106]

Also consider the fabricated panic over hydraulic fracturing, or "fracking." The fracking process entails injecting water, sand, and chemicals into a well at high pressure to loosen the shale and release gas, which is a safer and cleaner way to extract fossil fuels.

Not only does the process create hundreds of thousands of jobs, but it also provides cheaper energy for millions of Americans. Fracking has less of an environmental impact than other methods of extracting fuel. It also means less dependency on foreign oil.

A slew of panicky documentaries and investigations have been cooked up to warn Americans that fracking will bring ecological horrors on our land—fires, earthquakes, disaster. The *New York Times* claimed that "Drilling Is Making Oklahoma as Quake Prone as California."[107] CNN reported, "Fracking Fallout: 7.9 Million at Risk of Man-Made Earthquakes."[108]

None of this turned out to be true. But it was ironic that these outlets, then in the middle of spreading the Russia Collusion hoax, were repeating alarmism promoted by antifracking groups being financed by Russia. Putin knows that fracking gives the United States another advantage in the energy market.[109]

The alarmism worked. Polls generally show that 60 percent of Democrats oppose fracking. This is even though numerous scientific studies—one funded by the National Science Foundation that debunked the purported link between groundwater pollution and fracking—have assured us that there's nothing to fear.[110]

Nuclear power faces very similar PR difficulties. Democrats, while lately warming up to nuclear power in rhetoric, continue crippling the expansion of the cleanest power available. This has harmed the environmentalist cause. Nuclear is safer and cleaner than oil, natural gas, or coal extraction. It is also the only energy source we now have that could possibly come close to helping the United States reach "zero carbon emissions."

Yet Democrats in numerous states have been either standing in the way or dismantling nuclear power plants for decades over hysterical fears. After President Obama halted the development of Yucca

Mountain, Nevada, which made any real expansion of nuclear power unlikely, the Government Accountability Office found that it was done for political rather than scientific reasons.[111]

Then again, what are we to make of people who often mock religion as imaginary, but believe in fortune-telling? Democrats are twice as likely to believe in astrology as Republicans.[112] When the National Science Foundation released a report reviewing scientific knowledge, they found that 49 percent of Democrats, nearly half, had some level of trust in things like tarot cards, zodiac signs, and horoscopes. The group that believed in these things the least? Conservative Republicans, at 70 percent.

Democrats are also far more inclined to believe Eastern new age quackery than conservatives.[113] Need it be said that homeopathy is useless? Yet far more liberals believe in it than conservatives.

According to a HuffPost/YouGov poll, 48 percent of adults in the United States believe that alien spacecrafts are observing our planet right now. Among those who do believe extraterrestrials are hanging around, 69 percent are Democrats, a far higher number than Republicans.[114]

STEAL FROM THE POOR, GIVE
TO THE PLUTOCRATS

*People our age have never experienced American
prosperity in our adult lives—which is why so many
millennials are embracing Democratic socialism.*

—CHARLOTTE ALTER

For BlueAnon, every ordinary economic setback is akin to living through the famine of Holodomor.

In a mythmaking 2019 *Time* magazine profile of socialist sweetheart Alexandria Ocasio-Cortez, Charlotte Alter contended that the congresswoman's "adulthood" was "defined by financial crisis, debt & climate change. No wonder she and her peers are moving left."[1] This is a contention one often hears from Millennials. It is a chilling reality, no doubt.

Also, it isn't real. The truth is that AOC's formative years were no more defined by a recession than young adults who lived through 1928, 1937, 1945, 1949, 1953, 1958, 1960, 1969, 1973, 1980, 1981, 1990, or 2001. Maybe less so. Ocasio-Cortez, as of the writing of this book, had been alive exactly a single quarter of negative gross domestic product

(GDP) growth in her entire adult life—and seen eighteen quarters of above-average 3 percent growth. In the economic quarter she graduated from college, the United States economy grew by an impressive 4.7 percent.[2] Her formative adult experiences were many things, but economically traumatic is not one.

The reality is that today's young leftist has been bequeathed the healthiest, wealthiest, safest, and most peaceful world that human beings have ever known. But like millions of other indoctrinated young people, they act as if they live in a uniquely broken world.

Older than AOC, I happen to have been born in what is now her congressional district in New York. When I was a kid in the 1970s and '80s, New York was a crime-ridden hellhole that struggled with stagnation, bankruptcies, crushing energy prices, and retirement-destroying inflation. The year AOC was born, there were 2,245 murders for the year in NYC.[3] By the time Ocasio-Cortez turned twenty in 2009, New York saw a historic low of 461 murders. By the year she announced her candidacy in 2017, American's largest city, 8 million people, experienced only 286 homicides.[4]

While progressive policies are again helping to drag that great metropolitan area into the sewer, by the time AOC was elected to Congress, New York was again one of the richest and safest cities in the country.

Speaking of being safer, in the year Ocasio-Cortez was born, 45,582 Americans died in vehicular accidents (18.5 per 100,000). The year she graduated from college it had fallen to 32,479 (10.4). In 1970, around 14,000 workers were killed on the job. Although the workforce had more than doubled by the time Ocasio-Cortez went to Congress, the number of workplace deaths has dropped to 5,190, a rise from the historic low of 4,764 in 2020.[5] Fewer young Americans are forced to work dangerous jobs. These are all signs of an increasingly prosperous society.

Almost everything has gotten better.

In 1965, there were only 5.9 million Americans enrolled in college—mostly children of privilege. By the time Ocasio-Cortez was born, there were 13.5 million enrolled in institutions of higher education. The year AOC graduated, 21 million Americans were enrolled in college.[6] More minorities and women go to college than ever. According to the Federal Reserve study, Millennials are the most educated generation, with 65 percent possessing at least an associate's degree.[7]

Are kids in those schools often chasing useless degrees? Sure. Have those institutions of radicalism and Marxist twaddle pumped out ill-informed graduates like AOC who perpetuate fantasies about the economy? Yes. That too is a tragedy.

Left-wing outlets feed AOC's generation with a martyrdom complex, the sense of alarm about the world, claiming they have "lower earnings, fewer assets, and less wealth," as taxpayer-funded NPR claimed.[8] If they do, it is because many of them are still at the front end of their life's earning potential. Peak earnings for Americans happen in their late forties to late fifties. And the higher number of Americans getting a college education means more people defer financial success to later years.

Then again, even with spikes in inflation, almost everything is cheaper today due to technological advances. Especially the important things. In the last fifty years, spending on food and clothing as a share of family income has fallen from somewhere around 40 percent to somewhere around 10 percent. On an average night in the United States, a nation with a population of about 350 million, only 193,000 people have no access to nightly shelter.[9] Homeownership has remained incredibly stable at around 65 percent.[10]

Yes, health care costs have risen, especially for Millennials. But even this is a reflection of prosperity and technological advances, as Americans have generally enjoyed longer life expectancy (though it has fallen for a couple of years) and better health care in every imaginable way.

Yes, COVID killed many Americans. But Millennials have never had to worry about measles, rubella, mumps, diphtheria, polio, or a long list of other diseases that were often deadly. The cancer death rate has fallen over 27 percent since Ocasio-Cortez was born—which equals more than two million deaths averted.[11]

One can certainly disagree with or contextualize some of these facts, but the prevailing notion of the progressive left is that we live in a plutocracy. It's the narrative that fuels their Marxist efforts to radically change the American economy. Notwithstanding the genuine problems faced by society—and there are always many, I'm afraid—by almost every quantifiable *economic* standard, Alexandria Ocasio-Cortez has lived in a safer and more prosperous society than anyone in history. She has a higher standard of living than John D. Rockefeller.[12]

Young people are turning to "democratic socialism" because BlueAnon has ensured that they are inundated with myths regarding the state of the world to foster unhealthy apprehension among voters. It is true that we are not living anywhere close to a utopia. We never will. But only socialist conspiracy theorists can sip the sweet lemonade of a free economy and call for all lemon trees to be cut down because of the sourness of lemons.

ZERO-SUM FANTASIES

Why Republicans Hate It When Poor People Have Food to Eat
—TIMOTHY NOAH, *NEW REPUBLIC*

At the 2021 Met Gala in New York City, where guests selected by *Vogue*'s Anna Wintour ponied up around $35,000 a pop to hobnob with the rich and famous at the Metropolitan Museum of Art, Alexandria Ocasio-Cortez donned an elegant gown with the slogan "Tax the Rich" painted on the back.[13]

So stunning. So brave.

So brave, in fact, that the stunt was widely celebrated by the progressive media. Everyone knows that the wealthy pay little or nothing in taxes. It is an article of faith on the left. Democrats, happy to encourage class warfare and paranoia about the successful, often pin their electoral fortunes to the notion that our prosperous neighbors aren't paying their "fair share," and refuse to fund the basic functions of government.

Then again, it's not just your neighbors. The superwealthy often pay nothing as well. "Billionaires Barely Pay Taxes—Here's How They Get Away With It," explained *Teen Vogue* not long ago. ProPublica laid out the "Ten Ways Billionaires Avoid Taxes on an Epic Scale." "Think the rich don't pay their 'fair share'? Think again" and "Billionaires pay almost no tax. A global levy of just 2% could raise $250 billion," says CNN. And so on.

It's no surprise that most Americans support a wealth tax. And why not? Who wants to pay taxes? One recent poll found that 80 percent of voters were annoyed that corporations and the rich don't pay their "fair share."[14] Almost every poll shows that Americans would rather have rich people pay their taxes. Polls, however, rarely ask anyone what a "fair share" looks like. Is it a third of someone's earnings? Half? It is almost surely the case that most voters wildly underestimate the percentage paid by the rich, and wildly overestimate the amount their own strata pay.

Don't feel bad for the wealthy. I don't, but they have been shouldering an increasingly larger share of the cost of American government. Though very few people know it, the United States already has one of the most progressive tax systems in the free world. At the time AOC was wearing her fancy gown, a household making $207,350 was paying 35 percent in income tax. Those who make $518,400 or more pay a 37 percent income tax rate. The top 1 percent of earners make around 20 percent of all income but pay around 40 percent of all federal income taxes. The top 10 percent earned 48 percent and paid 71 percent of all federal income taxes.

Despite public perceptions, the lopsidedness of this equation has only gotten worse over the years.[15] Americans making less than $75,000 had, on average, no tax liability after deductions and credits in 2022. The average income tax rate for those making between $75,000 and $100,000 is less than 2 percent. More than 61 percent of Americans—around 107 million households—owe no federal income taxes in a normal year.[16]

You don't have to agree with me that taxing the wealthy undermines job creation and economic growth, or that a tax system that relies too heavily on the fortunes of a few creates more economic instability. But the idea that the rich or corporations don't pay their fair share is a myth. Unless by "fair share" the left means "all." (They probably do.)

In many ways this is another case of projection. It makes sense that the same people who believe they can regulate an economy (which entails *trillions* of decisions) and build a more equitable world also believe a small cabal of bad guys can control that economy to create destitution and unfairness for their own gain. It's been hammered into our consciousness since childhood.

Can you think of a single major Hollywood movie—where profit margins, incidentally, *far* exceed that of the oil industry or Big Pharma—that portrays free enterprise in a positive light? On the few occasions it does, it is almost always incidental or accidental.

The average movie villains are the venal real estate developers working to undermine a close-knit neighborhood to build condos for the wealthy, or stock traders who "produce nothing," or sociopathic bankers who snatched farms from hardmen and -women toiling the soil, or maybe the profit-mongering sports team owner who doesn't care about his community, or miners who are intent on decimating the planet for a dollar—or sometimes, as in the Avatar movies, other planets! Milburn Pennybags is always trying to rip off the workingman.

But you will rarely find a capitalist who works for his own benefit or the benefit of others. These tropes have informed the imaginations of generations of moviegoers. They are mainstays of the BlueAnon imagination.

In this age of populism, increasing numbers of Americans are accepting Marxist conceptions about the economy, in which the successful are omnipotent parasites and everyone else is a victim of their greed. Whereas not long ago, successful businesspeople and corporations were extolled as virtuous engines of American economic power and ingenuity, today they are nearly always slagged as corrupt and manipulative. The game is always rigged. They are always ripping you off. You are always the victim.

All this feeds into paranoia about meritocracy and the economy.

Anticapitalist, class-warfare conspiracy theories dominate the Democratic Party. We've convinced millions of Americans that a gaggle of billionaires trigger economic havoc for profit, control the economy to undermine the working class, and push commodity prices higher to reap the profits. The zero-sum fallacy that capitalism is inherently evil and rigged has been hammered into our conscience for decades.

The progressive left, for instance, is constantly overstating the power of "big" businesses over electoral outcomes. This is certainly not exclusively the bailiwick of the left wing, but it thrives in the BlueAnon era.

It has become the default norm to blame inflation and other economic tribulations on the Star Chambers of manipulative CEOs, who, for unexplained reasons, have a desire to see the country's economy destroyed. During the post-COVID inflation spike, which hit thirty-year highs, the likes of Elizabeth Warren, Bernie Sanders, and scores of other high-profile Democrats all attempted to deflect from the government's mismanagement and overspending by blaming the problem on corporate "price gouging."

"Any corporation that has not brought their prices back down, even as inflation has come down, even as the supply chains have been rebuilt, it's time to stop the price gouging," Joe Biden, sounding like some two-bit dictator, threatened companies near the end of 2023.[17]

Inflation, of course, had not "come down" at that point; the rate of the increase had merely slowed. But then, everything the Democrat had said surrounding the inflation crisis was infused with disinformation.

The idea that destructive, malevolent forces were behind inflation was a myth. Even as states were opening their economies after the misguided COVID shutdowns, Democrats (with the help of some Republicans) were still pumping trillions into the economy. And when economists began warning that doing so in a hot economy could trigger dangerous levels of inflation, Democrats treated this Economics 101 lesson with contempt and suspicion.

Whatever slight inflation was happening, they told us, was merely "transitory." President Biden even told the media that "no serious economist" was "suggesting there's unchecked inflation on the way," and the entire debate was a ruse invented by Republicans.

Democrats were engaged in a concerted political effort to ignore the problem long enough so they could try to cram through a $3.5 trillion agenda. When inflation suddenly became very much nontransitory, as well as politically problematic, the Biden administration argued that the prescription was even *more* spending. They changed the name of their Build Back Better bill to an equally misleading Inflation Reduction Act and pumped trillions more into the economy.

Finally, when unchecked inflation could no longer be ignored, Democrats revved up the old Marxist "price gouging" canard. Instead of grappling with their own role in the crisis, they held a series of congressional hearings to expose these "pandemic profiteers." Oligarchs were again scheming to undermine your choices.

Ocasio-Cortez, who, I am assured, graduated cum laude with a bachelor of arts degree in both international relations and economics from

Boston University, argued that inflation was actually "straight price gouging by corporations." And at various times, Democrats demanded that the government open investigations into Big Oil, Big Auto, Big Poultry, and Big Semiconductors for gouging consumers.

The word big *is* key. It conveys the impersonal and probably illegitimate nature of these powerful organizations. Of course, there is no "Small Auto" or "Small Pharma" because immense capital expenditures are needed to take on giant risks in those industries. The average cost of producing a new pharmaceutical product is around $3 billion. You don't bring a new drug to market pitching up a company with part-time workers making minimum wage in your garage.

In any case, Democrats wanted Americans to believe all these major industries had colluded at the very moment that supply-chain problems were hitting the world and Washington had devalued the dollar with a historic, partisan spending spree. We were supposed to believe that virtually every boogeyman industry of the left had suddenly raised their prices at once.

One of the worst offenders, according to the Democrats, was "Big Grocery." Warren blamed shortages on corporate greed and inflation on a lack of supermarket choices. "What happens when only a handful of giant grocery store chains like Kroger dominate an industry? They can force high food prices onto Americans while raking in record profits."

We don't know, because, despite Warren's contentions, the grocery game is one of the most competitive industries in the country. And the notion that Americans have fewer choices in venues is laughable.

There are numerous national chains (Kroger, Albertsons), regional chains (Meijers, Publix), higher-end markets (Trader Joe's, Wegmans, Whole Foods), big-box chains (Walmart and Target), and online shops (Amazon). There is more competition than ever. I live in a midsize American city in a purple state and we have, within a fifteen-minute drive from my house: Target grocery, Walmart grocery, two Harris Teeters, Food Lion, Publix, Aldi, Trader Joe's, Fresh Market, Earth Fare, and another half-dozen independent grocery stores, not including ethnic specialty-foods shops.

We have a ton of choices.

Now, granted, not everyone enjoys a similar number of selections. But in general, American consumers have more options for their food shopping than anyone else in the history of mankind—certainly more than our country has ever known. That is why, in part, Big Grocery is also one of the least profitable major businesses in the United States, with average margins coming in at a little over 2 percent.[18] Take Walmart, a favorite target of the political left for years. When consumers were asked, a few years back, "Just a rough guess, what percent profit on each dollar of sales do you think the average company makes after taxes?" they came up with a 36 percent profit margin on average.[19] In reality, Walmart's average net profit per quarter over the past decade has been under 3 percent. It was under 2 percent in 2023.[20]

Warren has good reason to believe that voters aren't aware of this fact.

Similar myths surround Big Oil.

Joe Biden spent most of his early presidency blaming Big Oil for high gas prices—while at the same time promising to destroy the fossil fuel industry and signing executive orders making production more expensive. Exxon, the president said, was making more money "than God."[21]

BlueAnon has concurrent but conflicting conspiracies running these days. The first is that conservatives are intent on destroying the world by doing nothing to stem the flow of fossil fuel, allowing cheap gas to flood the market. At same time, however, conservatives are also empowering a collection of powerful forces who were making gas more expensive to hurt consumers so that oil companies could get rich. Which one is it?

Strong earnings are good news not only for the oil barons but for the millions of people who depend on the industry for their employment, as well as the vast number of Americans who rely on investments in oil companies to bolster their pension funds, retirement funds, college funds, and so on. Exxon does not control the price of an international fungible commodity. There are high times and low in the industry. Oil corporations are indeed "highly" profitable some years, averaging around a 7–8 percent profit margin in 2023. But in 2021, Exxon Mobil had 2.7 profit margin, less than most industries. In 2022 it was 3.2. No one is crying for those companies in down years.

The same goes for Big Pharma, which, if you listened to progressives—and increasingly other populists—is the epitome of a scheming, unpatriotic, capitalist bloodsucker. "We talk about being a divided nation. In many ways, that's true. But, in some ways, we are absolutely united. For example, we all hate the drug companies," Bernie Sanders, who has spent decades spreading conspiracies about the pharmaceutical industry, quipped to *Late Night* host Stephen Colbert.[22]

Needless to say, no industry is chaste, but Big Pharma has done more to help mankind than all socialist and social justice initiatives combined. Big Pharma wants to make a buck, but while doing so has helped us alleviate pain, repel disease, mitigate depression, live longer, and live that life more actively, with more intimacy and less fear. It has transformed numerous once-deadly ailments that might have killed little Red Diaper Baby Bernie a long time ago, mitigating such plagues into footnotes of history. And one day, in the not-too-distant future, a pharma company will likely invent a drug to help people with Parkinson's and Alzheimer's, or effectively treat lung cancer, or cure autoimmune diseases.

We don't use a single lifesaving drug that was created in any socialist nation. They have never invented one. Big Pharma does it for money. Just like you do what you do for money.

Like all sectors, pharma lobbies Congress. Lots of the time, pharma, as well as every other industry, attempts to gain unfair advantages and rent-seeks. These days there is more widespread anger being ratcheted up over the vaccine wars. But COVID vaccine mandates aren't implemented by drug companies (even if they were happy to encourage them); they're implemented by a government that Bernie wants to make increasingly powerful and hegemonic.

Anyone who believes that rich lobbyists, in pursuit of their own special interests, exert too much influence over politics should be advocating for *less* government, not *more*. After all, the more the state intervenes in the economy (through subsidies and overregulation), the greater the influence that lobbyists can exert.

In truth, the fewer regulatory burdens a nation puts on its economy, the less corruption they experience. State power does not alleviate corruption; it exacerbates it. The influence that wealthy people exert on society is almost always achieved through access to politicians and government power.

We know this is true because, despite the left's paranoiac notions regarding free enterprise, nations with high levels of economic freedom have, without exception, lower levels of corruption than those that do not. When prosperity is created in open markets through entrepreneurship and merit rather than by access to bureaucrats and politicians, the rich have less power, not more. The modern left prefers the top-down economic model, which only ensures that the rich will have more power.

Moreover, zero-sum socialist notions are debunked by the existence of numerous lifesaving and improving ideas that make people billions. Having to choose between "people and profits" is a false dichotomy, but it's a belief that girds much of leftist economics. It is meant to invoke distrust and fear.

Big profits and big humanitarian efforts coexist most of the time. "I want to create something to help humanity" and "I want a boatload of cash for doing it" are perfectly compatible positions—and the latter is often necessary to make the former a reality.

Perhaps not in Conspiracyville, but definitely in the real world.

EPILOGUE:
YOU DON'T HAVE TO BE CRAZY TO WIN

The best revenge is not to be like your enemy.
—MARCUS AURELIUS

Contrarianism is good. Challenging sacred cows and conventional wisdom is fundamental to an open and healthy national debate.

Governments, need it even be said, lie. Corporations lie. The media lie. The mob lie. Academics lie. Your political party lies to you all the time. If for some reason you had any doubts that this is the way of the world, I hope the past few years have battered your trusting nature into submission.

As this book has detailed, the "conspiracy theory" accusation is often cynically thrown around to try to shut down open inquiry. Hillary Clinton, the godmother of BlueAnon, was a master of this ruse—though she is hardly alone. Democrats and their allies are quite adept at gaslighting the public by conflating conspiracy theories and genuine corruption. Why do you think the media incessantly covered "birtherism" or QAnon with bated breath? Why do you think the left lifts every fringy right-winger to prominence? They're trying to tether every nut to Republicans. But they also want to create the perception that everything, even genuine news stories—the Hunter Biden laptop, or concerns about Chinese involvement in the Wuhan virus come to mind—are just the ravings of a lunatic party.

"Democracy," they say. "Trust the science," they say. What they mean is shut up and do what we tell you.

You are under no obligation to immediately accept the veracity of every Democrat election victory, or every doomsday pronouncement regarding the environment, or every claim of "voter suppression," despite what the media demands of you.

That said, the reality of contemporary politics is so weird and ugly that we don't really need to make things up to be shocked.

Sometimes you do need to trust the science. Sometimes an election loss is just a loss. It's a downer, no doubt, but it's not the end of the world. Allowing emotions to dictate our positions, even after overwhelming proof has dispelled our initial suspicions, makes us no better than Al Gore or Stacey Abrams.

And we *really* need to be better than Al Gore and Stacey Abrams.

Due to the very real abuses of politicians and federal agencies over the past decade, the populist right has become increasingly reliant on conspiracies to explain political setbacks. It should be noted that much of the paranoia being normalized on the right-wing fringe has long been popular on the left: wars are fought to line pockets of greedy corporations; Jewish influences are pushing us into foreign policy; everyone's fortunes are controlled by greedy plutocrats; Big Pharma is out to make us sick; and so on.

It is a paranoiac worldview. To play into these tropes only strengthens the ability of the corrupt to hide the truth. And in the end, an unhinged skeptic is still unhinged.

Rank populism, left or right, appeals to the heart more than the mind. An all-purpose apocalyptic tone of partisan rhetoric and media coverage has permeated the left, and increasingly the right. The arms race in unhinged political rhetoric has convinced millions of Americans that we are on the precipice of some new disaster every day—

whether it's the climate change apocalypse or the destruction of the middle class or the rise of white supremacy, or any other such myth.

People with real principles, ideas, and good arguments do not need to find conspiratorial answers to problems.

Moreover, the new paranoia is not only bad for the soul, it tears at the fabric of American life. Perhaps the most destructive effect of the modern left's embrace of conspiracy is that it convinces millions of Americans to see their neighbors as fifth columnists—a hallmark of the authoritarian mindset. It's going to be difficult to sway your partisan adversary if you're convinced they want to murder you.

BlueAnon has personalized this kind of paranoia. Far too many Democrats are now incapable or unwilling to debate issues, turn to slandering political opponents as fascists and racists and misogynists and homophobes and transphobes and whatever "phobe" is next. Rather than debate, they engage in cloistered discussions, anointing themselves, quite ironically, as the defenders of American virtue and democratic values.

Neither side has a monopoly on thinking poorly of others, of course, but polls consistently find more Democrats see their fellow citizens as enemies. One 2023 Axios poll found that 61 percent of Democrats view the average Republican as racist, sexist, and bigoted. Far more Democrats contend that they would be disappointed if a family member married someone in the opposing party.

"Nearly a quarter of college students wouldn't be friends with someone who voted for the other presidential candidate—with Democrats far more likely to dismiss people than Republicans," according to another Axios poll.[1] And 71 percent of Democrats wouldn't go on a date with someone with opposing views, versus 31 percent of Republicans.

The political benefit of the villainization of partisan adversaries is that you can treat them as if they are beneath the dignity of your time. I'm not going to sit here and tell you naïvely that it never helps to achieve short-term political gain. But it's a disaster for the future of America.

Worse still, BlueAnon has created an environment that justifies authoritarianism. If stopping the opposition is the only way to protect the foundations of "democracy" and the future of the planet, then surely anything one does to prevail can be rationalized and justified.

This is an extraordinarily dangerous way to conceptualize politics in a free country. It is girded by anxieties created by BlueAnon. For Democrats, this means justifying un-American expansions of state power, weaponizing the Department of Justice to target political opponents, and pressuring private companies to censor political foes.

All of these are openly celebrated as necessary by the contemporary Democratic Party.

An arms race in conspiracy and hysteria leads to an arms race in authoritarianism. Many of us are considered "conservative" because we believe that the constitutional order is the best political system in protecting civil society and individual liberty. We should want to preserve our institutions, not destroy them.

As we've seen, BlueAnon's oeuvre is highly mockable. But there is a dark side to this trend, and the Republican Party should not be eager to follow. Conspiracy theories—the real ones—are dead ends. They are exhausting. Every time the left ignites another round of crazy talk, it will be less effective. Sooner or later, voters will wonder why none of their apocalyptic predictions ever come true.

Conservatives have a chance to do something revolutionary in modern American politics.

They can be normal.

NOTES

CHAPTER 1: THE VAST RIGHT-WING CONSPIRACY WILL NEVER DIE

1   https://www.nytimes.com/1998/01/28/us/president-under-fire-first-lady-first
    -lady-attributes-inquiry-right-wing.html

2   https://www.sfgate.com/politics/joegarofoli/article/The-Spinner-How-Chris
    -Lehane-revered-by-some-2679295.php

3   https://www.washingtonpost.com/wp-srv/politics/special/clinton/stories
    /hillary012898.htm

4   https://www.nbcnews.com/politics/2016-election/charles-koch-explains
    -donors-why-he-won-t-support-trump-n620621

5   https://www.realclearpolitics.com/articles/2016/11/24/democrats_and_the
    _nazi_card_132428.html

6   https://www.nationalreview.com/corner/a-50-year-history-of-the-worst
    -comparison/

7   https://www.tampabay.com/archive/2004/06/30/the-left-leaps-off-a-rhetorical
    -cliff/

8   https://www.salon.com/2005/05/26/absolute_power/

9   https://www.washingtonpost.com/archive/politics/2004/01/06/anti-bush-ad
    -contest-includes-hitler-images/950a0114-cc07-4538-a6e7-202bbb7a3c6e/

10 https://slate.com/news-and-politics/2003/12/whopper-of-the-week-howard
    -dean.html

11 https://www.politico.com/blogs/media/2015/06/nprs-diane-rehm-asks-bernie
    -sanders-about-israeli-citizenship-rumors-208583

12 https://slate.com/news-and-politics/2003/12/whopper-of-the-week-howard
    -dean.html

13 https://www.cnn.com/2003/ALLPOLITICS/12/12/column.novak.opinion.urban/

14 ibid.

15 https://www.politico.com/blogs/ben-smith/2011/04/more-than-half-of
    -democrats-believed-bush-knew-035224

16 https://www.aei.org/wp-content/uploads/2013/11/-public-opinion-on
    -conspiracy-theories_181649218739.pdf

17 https://freebeacon.com/politics/flashback-2007-ellison-compared-911-attacks
    -reichstag-fire/

18 https://blogs.chapman.edu/wilkinson/2016/10/11/what-arent-they-telling-us/

19 https://www.the-numbers.com/box-office-records/worldwide/all-movies
    /genres/documentary

20 https://ew.com/article/2003/03/27/michael-moore-defends-his-oscar-speech/

21   https://www.nytimes.com/2021/08/25/arts/television/spike-lee-911-conspiracy
      -theorists.html

22   https://www.politico.com/story/2011/08/sources-biden-likened-tea-partiers-to
      -terrorists-060421

23   https://www.wsj.com/articles/SB10001424052970204908604574336462379328406

24   https://www.nytimes.com/2011/07/27/opinion/27friedman.html?ref=opinion

25   https://www.nytimes.com/2011/08/02/opinion/the-tea-partys-war-on-america
      .html?_r=2

26   https://www.politico.com/story/2009/09/grayson-gop-wants-you-to
      -die-027726

27   https://www.nhregister.com/news/article/With-the-birther-issue-over-what
      -topic-should-11571247.php

28   https://www.theatlantic.com/politics/archive/2010/02/erick-erickson
      -excommunicates-birther-fringe/346653/

29   https://thehill.com/blogs/blog-briefing-room/news/403634-clip-of-mccain
      -defending-obama-after-supporter-called-him-arab/

30   https://www.politico.com/story/2011/04/mitt-obama-born-here-period
      -053073

31   https://www.telegraph.co.uk/news/worldnews/barackobama/8478044/Birther
      -row-began-with-Hillary-Clinton-supporters.html

32   https://www.politico.com/story/2016/09/sid-blumenthal-birthers-clinton
      -obama-228388

33   https://www.nbcnews.com/id/wbna23415028

34   https://news.harvard.edu/gazette/story/2016/02/a-question-of
      -citizenship/#:~:text=During%20a%20forum%20at%20Harvard,strict
      %20interpretation%20of%20the%20Constitution.

35   https://www.foxnews.com/politics/hillary-clinton-accuses-gop-scheming
      -literally-steal-next-presidential-election

36   https://www.nytimes.com/2023/03/18/us/politics/jimmy-carter-october
      -surprise-iran-hostages.html

37   https://jacobin.com/2020/01/ronald-reagan-october-surprise-carter-iran
      -hostage-crisis-conspiracy

38   https://nymag.com/intelligencer/2023/03/lawmaker-admits-1980-gop-plot-to
      -prolong-iran-hostage-crisis.html

39   https://www.telegraph.co.uk/world-news/2023/03/19/ronald-reagan-allies
      -sabotaged-jimmy-carters-re-election-telling/

40   https://www.pbs.org/newshour/show/expert-analyzes-new-account-of-gop
      -deal-that-used-iran-hostage-crisis-for-gain

41   https://newrepublic.com/article/172324/its-settled-reagan-campaign-delayed
      -release-iranian-hostages

42   https://twitter.com/JamesFallows/status/1637225067326103552

43   https://www.newsweek.com/making-myth-201934

44   https://www.latimes.com/archives/la-xpm-1986-03-20-mn-21558-story.html

45   https://news.google.com/newspapers?id=p54rAAAAIBAJ&sjid=PvwFAAAAIBAJ
      &pg=3574,4204889&dq=lyndon-larouche+perennial+candidate&hl=en

46   https://www.meforum.org/4134/the-october-surprise-theory

47   https://www.newsweek.com/making-myth-201934

48 https://books.google.com/books?id=WRVj7Rvhvu8C&pg=PA8&lpg=PA8&dq=
%22wholly+insufficient+credible+evidence%22+of+any+communications
+between+Reagan+campaign+officials+and+the+Iranian+government
+and+%22no+credible+evidence%22&source=bl&ots=9nh2u4PWIx&sig
=ACfU3U2TUNPMiO3thq5-kkjy9nUtwOGuWg&hl=en&sa=X&ved
=2ahUKEwjNjtvss__-AhVmFVkFHfXKCkUQ6AF6BAgFEAM#v=onepage
&q=%22wholly%20insufficient%20credible%20evidence%22%20of
%20any%20communications%20between%20Reagan%20campaign
%20officials%20and%20the%20Iranian%20government%20and
%20%22no%20credible%20evidence%22&f=false

49 https://books.google.com/books?id=YY3vCgAAQBAJ&pg=PA324&lpg
=PA324&dq=,+%22by+any+standard,+the+credible+evidence+now+known+falls
+far+short+of+supporting+the+allegation+of+an+agreement+between+the+Reagan
+campaign+and+Iran+to+delay+the+release+of+the+hostages.%22&source=bl
&ots=ck5aWSrHEc&sig=ACfU3Uobb_whtM8tYHaD6XO93Nkxxyr0Aw&hl
=en&sa=X&ved=2ahUKEwi45basrbCDAxUNEGIAHXd_Cfs4ChDoAX0ECAQQAw
#v=onepage&q=%2C%20%22by%20any%20standard%2C%20the%20credible
%20evidence%20now%20known%20falls%20far%20short%20of%20supporting
%20the%20allegation%20of%20an%20agreement%20between%20the
%20Reagan%20campaign%20and%20Iran%20to%20delay%20the%20release
%20of%20the%20hostages.%22&f=false

50 https://studylib.net/doc/7705309/belief-in-conspiracy-theories

51 https://www.nytimes.com/2000/11/10/us/the-2000-election-confused-by
-ballot-anger-and-chagrin-after-an-oops-on-a-ballot.html

52 https://www.washingtonpost.com/archive/politics/2001/01/31/for-bush-camp
-some-momentum-from-a-memo/8c319870-8e1a-4062-b33e-b31a2afa5c9b/

53 https://www.cnn.com/2015/11/02/politics/bush-gore-military-ballots/index
.html

54 https://www.nytimes.com/2001/04/04/us/analysis-of-florida-ballots-proves
-favorable-to-bush.html

55 https://www.nytimes.com/2001/11/12/us/examining-vote-overview-study
-disputed-florida-ballots-finds-justices-did-not.html

56 https://www.nationalreview.com/corner/hillary-clinton-2002-george-w-bush
-was-selected-not-elected/

57 https://www.newsweek.com/first-families-square-142141

58 https://www.usatoday.com/story/theoval/2013/06/12/biden-gore-george-w
-bush-2000-election/2414933/

59 https://www.politico.com/story/2016/06/biden-orlando-gun-control-224401

60 https://nymag.com/intelligencer/2012/06/yes-bush-v-gore-did-steal-the
-election.html

61 https://www.nbcnews.com/id/wbna7456686

62 https://www.democracynow.org/2005/11/4/mark_crispin_miller_kerry_told_me

63 https://www.cnn.com/2005/ALLPOLITICS/01/06/electoral.vote.1718/

64 https://clerk.house.gov/evs/2005/roll007.xml

65 https://nypost.com/2004/01/22/deans-ballot-box-conspiracy-theory/

66 https://www.c-span.org/video/?c4932630/user-clip-2005-pelosi-voter
-suppression

67 https://www.nationalreview.com/2021/10/terry-mcauliffes-election
    -trutherism-shouldnt-be-excused/
68 https://www.dispatch.com/story/news/politics/elections/2018/04/27/kucinich
    -has-colorful-history-with/12363909007/
69 https://abcnews.go.com/WNT/story?id=239735&page=1
70 http://publicmind.fdu.edu/2013/outthere/final.pdf
71 https://www.c-span.org/video/?185006-2/senate-session

CHAPTER 2: THE GREATEST HOAX IN AMERICAN HISTORY

1   https://www.washingtonpost.com/politics/hillary-clinton-trump-is-an
    -illegitimate-president/2019/09/26/29195d5a-e099-11e9-b199-f638bf2c340f
    _story.html
2   https://www.cbsnews.com/news/jimmy-carter-says-president-trump
    -illegitimate-president-russian-interference-2019-06-28/
3   https://www.washingtonexaminer.com/opinion/editorials/harry-reid-strikes
    -again
4   https://nymag.com/intelligencer/2016/11/activists-urge-hillary-clinton-to
    -challenge-election-results.html
5   https://www.nytimes.com/2016/11/07/opinion/how-to-rig-an-election.html
6   https://www.theguardian.com/us-news/2015/sep/27/hillary-clinton-email
    -scandal-conspiracy-theory-interview
7   https://www.fbi.gov/news/press-releases/statement-by-fbi-director-james
    -b-comey-on-the-investigation-of-secretary-hillary-clinton2019s-use-of-a
    -personal-e-mail-system
8   https://www.justice.gov/storage/report-from-special-counsel-robert-k-hur
    -february-2024.pdf
9   https://abcnews.go.com/Politics/hillary-clinton-emailed-gefilte-fish/story
    ?id=33457042
10 https://www.nytimes.com/2016/07/06/us/politics/fbi-findings-damage-many-
    of-hillary-clintons-claims.html
11 https://www.nytimes.com/2016/07/07/us/hillary-clintons-email-was-probably
    -hacked-experts-say.html?_r=0
12 https://www.motherjones.com/politics/2021/11/the-steele-dossier-and-donald
    -trumps-betrayal-of-america/
13 https://www.scribd.com/document/336226994/The-Trump-Russia-Dossier-as
    -Released-By-Buzzfeed
14 https://www.cnn.com/2018/04/12/politics/comey-book-golden-showers/index
    .html
15 https://www.washingtonpost.com/politics/real-or-fake-news-either-way-lewd
    -tape-allegations-pose-a-challenge-for-trump/2018/04/13/098cdedc-3f2b-11e8
    -8d53-eba0ed2371cc_story.html
16 https://www.nytimes.com/2018/04/16/opinion/comey-book-steele-dossier.html
17 https://www.cnn.com/2017/08/31/politics/michael-cohen-russia-letter
    -congress/index.html
18 https://www.mcclatchydc.com/news/investigations/article219016820.html
19 https://townhall.com/tipsheet/juliorosas/2019/12/11/ig-michael-horowitz-fisa
    -applications-relied-entirely-on-information-from-steele-dossier-n2557851

20 https://www.youtube.com/watch?v=7vkdmotNfK4&t=124s
21 https://www.washingtonpost.com/politics/lindsey-graham-seeks-obama
    -officials-who-unmasked-trump-allies/2020/05/19/d72c434a-9a0b-11ea-a282
    -386f56d579e6_story.html
22 https://www.slate.com/articles/news_and_politics/cover_story/2016/10/was_a
    _server_registered_to_the_trump_organization_communicating_with_russia
    .html
23 https://www.presidency.ucsb.edu/documents/hillary-clinton-campaign-press
    -release-statement-from-jake-sullivan-new-report-exposing
24 https://www.cnn.com/2021/11/18/politics/steele-dossier-reckoning/index.html
25 https://www.washingtonexaminer.com/news/76426/fbi-agent-at-sussmann
    -trial-says-he-rejected-alfa-bank-claims-within-days/
26 https://www.foxnews.com/media/slate-writer-draft-trump-fusion-gps
27 https://www.washingtonpost.com/blogs/erik-wemple/wp/2017/01/18/c-span
    -no-we-werent-hacked/
28 https://money.cnn.com/2017/06/26/media/cnn-announcement-retracted-article/
29 https://www.cbsnews.com/news/brian-ross-abc-news-suspends-reporter-four
    -weeks-without-pay-for-botched-flynn-report/
30 https://www.washingtonpost.com/politics/attorney-for-michael-cohen-backs
    -away-from-confidence-that-cohen-has-information-about-trumps-knowledge
    -on-russian-efforts/2018/08/26/09d7f26e-a876-11e8-97ce-cc9042272f07_story
    .html
31 https://nymag.com/intelligencer/2016/12/trump-denies-thing-that-66-million
    -people-saw-happen.html
32 https://nymag.com/intelligencer/2018/07/trump-putin-russia-collusion.html
33 https://nymag.com/intelligencer/article/ex-kgb-agent-trump-russian-asset
    -mueller-putin-kompromat-unger-book.html
34 https://thehill.com/blogs/blog-briefing-room/news/312398-dems-trump
    -spokesman-a-shill-for-putin/
35 https://www.politico.com/magazine/story/2019/03/27/rachel-maddows-deep
    -delusion-226266/
36 https://www.washingtonpost.com/world/national-security/sessions-spoke
    -twice-with-russian-ambassador-during-trumps-presidential-campaign-justice
    -officials-say/2017/03/01/77205eda-feac-11e6-99b4-9e613afeb09f_story.html
37 https://www.politico.com/story/2009/02/biden-time-to-hit-the-reset
    -button-018533
38 https://www.sandiegouniontribune.com/sdut-biden-to-medvedev-russian
    -wto-bid-is-top-priority-2011mar09-story.html
39 https://www.nytimes.com/2012/03/27/us/politics/obama-caught-on
    -microphone-telling-medvedev-of-flexibility.html
40 https://www.nbcnews.com/news/world/first-thoughts-were-flna624185
41 https://www.youtube.com/watch?v=ZOcfIfrTOnU
42 https://www.breitbart.com/clips/2017/04/07/msnbcs-odonnell-maybe-putin
    -masterminded-chemical-attack-so-trump-could-look-good-by-striking-syria/
43 https://www.washingtonpost.com/opinions/mitch-mcconnell-is-a-russian
    -asset/2019/07/26/02cf3510-afbc-11e9-a0c9-6d2d7818f3da_story.html
44 https://www.washingtonpost.com/blogs/plum-line/wp/2018/07/20/the-entire

-republican-party-is-becoming-a-russian-asset/

45 https://twitter.com/tribelaw/status/825498030942121984?lang=en

46 https://www.npr.org/sections/thetwo-way/2013/07/02/198118060/clapper
-apologizes-for-answer-on-nsas-data-collection

47 https://time.com/4808685/trump-russia-watergate-james-clapper/

48 https://thehill.com/homenews/administration/365539-former-intel-chief
-putin-is-handling-trump-like-an-asset/

49 https://www.wsj.com/articles/all-the-adam-schiff-transcripts-11589326164

50 https://www.cnn.com/2023/12/18/politics/china-russia-iran-cuba-2022
-midterm-election-meddling/index.html

51 https://bloggingwizard.com/facebook-video-statistics/

52 https://www.nytimes.com/interactive/2018/05/14/technology/facebook-ads
-congress.html

53 https://www.bloomberg.com/news/articles/2018-03-20/cambridge-analytica-s
-global-election-bombshell-balance-of-power

54 https://www.theatlantic.com/magazine/archive/2020/03/the-2020
-disinformation-war/605530/

55 https://www.cnet.com/tech/services-and-software/cambridge-analytica-says
-kogans-facebook-data-was-ineffectual/

CHAPTER 3: NO EVIDENCE? NO MATTER

1 https://www.axios.com/2021/11/14/steele-dossier-discredited-media
-corrections-buzzfeed-washington-post

2 https://today.yougov.com/politics/articles/17286-belief-conspiracies-largely
-depends-political-iden

3 https://www.washingtonexaminer.com/opinion/whoever-convinced-most
-democrats-that-putin-hacked-the-election-tallies-is-doing-putins-bidding

4 https://www.intelligence.senate.gov/sites/default/files/documents/Report
_Volume1.pdf

5 https://www.rasmussenreports.com/public_content/politics/general_politics
/april_2022/democrats_still_believe_russia_changed_2016_election?s=03

6 https://thehill.com/homenews/house/4483740-comer-says-indicted-fbi
-informant-wasnt-an-important-part-of-this-investigation/

7 https://www.foxnews.com/media/matt-taibbi-msnbc-joe-scarborough-russia
-hoax

8 https://www.axios.com/2021/11/14/steele-dossier-discredited-media
-corrections-buzzfeed-washington-post

9 https://news.grabien.com/story-dan-goldman-republicans-are-knowingly
-assisting-putin-to-install-donal

10 https://nypost.com/2024/06/04/us-news/hunter-biden-gun-trial-jurors-shown
-infamous-laptop-first-exposed-by-the-post-in-dramatic-courtroom-reveal/

11 https://www.theatlantic.com/politics/archive/2020/09/trump-americans-who
-died-at-war-are-losers-and-suckers/615997/

12 https://www.nbcnews.com/think/opinion/trump-s-losers-suckers-troops
-scandal-call-action-america-s-ncna1239433

13 https://www.washingtonpost.com/politics/2020/09/15/trump-says-there-are
-25-witnesses-disputing-atlantic-nope/

14 https://www.politico.com/story/2019/08/28/biden-brother
    -business-2020-1476815
15 https://apnews.com/article/joe-biden-europe-adam-schiff
    -fffd9b7265b09e75d8da24087b6623bb
16 https://www.politico.com/news/2020/10/19/hunter-biden-story-russian
    -disinfo-430276
17 https://www.cnn.com/factsfirst/politics/factcheck_036fb62c-377f-4c68-8fa5
    -b98418e4bb9c
18 https://www.washingtonexaminer.com/news/2717999/john-ratcliffe
    -rejects-adam-schiff-claims-that-hunter-biden-laptop-is-part-of-russian
    -disinformation-operation/
19 https://www.foxnews.com/politics/former-obama-official-one-word-answer
    -asked-retract-attack-hunter-biden-laptop
20 https://twitter.com/RepJeffries/status/964581721088897025
21 https://twitter.com/RepJeffries/status/1580876081611128833
22 https://www.usatoday.com/story/news/politics/elections/2020/09/02/biden
    -leads-trump-narrower-7-points-post-conventions-suffolk-poll/3446536001/
23 https://nypost.com/2020/08/25/clinton-biden-should-not-concede-under-any
    -circumstances/
24 https://www.washingtonpost.com/outlook/2020/09/03/trump-stay-in-office/
25 Ibid.
26 https://twitter.com/chrislhayes/status/1299037934121816066
27 https://www.nytimes.com/2020/08/02/business/media/election-coverage
    .html?smid=tw-share
28 https://nypost.com/2020/01/22/house-democrats-to-present-case-in-trumps
    -senate-impeachment-trial/
29 https://apnews.com/article/top-officials-elections-most-secure
    -66f9361084ccbc461e3bbf42861057a5
30 https://www.whitehouse.gov/briefing-room/speeches-remarks/2022/11/03
    /remarks-by-president-biden-on-standing-up-for-democracy/

CHAPTER 4: THE PLOT AGAINST AMERICA

1   https://www.nytimes.com/2022/01/29/us/politics/democrats-dark-money
    -donors.html
2   https://www.politico.com/gallery/2013/02/10-famous-lines-from-sotu
    -history/000776-011043.html
3   https://www.theguardian.com/us-news/2019/mar/10/democrats-small-dollar
    -donors-essential-bernie-sanders
4   https://fortune.com/2016/09/19/donald-trump-small-donors/
5   https://fortune.com/2024/06/26/fortune-100-ceos-trump-small-businesses/
6   https://www.forbes.com/sites/michelatindera/2020/02/01/billionaire-tom
    -steyer-spent-200-million-on-his-own-presidential-campaign-last-year/
7   https://www.nytimes.com/2000/02/10/us/the-2000-campaign-the-end-forbes
    -spent-millions-but-for-little-gain.html
8   https://docquery.fec.gov/cgi-bin/forms/C00728154/1402692/
9   https://www.nytimes.com/interactive/2020/02/01/us/elections/democratic-q4
    -fundraising.html

10 https://www.opensecrets.org/orgs/summary?topnumcycle=A&toprecipcycle
=All%20cycles&contribcycle=All%20cycles&lobcycle=All%20cycles
&outspendcycle=All%20cycles&id=d000000082

11 https://www.opensecrets.org/federal-lobbying/industries

12 https://sfbos.org/sites/default/files/19%20NRA%20Domestic%20Terrorist
%20Resolution%20Press%20Release.pdf

13 https://www.opensecrets.org/federal-lobbying/clients/summary
?cycle=2021&id=d000000082

14 https://www.upi.com/Top_News/US/2018/04/25/NRA-sets-fundraising-record
-mostly-from-small-donors/3321524635020/

15 https://www.rollingstone.com/politics/politics-news/the-trump-russia-nra
-connection-heres-what-you-need-to-know-205458/

16 https://www.npr.org/2018/04/11/601534305/nra-in-new-document
-acknowledges-more-than-20-russian-linked-contributors

17 https://volokh.com/2010/05/10/elena-kagan-i-love-the-federalist-society-i
-love-the-federalist-society/

18 https://www.wsj.com/articles/justice-ginsburg-and-the-value-of
-anonymity-11602797350

19 https://medium.com/senator-sheldon-whitehouse/the-third-federalist-society
-f8a3ff2e19fd

20 https://www.whitehouse.senate.gov/news/speeches/the-scheme-speech-5-the
-federalist-society

21 https://x.com/AOC/status/1685039393860448256

22 https://www.businessinsider.com/aoc-impeachment-articles-supreme-court
-trump-immunity-ruling-2024-7

23 https://www.opensecrets.org/news/2018/10/only-a-fraction-of-dark-money
-spending-on-kavanaugh-disclosed/

24 https://nypost.com/2021/04/29/biden-calls-capitol-riots-worst-attack-on
-our-democracy-since-the-civil-war/#:~:text=President%20Biden%20is%20
being%20ripped,democracy%20since%20the%20Civil%20War.%E2%80%9D

25 https://www.washingtonexaminer.com/opinion/msnbc-jan-6-was-worse
-than-9-11

26 https://www.politico.com/news/2021/07/27/bennie-thompson-opening
-statement-jan-6-hearing-500827

27 https://billmoyers.com/story/the-putsch-of-january-6-2021/

28 https://twitter.com/donnabrazile/status/1420401432650469389

29 https://www.nytimes.com/2021/07/28/opinion/jan-6-coup-general-milley
.html?referringSource=articleShare

30 https://www.washingtonpost.com/nation/2021/01/19/lauren-boebert-tour
-capitol-riots/

31 https://www.washingtonpost.com/nation/2021/01/13/mikie-sherrill
-reconnaissance-capitol-attack/

32 https://www.foxnews.com/media/rep-maxine-waters-trump-supporters
-training-in-hills-election-attack

33 https://www.npr.org/2016/11/20/502719871/energized-by-trumps-win-white
-nationalists-gather-to-change-the-world

34 Ibid.

35   Ibid.

36   https://www.denverpost.com/2018/10/29/colorado-flat-earth-conference-denver/

37   https://www.cnn.com/2018/08/12/us/unite-the-right-charlottesville
     -anniversary/index.html

38   https://www.cnn.com/2019/10/30/us/white-supremacist-woman-reeve/index
     .html

39   https://www.msnbc.com/opinion/msnbc-opinion/pandemic-fitness-trends
     -have-gone-extreme-literally-n1292463

40   https://www.theguardian.com/politics/2022/mar/06/fascist-fitness-how-the
     -far-right-is-recruiting-with-online-gym-groups

41   https://www.foxnews.com/politics/white-house-staff-relocated-pro
     -palestinian-rioters-damage-exterior-fencing-hurl-objects-cops

42   https://www.cbsnews.com/newyork/news/alexandria-shooter-bernie-sanders
     -campaign-volunteer/

43   https://abcnews.go.com/Politics/calif-man-indicted-attempting-assassinate
     -brett-kavanaugh-arrest/story?id=85423002

44   https://www.axios.com/2020/09/16/riots-cost-property-damage

45   https://apnews.com/article/donald-trump-ap-top-news-george-floyd-politics
     -a2326518da6b25b4509bef1ec85f5d7f

46   https://twitter.com/chriscuomo/status/897820041273626626?lang=en

47   https://www.teenvogue.com/story/antifa-history-and-politics-explained

48   https://www.jpost.com/opinion/behind-antifas-mask-504636

49   https://twitter.com/nytimes/status/1300755299339513858

50   https://www.realclearpolitics.com/video/2020/08/31/rep_adam_schiff
     _president_trump_and_the_russians_are_fanning_the_flames_of_violence
     _in_us.html

51   https://twitter.com/joyannreid/status/1300114584859299841

52   https://thehill.com/homenews/media/508265-msnbcs-heilemann-trump
     -deploying-feds-to-portland-as-trial-run-to-steal-this/

53   https://www.nytimes.com/2020/07/20/opinion/portland-protests-trump.html

54   https://www.politico.com/news/2020/07/28/barr-pelosi-comments
     -endangered-law-enforcement-384238

55   https://www.thewrap.com/the-view-constitution-trash-elie-mystal-video/

56   https://www.theguardian.com/us-news/2022/apr/18/jamie-raskin-climate
     -crisis-democracy

57   https://twitter.com/allinwithchris/status/1582887592277991425

58   https://www.cnn.com/2020/10/21/opinions/court-packing-will-save
     -democracy-w-kamau-bell/index.html

59   https://www.warren.senate.gov/imo/media/doc/warren_letter_to_judicial
     _conference_re_cfpb_credit_card_recusal_issue.pdf

60   https://www.nbcnews.com/politics/supreme-court/democrats-introduce-bill
     -expand-supreme-court-9-13-justices-n1264132

61   https://publicpolicy.pepperdine.edu/academics/research/faculty-research/new
     -deal/legislation/sen060737.htm

62   https://slate.com/human-interest/2016/11/the-electoral-college-is-an
     -instrument-of-white-supremacy-and-sexism.html

63   https://www.washingtonpost.com/opinions/abolish-the-electoral

-college/2020/11/15/c40367d8-2441-11eb-a688-5298ad5d580a_story.html

64 https://www.cbsnews.com/news/biden-voting-rights-speech-filibuster-atlanta/

65 https://www.politico.com/news/2020/06/08/senate-record-breaking
-gridlocktrump-303811

66 https://www.usatoday.com/story/opinion/2021/04/02/kill-senate-filibuster
-save-american-democracy-column/7060951002/

67 https://www.nytimes.com/2021/03/11/opinion/us-filibuster-senate.html

68 https://www.klobuchar.senate.gov/public/index.cfm/2021/3/for-the-people-act
-is-one-reason-we-must-eliminate-the-filibuster-amy-klobuchar-says

69 https://www.usatoday.com/story/opinion/2021/04/02/kill-senate-filibuster
-save-american-democracy-column/7060951002/

70 https://www.foxnews.com/politics/senate-abolish-filibuster-dick-durbin-flip
-flop

71 http://obamaspeeches.com/010-The-Nuclear-Option-Obama-Speech.htm

72 https://www.cnn.com/2020/07/30/politics/obama-filibuster-jim-crow-voting
-rights/index.html

73 https://www.theguardian.com/us-news/2023/apr/15/republicans-minority-rule
-tennessee-race-gun-control

74 https://www.theatlantic.com/ideas/archive/2020/12/minority-rule-cannot-last
-america/617272/

75 https://www.npr.org/2021/06/09/1002593823/how-democratic-is-american
-democracy-key-pillars-face-stress-tests#:~:text=Right%20now%2C
%20the%20Senate%20is,of%20Americans%20by%2070%20senators.

76 https://www.pbs.org/newshour/show/tyranny-of-the-minority-writers-say
-constitution-not-strong-enough-to-protect-democracy

77 https://www.politico.com/news/magazine/2022/01/05/democracy-january-6
-coup-constitution-526512

78 https://www.johnlocke.org/mislabeling-natural-law-as-white-nationalism/

CHAPTER 5: THE HANDMAID'S TALE

1 https://www.theguardian.com/us-news/2023/nov/04/mike-johnson-theocrat
-house-speaker-christian-trump

2 https://www.washingtonpost.com/politics/2023/10/04/republican-votes-kevin
-mccarthy-ousted/

3 https://www.facebook.com/AdamSchiffCA/videos/2334537000039701/

4 https://thehill.com/homenews/house/4266729-jeffries-blasts-jim-jordan-as
-clear-and-present-danger-ahead-of-third-vote/

5 https://auburnpub.com/partners/cnn/video_a80e966d-2f4d-532e-b797
-ofcee162b28e.html

6 https://www.dailysignal.com/2023/11/06/to-many-on-far-left-maga
-republicans-are-greater-threat-than-hamas/

7 https://www.nytimes.com/2023/11/01/opinion/mike-johnson-christian
-nationalism-speaker.html

8 https://www.realclearpolitics.com/video/2024/02/23/heidi_przybyla
_extremist_conservative_christian_nationalists_believe_your_rights_come
_from_god_not_government.html

9 https://www.newsweek.com/mike-johnson-house-speaker-christian

-nationalism-1838148#:~:text=While%20Johnson%20has%20made%20no ,presidency%20obehind%20the%20vice%20president.

10   https://www.nytimes.com/2024/05/22/us/justice-alito-flag-appeal-to-heaven .html

11   https://www.theblaze.com/news/justice-alito-told-democrats-to-pound-sand -now-raskin-wants-the-biden-doj-to-pressure-the-court

12   https://sfist.com/2024/05/29/appeal-to-heaven-flag-part-of-city-collection-for -decades-quietly-removed-from-sfs-civic-center-plaza/

13   https://www.sourcewatch.org/index.php/The_Bush_Theocracy

14   https://www.politico.com/news/magazine/2022/09/21/most-republicans -support-declaring-the-united-states-a-christian-nation-00057736

15   https://criticalissues.umd.edu/sites/criticalissues.umd.edu/files/American %20Attitudes%20on%20Race%2CEthnicity%2CReligion.pdf

16   https://www.miamiherald.com/news/politics-government/article265261411 .html

17   https://www.c-span.org/video/?c4681442/user-clip-durbin-orthodox-catholic

18   https://www.c-span.org/video/?c4681521/user-clip-al-franken-roasted-amy -barrett

19   https://catholicherald.co.uk/fbi-spied-on-traditionalist-u-s-catholics-from -coast-to-coast-new-evidence-reveals/

20   https://www.newsweek.com/mike-johnson-handmaids-tale-comparisons -speaker-1838056

21   https://pro.morningconsult.com/articles/is-the-handmaids-tale-rooted-in -reality-it-depends-on-your-party-affiliation

22   https://www.cnn.com/2019/06/02/media/handmaids-tale-gilead/index.html

23   https://www.foxnews.com/story/debate-reaction

24   https://www.cnn.com/2017/05/04/health/pre-existing-condition-rape -domestic-violence-insurance/index.html

25   https://www.thedailybeast.com/is-the-gops-war-on-women-now-pro-rapist

26   https://www.cbsnews.com/news/from-the-vault-abortion-and-the-law/

27   https://slate.com/news-and-politics/2023/04/birth-control-is-next -republicans-abortion.html

28   https://www.youtube.com/watch?v=RyKo2em7Nic

29   https://www.cnn.com/2015/11/30/politics/ted-cruz-condoms-iowa/index.html

30   https://www.washingtonpost.com/news/wonk/wp/2015/06/15/why-republicans -are-pushing-for-over-the-counter-birth-control/

31   https://news.gallup.com/poll/245618/abortion-trends-gender.aspx

32   https://www.hks.harvard.edu/faculty-research/policy-topics/fairness-justice /roe-v-wade-has-been-overturned-what-does-mean

33   https://www.opensocietyfoundations.org/newsroom/the-overturning-of-roe-v -wade-is-an-assault-on-women-and-democracy-globally

34   https://www.bloomberg.com/opinion/articles/2022-05-05/abortion-rights -falter-as-democracy-slides#xj4y7vzkg

35   https://x.com/JeffreyToobin/status/1173331982689996802

36   https://x.com/tomselliott/status/1235326137120755718

37   https://www.commentary.org/articles/terry-eastland/the-case-against-anita -hill/

38 https://www.commentary.org/articles/terry-eastland/the-case-against-anita
    -hill/

39 https://anitahillcase.com/wp-content/themes/anita/pdf/FBI-Affadavit-Jolene
    -Smith-Jameson.pdf

40 https://thefederalist.com/2019/09/15/new-book-christine-blasey-fords-friend
    -leland-keyser-doesnt-believe/

41 https://www.foxnews.com/politics/christine-blasey-ford-attorney-says-she
    -came-forward-to-get-asterisk-on-kavanaughs-name-ahead-of-abortion-rulings

42 https://twitter.com/cnnbrk/status/1043861491957596161

43 https://www.newyorker.com/news/news-desk/senate-democrats-investigate
    -a-new-allegation-of-sexual-misconduct-from-the-supreme-court-nominee
    -brett-kavanaughs-college-years-deborah-ramirez

44 https://www.washingtonpost.com/opinions/the-anatomy-of-a-smear
    /2018/09/25/fdee68ea-c0d8-11e8-9005-5104e9616c21_story.html

45 https://www.nytimes.com/2018/09/25/us/politics/deborah-ramirez-brett
    -kavanaugh-allegations.html?action=click&module=Intentional&pgtype=Article

46 https://www.washingtonpost.com/local/who-is-julie-swetnick-the-third
    -kavanaugh-accuser/2018/09/26/91e16ed8-c1bc-11e8-97a5-ab1e46bb3bc7_story
    .html

47 https://www.cnn.com/2018/09/26/politics/who-is-julie-swetnick/index.html

48 https://www.nytimes.com/2018/09/26/us/politics/julie-swetnick-avenatti
    -kavanaugh.html

49 https://www.nbcnews.com/politics/supreme-court/kavanaugh-accuser-julie
    -swetnick-speaks-out-sexual-abuse-allegations-n915641

50 https://www.cbsnews.com/news/3rd-brett-kavanaugh-accuser-julie-swetnick
    -has-history-of-legal-disputes/

51 https://www.cbsnews.com/news/3rd-brett-kavanaugh-accuser-julie-swetnick
    -has-history-of-legal-disputes/

52 https://thefederalist.com/2019/09/15/alleged-victim-in-new-york-times
    -kavanaugh-story-doesnt-remember-incident/

53 https://www.cbsnews.com/news/boofed-devils-triangle-fffffourth-of-july
    -how-brett-kavanaugh-explained-yearbook-jokes/

54 https://www.politico.com/magazine/story/2018/10/01/kavanaugh-boofing-fbi
    -investigation-220808/

55 https://slate.com/news-and-politics/2018/09/brett-kavanaugh-yearbook-devils
    -triangle-boofing-renate-ralph-club.html

56 https://www.washingtonpost.com/politics/2018/09/25/what-we-know-about
    -allegations-surrounding-brett-kavanaugh/

CHAPTER 6: THE FASCIST STATE

1   https://www.project2025.org/

2   https://x.com/JoeBiden/status/1811509522403352669

3   https://www.washingtonpost.com/elections/2024/07/08/project-2025-trump
    -election/

4   Ibid.

5   https://www.tvinsider.com/1143477/the-view-july-12-project-2025/

6   Ibid.

7   https://tribune.com.pk/story/2476260/mark-ruffalo-slams-us-right-wing
    -project-2025-gets-slammed-right-back-for-calling-it-sharia-law

8   https://wlos.com/news/nation-world/nbc-historian-says-children-will-be
    -arrested-and-conceivably-killed-if-gop-wins-congress-biden-makes
    -midterm-plea-saying-republicans-are-a-threat-to-democracy-president-joe
    -biden-democrats-republicans-midterms-one-week-election-day-blue-states
    -dems

9   https://x.com/MaddowBlog/status/1309314716788031489

10 https://twitter.com/MaddowBlog/status/1309314716788031489

11 https://www.cnn.com/2019/03/20/politics/james-clyburn-trump-hitler
    -comparison/index.html

12 https://www.nbcnews.com/politics/national-security/dem-rep-hank-johnson
    -compares-trump-hitler-naacp-speech-n954316

13 https://www.politico.com/news/2020/09/26/joe-biden-trump-joseph
    -goebbels-422047

14 https://www.dallasnews.com/news/politics/2021/01/08/biden-likens-ted
    -cruz-to-nazi-propagandist-goebbels-for-helping-trump-spread-big-lie-about
    -election-fraud/

15 https://www.cbsnews.com/video/donald-trump-increasingly-compared-to
    -adolf-hitler/

16 https://www.washingtonpost.com/posteverything/wp/2016/09/13/dont
    -compare-donald-trump-to-adolf-hitler-it-belittles-hitler/

17 https://www.inquirer.com/opinion/commentary/trump-hitler-insurrection
    -autocracy-holocaust-january-6-20210127.html

18 https://twitter.com/tomselliott/status/1727333738428706939

19 https://x.com/BruceBartlett/status/1054788112193331200

20 https://thehill.com/homenews/media/4263050-rachel-maddow-trump-wants
    -to-execute-us-at-msnbc/

21 https://www.youtube.com/watch?v=mRne69l__j8

22 https://www.allsides.com/news/2021-03-02-1324/nod-or-blunder-no-cpac
    -2021-apology-stage-shaped-white-supremacist-symbol

23 https://twitter.com/joebiden/status/1009472212456308737?lang=en

24 https://www.washingtonexaminer.com/tag/msnbc?source=%2Fnews%2Fwhite
    -house-dhs-rip-joe-scarborough-for-comparing-border-officials-to-nazis

25 https://www.nytimes.com/2018/06/17/opinion/trump-and-the-baby-snatchers.html

26 https://www.cnn.com/2019/06/18/politics/alexandria-ocasio-cortez
    -concentration-camps-migrants-detention

27 https://www.cbsnews.com/news/migrant-children-border-patrol-custody-past
    -legal-limit/?ftag=CNM-00-10aab7e&linkId=112932380

28 https://www.axios.com/2023/12/20/trump-hitler-biden-campaign-comparison

29 https://www.washingtonpost.com/politics/2022/08/25/fiery-midterm-speech
    -biden-says-gops-turned-toward-semi-fascism/

30 https://twitter.com/maxboot/status/1524345353545388032

31 https://thehill.com/media/4437923-taylor-swift-conspiracy-theories-engulf
    -conservative-social-media/

32 https://thehill.com/homenews/administration/512172-taylor-swift-trumps
    -calculated-dismantling-of-usps-proves-hes-trying/

33 https://www.salon.com/2021/08/09/the-gops-death-cult-comes-for-the
    -children/

34 https://newrepublic.com/article/164619/ron-desantis-freedom-anti-vaccine

35 https://www.mediaite.com/tv/mika-brzezinski-goes-off-on-desantis-for
    -fueling-anti-vaccine-death-cult-he-owns-floridas-medical-crisis/

36 https://nymag.com/intelligencer/2022/07/ron-desantis-authoritarian
    -democracy-trump-2024-republican.html

37 https://newrepublic.com/article/170441/ron-desantis-presidency-even-worse
    -trump

38 https://www.msnbc.com/opinion/msnbc-opinion/florida-gov-ron-desantis-far
    -more-dangerous-donald-trump-n1294862

39 https://thehill.com/opinion/campaign/4030670-desantis-is-the-greatest-threat
    -to-america-ever-until-the-next-guy/

40 https://www.whitehouse.gov/briefing-room/speeches-remarks/2024/01/05
    /remarks-by-president-biden-on-the-third-anniversary-of-the-january-6th
    -attack-and-defending-the-sacred-cause-of-american-democracy-blue-bell-pa/

41 https://www.wsj.com/politics/elections/biden-d-day-normandy-speec
    h-democracy-9de16276

42 https://www.foxnews.com/media/biden-campaign-complains-ny-times
    -coverage-urges-paper-more-critical-trump

43 https://www.washingtonpost.com/opinions/2023/11/30/trump-dictator-2024
    -election-robert-kagan/

44 https://www.nytimes.com/2023/12/04/us/politics/trump-2025-overview.html

45 https://theatln.tc/F7S97eqG

46 https://money.cnn.com/2016/02/12/media/joe-scarborough-donald-trump-nbc/

47 https://www.theblaze.com/news/video-joe-scarborough-declares-without
    -evidence-that-trump-will-execute-and-will-imprison-people-if-hes-elected
    -again

48 https://t.co/IcE9rtRfM5

49 https://www.nbcnews.com/think/opinion/ending-net-neutrality-will-destroy
    -everything-makes-internet-great-ncna823301

50 https://pelosi.house.gov/news/press-releases/pelosi-remarks-at-press
    -conference-following-the-senate-vote-to-save-net

51 https://kotaku.com/the-fcc-is-trying-to-destroy-the-internet-1820643768

52 https://www.salon.com/2017/11/28/the-fcc-will-destroy-innovation-if-it-kills
    -net-neutrality/

53 https://www.popularmechanics.com/technology/infrastructure/a13817671/fcc
    -net-neutrality-full-repeal-2017/

54 https://x.com/SenateDems/status/968525820410122240

55 https://www.bostonglobe.com/opinion/2018/12/28/year-after-net-neutrality-repeal
    -internet-alive-and-well-and-faster-than-ever/AoVm2iZI9Jxs0ZzZFXsOfM/story
    .html

56 https://www.cnn.com/2016/11/22/politics/conway-no-clinton-charges-donald
    -trump/index.html

57 https://www.investopedia.com/what-biden-s-vaccine-mandate-means-for
    -business-5200907

58 https://www.nytimes.com/2021/01/27/opinion/biden-executive-orders.html

59   https://www.nbcnews.com/politics/2024-election/trump-military-fears
     -rcna129159?cid=sm_npd_nn_tw_ma&taid=65a3fdfdbfa495000187e4e9&utm
     _campaign

60   https://www.miamiherald.com/opinion/op-ed/article266573856.html

61   https://www.kff.org/report-section/kff-thegrio-survey-of-black-voters
     -findings/

62   https://www.whitehouse.gov/briefing-room/speeches-remarks/2022/01/11
     /remarks-by-president-biden-on-protecting-the-right-to-vote/

63   https://www.cato.org/commentary/no-its-not-easier-get-rifle-vote

64   https://lawyersdemocracyfund.org/voter-id/broad-support/

65   https://www.politifact.com/factchecks/2020/aug/17/facebook-posts/no
     -wisconsin-mailbox-picture-isnt-proof-massive-vo/

66   https://www.cnn.com/2020/08/08/politics/usps-postal-service-democrats
     -allegations-sabotage/index.html

67   https://www.foxnews.com/media/msnbcs-nicolle-wallace-asks-foreign
     -countries-should-monitor-us-midterm-elections

68   https://www.washingtonpost.com/politics/2020/11/09/us-election-is-over
     -what-did-international-observers-think/

69   https://www.wsj.com/podcasts/opinion-potomac-watch/why-stacey-abrams
     -owes-georgia-an-apology/091051ab-adcf-436e-93c9-33d67041d9f0

70   https://www.c-span.org/video/?457208-1/health-action-conference-stacey
     -abrams-remarks

71   https://gop.com/rapid-response/35-times-stacey-abrams-denied-the-results
     -of-her-2018-race/

72   https://transcripts.cnn.com/show/cg/date/2022-08-17/segment/01

73   https://www.chicagohumanities.org/events/attend/stacey-abrams/

74   https://dailycaller.com/2019/03/04/clinton-lied-georgia-2018-election/

75   https://www.nationalreview.com/2019/06/stacey-abrams-stolen-election
     -myth-endures-democratic-party/

76   https://www.nationalreview.com/2019/06/stacey-abrams-stolen-election
     -myth-endures-democratic-party/

77   https://www.foxnews.com/politics/kamala-harris-claims-gillum-abrams

78   https://freebeacon.com/politics/obama-ag-eric-holder-says-stacey-abrams
     -won-georgia-gov-election/

79   https://www.yahoo.com/news/cory-booker-says-georgia-election-stolen
     -stacey-abrams-012932105.html

80   https://thehill.com/homenews/campaign/416675-sherrod-brown-if-stacey
     -abrams-doesnt-win-republicans-stole-it/#:~:text=Sen.,%E2%80%9CIt's
     %20clear.%E2%80%9D

81   https://freebeacon.com/politics/warren-evidence-suggests-abrams-had-race
     -stolen-from-her-in-georgia/

82   https://www.axios.com/2021/04/04/mlb-star-game-cost-georgia-100-million

83   https://www.foxnews.com/media/usa-today-under-fire-for-allowing-stacey
     -abrams-to-retroactively-edit-op-ed-to-downplay-boycott-support

84   https://www.espn.com/mlb/story/_/id/31183822/mlb-moving-all-star-game
     -atlanta-georgia-voting-law

85   https://www.washingtonpost.com/politics/2022/09/29/stacey-abramss

-rhetorical-twist-being-an-election-denier/

86 https://www.facebook.com/watch/live/?ref=watch_permalink
    &v=1525254621323691

87 https://nypost.com/2022/08/18/ex-cia-director-michael-hayden-calls-gop
    -nihilistic-dangerous/

88 https://twitter.com/GenMhayden/status/1560027626626072577

89 https://www.washingtonpost.com/politics/2023/05/14/biden-white-supremacy
    -howard-university/

90 https://www.nytimes.com/2019/10/01/us/politics/white-supremacy-homeland
    -security.html

91 https://www.nytimes.com/2019/02/22/opinion/christopher-hasson-extremism
    .html

92 https://www.politico.com/news/2020/09/04/white-supremacists-terror-threat
    -dhs-409236

93 https://www.cnn.com/2020/10/06/politics/white-supremacists-anarchists-dhs
    -homeland-threat-assessment/index.html

94 https://www.nytimes.com/2020/10/24/us/domestic-terrorist-groups.html

95 https://apnews.com/article/fbi-chris-wray-testify-capitol-riot
    -9a5539af34b15338bb5c4923907eeb67

96 https://www.reuters.com/article/us-usa-terrorism-idUSKBN2B92SG/

97 https://www.nytimes.com/2021/05/12/us/politics/domestic-terror-white
    -supremacists.html

98 https://www.nbcnews.com/politics/national-security/fbi-dhs-meta-tiktok
    -threat-domestic-extremists-rcna57458

99 https://www.theguardian.com/world/2023/may/28/lone-wolf-far-right-terror
    -attack-warning

100 https://nymag.com/intelligencer/2023/05/white-supremacy-most-dangerous
    -terrorist-threat-biden-howard-republicans-proud-boys-fbi-gosar-fuentes
    .html

101 https://www.pbs.org/newshour/show/far-right-violence-a-growing-threat-and
    -law-enforcements-top-domestic-terrorism-concern

102 https://www.newsweek.com/2023/10/13/exclusive-fbi-targets-trump-followers
    -as-2024-election-nears-1831836.html

103 Ibid.

104 https://www.cdc.gov/disasters/lightning/victimdata/infographic.html

105 https://twitter.com/shellenberger/status/1679548017865637889

106 https://www.start.umd.edu/gtd/search/Results.aspx?chart=fatalities&casualties
    _type=&casualties_max=&country=217

107 https://www.dhs.gov/sites/default/files/publications/US%20White
    %20Supremacist%20Extremists_CVE%20Task%20Force_Final.pdf

108 https://thefederalist.com/2022/05/17/congrats-to-the-media-for-finally
    -finding-a-white-supremacist/

109 https://www.njohsp.gov/threat-landscape/domestic-threats

110 https://thefederalist.com/2022/05/17/congrats-to-the-media-for-finally
    -finding-a-white-supremacist/

111 https://www.npr.org/2021/10/21/1047334766/school-board-threats-race-masks
    -vaccines-protests-harassment

112 https://reason.com/2021/10/29/2-big-things-the-media-get-wrong-about
-school-board-protests/

113 https://www.nationalreview.com/news/memo-confirms-national-school
-board-group-actively-engaged-with-white-house-while-drafting-domestic
-terrorists-letter/

114 https://www.nytimes.com/2021/10/27/us/politics/merrick-garland-justice
-department-schools-memo.html

115 https://www.washingtonpost.com/technology/2024/07/14/blueanon
-conspiracy-theories-trump-rally-shooting/; see also: https://www.semafor
.com/article/07/14/2024/top-democrat-pushed-reporters-to-consider-staged
-shooting

116 https://www.newsweek.com/trump-shooting-assassination-conspiracy
-theory-staged-biden-poll-1925723

117 https://www.vox.com/recode/21451481/linkedin-reid-hoffman-billionaire
-democratic-party-tension-silicon-valley

118 https://www.cnn.com/2024/07/14/media/msnbc-morning-joe-pulled-trump
-assassination

119 https://twitter.com/EndWokeness/status/1684647143728914433

120 https://www.foxnews.com/media/elon-musks-criticism-debunked-hands-up
-dont-shoot-mantra-triggers-cnns-don-lemon-needs-context

121 https://www.cnn.com/2020/08/26/politics/joe-biden-kamala-harris-jacob
-blake-family/index.html

122 https://www.capitalgazette.com/2021/01/05/police-officer-wont-face-charges
-in-jacob-blake-police-shooting-kenosha-prosecutor-says-rittenhouse-pleads
-not-guilty/

123 https://apnews.com/article/police-shooting-chicago-officers-investigation
-ca147a5ea386e70190f23bd6912445f0

124 https://www.wsj.com/articles/the-myth-of-systemic-police-racism-11591119883

125 https://www.obama.org/stories/this-shouldnt-be-normal/

126 https://manhattan.institute/article/perceptions-are-not-reality-what
-americans-get-wrong-about-police-violence

127 https://nypost.com/2021/02/27/cases-of-police-brutality-against-black-people
-are-overestimated/

128 https://manhattan.institute/article/perceptions-are-not-reality-what
-americans-get-wrong-about-police-violence

129 https://www.foxnews.com/media/buttigieg-points-roads-designed-built
-reason-racial-disparities-road-fatalities

130 https://www.foxnews.com/politics/buttigieg-pressured-democrats-reform
-racist-traffic-enforcement

131 https://www.washingtonpost.com/outlook/2020/10/16/barrett-children
-adopted-racist-slur/

132 https://twitter.com/POTUS/status/1683886831396442113

133 https://x.com/KamalaHarris/status/1744050013137752493?s=20

134 https://x.com/joshtpm/status/1682526060900909059?s=20

135 https://www.washingtonpost.com/politics/2023/07/27/desantis-black-history/

136 https://www.the-express.com/entertainment/tv/106562/The-View-Whoopi
-Goldberg-Ron-DeSantis

137 https://www.fldoe.org/core/fileparse.php/20653/urlt/6-4.pdf
138 https://www.nationalreview.com/corner/kamala-harris-is-brazenly-lying
     -about-floridas-slavery-curriculum/
139 https://www.nationalreview.com/corner/kamala-harris-is-brazenly-lying
     -about-floridas-slavery-curriculum/
140 https://www.nationalreview.com/news/ap-curriculum-touted-by-progressives
     -also-includes-section-on-slaves-learning-skills/
141 https://nypost.com/2023/07/27/vp-harris-praised-ap-lesson-about-slaves-skills
     -before-florida-drama/?utm_source=twitter&utm_medium=social&utm
     _campaign=nypost_sitebuttons
142 https://www.nationalreview.com/news/ap-curriculum-touted-by-progressives
     -also-includes-section-on-slaves-learning-skills/
143 https://www.washingtonpost.com/education/2023/03/06/slavery-was-wrong
     -5-other-things-educators-wont-teach-anymore/
144 https://www.edweek.org/policy-politics/heres-the-long-list-of-topics
     -republicans-want-banned-from-the-classroom/2022/02
145 https://apnews.com/article/race-and-ethnicity-racial-injustice-business
     -education-government-and-politics-905c354a805cec1785160cf21f04c7ec
146 https://billstatus.ls.state.ms.us/documents/2022/html/HB/1400-1499
     /HB1494IN.htm
147 https://www.nytimes.com/2021/11/09/magazine/1619-project-us-history.
     html

CHAPTER 7: CULTURE OF PARANOIA

1   https://time.com/6155905/florida-dont-say-gay-passed/
2   https://abcnews.go.com/Politics/dont-gay-bill-passes-florida-senate/story
    ?id=83301889
3   https://www.nbcnews.com/nbc-out/out-politics-and-policy/florida-house
    -passes-dont-say-gay-bill-rcna17532
4   https://www.cbsnews.com/news/florida-lgbtq-bill-controversy-dont-say-gay/
5   https://www.npr.org/2022/02/24/1082969036/florida-house-passes
    -controversial-measure-dubbed-the-dont-say-gay-bill-by-criti
6   https://www.myfloridahouse.gov/Sections/Bills/billsdetail.aspx?BillId=76545
7   https://www.washingtonexaminer.com/news/1680253/ana-navarro-says-she
    -yells-like-a-dog-with-its-head-outside-of-her-car-when-in-florida-we-say-gay/
8   https://www.politico.com/f/?id=0000017f-9034-d137-abff-f0f410670000
9   https://pos.org/wp-content/uploads/2022/03/POS-National-Poll-Release
    -Memo.pdf
10 https://www.hrc.org/press-releases/for-the-first-time-ever-human-rights-campaign
    -officially-declares-state-of-emergency-for-lgbtq-americans-issues-national
    -warning-and-guidebook-to-ensure-safety-for-lgbtq-residents-and-travelers
11 https://www.tampabay.com/news/florida-politics/2023/04/24/florida-lgbtq
    -transgender-laws-bills-desantis/
12 https://www.washingtonpost.com/nation/2023/06/10/florida-anti-lgbtq-laws/
13 https://money.yahoo.com/lgbtq-people-fleeing-florida-mass-155026109.html
14 https://www.npr.org/sections/health-shots/2023/05/11/1172589936/as
    -conservative-states-target-trans-rights-a-florida-teen-flees-for-a-better-lif

15 https://www.southwestjournal.com/florida-why-more-americans-are
    -choosing-to-move-south/#:~:text=A%20significant%20increase%20in
    %20migration,not%20simply%20there%20for%20relaxation.

16 https://www.statista.com/statistics/1378808/most-visited-states-us/

17 https://www.pbs.org/newshour/politics/tens-of-thousands-of-lgbtq-people
    -flock-to-florida-for-gay-days-festival

18 https://www.nationalreview.com/2023/11/there-is-no-trans-genocide/

19 https://www.lapdonline.org/newsroom/shooting-investigation-nr23231ti/

20 https://www.washingtonexaminer.com/restoring-america/fairness-justice/the
    -false-myth-of-transgender-oppression

21 https://www.whitehouse.gov/briefing-room/presidential-actions/2024/03/29/a
    -proclamation-on-transgender-day-of-visibility-2024/

22 https://www.foxnews.com/media/biden-called-claims-banning-books-history
    -course-lie

23 https://www.cbsnews.com/news/biden-anti-book-ban-coordinator-new-lgbtq
    -protections/

24 https://prufrock.substack.com/p/those-ala-book-b

25 https://www.npr.org/2023/03/23/1164284891/book-bans-school-libraries-florida

26 https://www.npr.org/2023/06/08/1180941627/biden-pride-month-book-bans

27 https://www.slj.com/review/lawn-boy

28 https://reduxx.info/pornographic-gender-book-aimed-at-minors-allowed-to
    -continue-sale-in-virginia/

29 https://nypost.com/2021/04/29/jeopardy-winner-accused-of-flashing-white
    -power-symbol

30 https://www.vice.com/en/article/qj8pnb/jeopardy-should-probably-speak-up
    -about-kelly-donohue-hand-gesture

31 https://www.hollywoodreporter.com/tv/tv-news/jeopardy-slammed-winner
    -alleged-white-power-hand-gesture-4175660/

32 https://medium.com/@j.contestants.letter/letter-from-former-jeopardy
    -2eda854efdf1

33 https://www.splcenter.org/fighting-hate/extremist-files/group/three
    -percenters

34 https://www.splcenter.org/fighting-hate/extremist-files/group/three
    -percenters

35 https://today.yougov.com/politics/articles/24783-white-supremacy-trump-fox
    -news-poll

36 https://www.forbes.com/sites/alexreimer/2019/12/23/medias-rush-to-judgment
    -over-hand-gestures-at-army-navy-game-is-mortifying-sign-of-the-times/

37 https://www.ksbw.com/article/investigators-find-no-racist-intent-in-ok-hand
    -sign-say-they-were-playing-sophomoric-game/30299021

38 https://www.politico.com/magazine/story/2018/09/05/kavanaugh-white-power
    -zina-bash-219733/

39 https://mashable.com/article/ok-hand-gesture-hate-symbol-anti-defamation
    -league-white-sumpremacy

40 https://www.theatlantic.com/ideas/archive/2022/03/taxonomy-right-wing-dog
    -whistles/622930/

41 https://time.com/6250153/woke-convenient-republican-dog-whistle/

42 https://www.washingtonpost.com/magazine/2022/09/26/damon-young-woke
    -is-now-dog-whistle-black-whats-next/

43 https://www.vox.com/the-big-idea/2016/11/7/13549154/dog-whistles-campaign
    -racism

44 https://www.theatlantic.com/ideas/archive/2022/03/taxonomy-right-wing-dog
    -whistles/622930/

45 https://theconversation.com/when-trump-calls-someone-a-dog-hes-tapping
    -into-ugly-history-128589

46 https://www.washingtonpost.com/politics/like-a-dog-trump-has-a-long
    -history-of-using-canine-insults-to-dehumanize-enemies/2018/08/14
    /doc67fb8-9fce-11e8-83d2-70203b8d7b44_story.html

47 https://twitter.com/marcorubio/status/1556238074828320768

48 https://twitter.com/rweingarten/status/1556287754765570049

49 https://twitter.com/maxboot/status/1556274097767718914

50 https://www.nytimes.com/2023/04/04/us/politics/george-soros-bragg-trump
    .html

51 https://www.washingtonexaminer.com/opinion/2074818/new-group-jews
    -against-soros-aims-to-fight-the-lefts-antisemitism-claims/

52 https://www.politico.com/story/2016/08/george-soros-criminal-justice
    -reform-227519

53 https://www.wsj.com/articles/why-i-support-reform-prosecutors-law
    -enforces-jail-prison-crime-rate-justice-police-funding-11659277441

54 https://www.city-journal.org/article/randi-weingartens-mixed-record-on-anti
    -semitism

55 https://freebeacon.com/campus/teachers-union-head-rips-jews-in-interview
    -on-school-reopening/

56 https://finance.yahoo.com/news/sarah-palin-catching-heat-tweeting-211946314
    .html

57 https://twitter.com/tomselliott/status/1706624888172142721

58 https://waters.house.gov/media-center/press-releases/rep-waters-slams
    -surgeon-general-jerome-adams-offensive-comments-during

59 https://time.com/5849163/why-describing-george-floyd-protests-as-riots-is
    -loaded/

60 https://dailycaller.com/2016/10/11/prominent-liberal-under-a-trump
    -administration-mobs-could-kill-minorities-with-impunity/

61 https://www.facebook.com/santamonicapd/posts/1248837835137297

62 https://abc11.com/mebane-kkk-march-is-the-photo-real/1598666/

63 https://www.13abc.com/content/news/BG-police-say-student-lied-about
    -politically-driven-attack-401814426.html

64 https://www.snopes.com/news/2016/11/10/students-use-blackface-to-celebrate
    -trump-victory/

65 https://www.cbsnews.com/news/heil-trump-swastika-gay-slur-spray-painted
    -on-indiana-church/

66 https://fox59.com/news/police-organist-spray-painted-heil-trump-swastika
    -gay-slur-on-brown-county-church/

67 https://www.washingtonpost.com/news/morning-mix/wp/2016/11/10/women-in
    -hijabs-on-2-campuses-say-they-were-attacked-by-men-invoking-donald-trump/

68 https://www.cbsnews.com/news/yasmin-seweid-teen-accused-of-making-up
-story-of-anti-muslim-harassment-on-nyc-subway/
69 https://www.justice.gov/crs/highlights/2022-hate-crime-statistics
70 https://apnews.com/arts-and-entertainment-general-news-television-
programs-1eb82717d12743d4b86b519a6a902cfa
71 https://twitter.com/CoryBooker/status/1090341255786184704
72 https://www.newsweek.com/joe-biden-kamala-harris-tweets-supporting
-jussie-smollett-remain-jail-1687101
73 https://twitter.com/JoeBiden/status/1090422326783606784?lang=en
74 https://twitter.com/ABC/status/1091036056902758400
75 https://www.tennessean.com/story/opinion/2019/01/30/covington-kids
-intimidated-native-americans-who-taught-them-that/2716469002/
76 https://www.nytimes.com/2019/01/20/us/nathan-phillips-covington.html
77 https://abcnews.go.com/US/viral-video-catholic-school-teens-taunting-native
-americans/story?id=60498772
78 https://thehill.com/blogs/blog-briefing-room/news/426160-haaland-condemns
-students-behavior-toward-native-elder-at/
79 https://www.wbal.com/viral-video-of-teens-taunting-native-americans-draws
-widespread-condemnation/
80 https://www.washingtontimes.com/news/2020/jan/13/reza-aslan-likely-be
-sued-over-now-deleted-punchab/
81 https://www.usatoday.com/story/opinion/2019/01/22/covington-catholic-boys
-native-american-video-stop-social-media-mobs-column/2637669002/
82 https://www.buzzfeednews.com/article/juliareinstein/teens-taunted-native
-american-elder-indigenous-peoples-march
83 https://www.wlwt.com/article/prosecutor-hundreds-of-threats-made-against
-covington-catholic-after-dc-march-firestorm/26014571
84 https://time.com/5508226/covington-catholic-native-american-video/
85 https://www.nydailynews.com/2019/01/21/see-it-covington-catholic-high
-students-in-blackface-at-past-basketball-game/
86 https://www.nbcnews.com/feature/nbc-out/gay-valedictorian-banned
-speaking-covington-graduation-not-surprised-d-c-n961446
87 https://www.nbcnews.com/feature/nbc-out/gay-valedictorian-banned
-speaking-covington-graduation-not-surprised-d-c-n961446
88 https://www.aol.com/article/entertainment/2019/01/22/jim-carrey-labels
-covington-catholic-students-as-baby-snakes-in-new-artwork/23650004/
89 https://www.washingtonexaminer.com/politics/native-american-activist
-nathan-phillips-has-violent-criminal-record-and-escaped-from-jail-as
-teenager
90 https://www.washingtonpost.com/local/social-issues/picture-of-the-conflict
-on-the-mall-comes-into-clearer-focus/2019/01/20/c078f092-1ceb-11e9-9145
-3f74070bbdb9_story.html
91 https://www.washingtonpost.com/local/social-issues/picture-of-the-conflict
-on-the-mall-comes-into-clearer-focus/2019/01/20/c078f092-1ceb-11e9-9145
-3f74070bbdb9_story.html
92 https://www.nationalreview.com/2019/01/nathan-phillips-lied-the-media
-bought-it/

93   https://www.militarytimes.com/news/your-military/2019/01/23/tribal-elder-in
      -viral-standoff-video-was-not-a-vietnam-veteran-military-records-show/

CHAPTER 8: THE JEWS!

1   https://www.jewishpress.com/indepth/editorial/nys-assemblywoman-diana
      -richardson-should-resign/2018/04/11/
2   https://www.nytimes.com/article/kyrie-irving-antisemitic.html
3   https://www.adl.org/resources/blog/hebrews-negroes-what-you-need-know
4   https://twitter.com/JerryDunleavy/status/1506670935344132101
5   https://www.washingtonpost.com/local/dc-politics/dc-lawmaker-says-recent
      -snowfall-caused-byrothschilds-controlling-the-climate/2018/03/18/daeb0eae
      -2ae0-11e8-911f-ca7f68bff0fc_story.html
6   https://twitter.com/JustinGrayWSB/status/1354870334655262724?s=20&t=R
      -kD8tYIXI2FDxqSF50DOA
7   https://freebeacon.com/culture/black-americas-anti-semitism-problem/
8   https://www.inss.org.il/publication/black-antisemitism/
9   https://books.google.com/books?id=dukCAAAAMBAJ&pg=PA28&lpg=PA28
      &dq=%E2%80%9Cplaced+Gavin+Cato+in+a+heavenly+pantheon+of+the
      +victims+of+white-racist+violence.%E2%80%9D&source=bl&ots=pufrlduznt
      &sig=ACfU3U3dFo2AWijECE7le7_RoENko_Yf_A&hl=en&sa=X&ved
      =2ahUKEwiX7aHo77-GAxUoEVkFHTO_BusQ6AF6BAgPEAM#v=onepage
      &q=%E2%80%9Cplaced%20Gavin%20Cato%20in%20a%20heavenly
      %20pantheon%20of%20the%20victims%20of%20white-racist%20violence
      .%E2%80%9D&f=false
10   https://www.congress.gov/116/meeting/house/109952/documents/HHRG-116
      -JU00-20190919-SD033.pdf
11   https://www.history.com/this-day-in-history/a-jewish-youth-is-killed-by-a-mob
12   https://www.jewishpost.com/archives/news/reverend-sharptons-anti-semitic
      -and-racist-broadcast.html
13   https://www.jewishpost.com/archives/news/reverend-sharptons-anti-semitic
      -and-racist-broadcast.html
14   https://www.washingtonpost.com/archive/politics/1995/12/14/did-angry
      -words-ignite-a-tragedy-fiery-protest-preceding-arson-has-ny-looking-for
      -links/1ba5aecf-2200-4936-ad31-3fb9c833b8e0/
15   https://slate.com/news-and-politics/2003/09/a-troubling-story-about-al
      -sharpton.html
16   https://archive.nytimes.com/www.nytimes.com/library
      /national/021198brawley-suit.html
17   https://www.politico.com/magazine/story/2014/08/al-sharpton-obama-race
      -110249/#:~:text=If%20anything%2C%20the%20Ferguson%20crisis,many
      %20in%20his%20own%20party.
18   https://www.washingtonpost.com/archive/politics/1996/10/04/conspiracy
      -theories-can-often-ring-true/3960d4c5-593e-4b4d-b3c9-a2f9f4148c9d/
19   https://www.thelancet.com/journals/laninf/article/PIIS1473309905012934
      /fulltext
20   https://www.timesofisrael.com/black-lives-matter-platform-author-defends
      -israel-genocide-claim/

21 https://medium.com/@jewishorgssayblacklivesmatter/jewish-organizations
-and-synagogues-say-black-lives-matter-a1a0f7ea6da7

22 https://deadlyexchange.org/

23 https://docs.google.com/document/u/1/d
/11gCI2Xl32dcv9kVa32SRInNNM1w0OlA8Pxb9Cfidbvo
/mobilebasic?fbclid=IwAR2AyIIemGfMndXJl5EGWdWtKlB3eKOtH
-8dSdskyz1Eh32Y3MYcalr5MbM&usp=gmail

24 https://twitter.com/canarymission/status/1723755033609515324

25 https://www.instagram.com/p/BT9wDcUBShs/?hl=en

26 https://www.nytimes.com/2018/12/23/us/womens-march-anti-semitism.html

27 https://hotair.com/john-s-2/2018/03/09/valerie-jarrett-compares-meeting
-farrakhan-meeting-koch-brothers-n255477

28 https://www.nytimes.com/1984/07/17/us/farrakhan-again-describes-hitler-as-a
-very-great-man.html

29 https://www.ajc.com/news/local/could-this-long-lost-photo-have-derailed
-obama-2008-campaign/jC8NKhQr6a72VjRYY90oEM/

30 https://www.nytimes.com/1988/07/29/us/black-jewish-hostility-rouses-leaders
-in-chicago-to-action.html

31 https://abcnews.go.com/Politics/republican-jewish-coalition-calls-resignation
-democrats-ties-farrakhan/story?id=53601481

32 https://www.tabletmag.com/sections/news/articles/democratic-rep-danny
-davis-calls-louis-farrakhan-an-outstanding-human-being-farrakhan-says-jews
-are-satanic-and-did-911

33 https://www.indystar.com/story/opinion/columnists/tim-swarens/2018/03/13
/swarens-andre-carson-wont-rule-out-future-meetings-louis-
farrakhan/415971002/

34 https://dailycaller.com/2018/03/05/house-democrats-ties-to-louis
-farrakhan/

35 https://www.timesofisrael.com/senior-democrat-keith-ellison-dined-with
-iranian-president-louis-farrakhan/

36 https://www.jpost.com/diaspora/antisemitism/article-775776

37 https://www.foxnews.com/politics/speakers-oakland-city-council-meeting
-defend-hamas-some-deny-oct-7-atroscities

38 https://variety.com/2023/tv/news/anti-defamation-league-director-slams
-msnbc-israel-attacks-hamas-1235749595/

39 https://www.foxnews.com/media/liberal-msnbc-host-mehdi-hasan-history
-controversial-rhetoric-in-spotlight-amid-hostile-coverage-israel

40 https://www.economist.com/united-states/2023/12/07/one-in-five-young
-americans-thinks-the-holocaust-is-a-myth

41 https://www.pewresearch.org/politics/2018/01/23/republicans-and-democrats
-grow-even-further-apart-in-views-of-israel-palestinians/

42 https://harvardharrispoll.com/wp-content/uploads/2023/10/HHP_Oct2023
_Crosstabs.pdf

43 https://www.nationalreview.com/news/indianapolis-woman-arrested-for
-plowing-car-into-building-she-though-was-a-jewish-school/

44 https://www.news5cleveland.com/news/local-news/jewish-cemetery-vandalized
-with-swastika-graffiti-in-brooklyn-oh-volunteers-help-with-clean-up

45 https://freebeacon.com/author/stiles/politics/this-is-the-future-liberals-want
-pro-hamas-mob-attacks-jews-outside-museum-of-tolerance-in-la/

46 https://www.cbsnews.com/baltimore/news/maryland-college-students-speak
-about-antisemitism-on-campus-as-hate-incidents-rise-baltimore-hamas-israel/

47 https://www.nbcnews.com/news/us-news/man-dies-hitting-head-israel
-palestinian-rallies-california-officials-rcna123942

48 https://nypost.com/2023/10/14/jewish-students-dorm-room-set-on-fire-at
-drexel-university-report/

49 https://nypost.com/2023/11/07/news/israel-hamas-war-live-updates-and
-analysis-on-gaza-invasion/

50 https://www.timesofisrael.com/umass-student-arrested-for-punching-jewish
-student-at-hillel-vigil/

51 https://www.latimes.com/california/story/2022-11-24/uc-berkeley-law-student
-groups-ban-zionist-speakers

52 https://jewishjournal.com/commentary/opinion/351854/berkeley-develops
-jewish-free-zones/

53 https://www.wsj.com/articles/dont-hire-my-anti-semitic-law-students
-protests-colleges-universities-jews-palestine-6ad86ad5

54 https://www.thecrimson.com/article/2023/10/10/psc-statement-backlash/

55 https://freebeacon.com/campus/anti-israel-upenn-faculty-group-blocks
-access-to-campus-building-during-die-in-protest/

56 https://www.politico.com/story/2019/02/10/ilhan-omar-israel-aipac
-money-1163631

57 https://pjmedia.com/davidsteinberg/2018/11/08/105-articles-cover-ilhan
-omars-win-zero-cover-her-anti-semitism-finance-investigations-or-perjury
-evidence-n120274

58 https://freebeacon.com/politics/dem-candidate-voted-minnesota-bill-stop
-insurance-payments-convicted-terrorists/

59 https://www.usatoday.com/story/news/politics/2021/06/10/ilhan-omar
-rebuked-lumping-u-s-and-israel-hamas-and-taliban/7633680002/

60 https://www.rollingstone.com/politics/politics-features/nancy-pelosi-trump
-interview-797209/

61 https://thehill.com/homenews/house/433263-pelosi-omar-not-anti-semitic
-has-different-use-of-words/

62 https://www.timesofisrael.com/woman-running-for-congress-in-minnesota
-rejects-anti-semitism-accusations/

63 https://www.haaretz.com/us-news/2019-03-01/ty-article/ilhan-omar
-influential-americans-push-for-allegiance-to-foreign-country/0000017f-f033
-df98-a5ff-f3bfea4a0000

64 https://www.mediaite.com/online/rep-ilhan-omar-retweets-post-accusing-her
-of-anti-semitism-she-might-as-well-call-us-hook-nosed/

65 https://www.opensecrets.org/news/2019/02/aipac-dont-contribute-which-pro
-israel-groups-do/

66 https://www.opensecrets.org/industries/background?cycle=All&ind=Q05

67 https://www.thejc.com/news/usa/florida-congresswoman-blames-israel-lobby
-for-democrat-vote-to-ban-tiktok-lbek8s6l

68 https://www.axios.com/2019/03/07/bernie-sanders-kamala-harris-elizabeth -warren-defend-ilhan-omar

69 https://nypost.com/2023/10/16/ilhan-omar-falsely-claims-photo-is-of-dead -palestinian-kids/

70 https://www.adl.org/resources/press-release/adl-statement-concerning-rep -rashida-tlaibs-tweet-pending-bds-bill-congress

71 https://www.washingtonexaminer.com/opinion/2055423/unrepentant-ilhan -omar-suggests-jews-who-criticize-her-anti-semitic-statements-are-doing-so -because-shes-muslim-revives-dual-loyalty-smear/

72 https://www.nationalreview.com/corner/rashida-tlaib-says-certain-people-are -exploiting-america/

73 https://www.businessinsider.com/rashida-tlaib-wrote-column-louis -farrakhans-blog-2019-2

74 https://twitter.com/RashidaTlaib/status/1720574880557539763?lang=en

75 https://twitter.com/RashidaTlaib/status/1714342122185191596

76 https://www.nytimes.com/2023/11/13/us/politics/democratic-aides-congress -israel-hamas.html

77 https://www.tabletmag.com/sections/arts-letters/articles/soviet-anti-semitic- cartoons

CHAPTER 9: APOCALYPSE NOW-ISH

1 https://nypost.com/2023/12/19/news/humans-may-be-fueling-global-warming -by-breathing-new-study/

2 https://www.theguardian.com/environment/2022/sep/21/brain-eating-amoeba -climate-crisis-naegleria-fowleri

3 https://www.cdc.gov/parasites/naegleria/state-map.html

4 https://twitter.com/abcnews/status/1537537988824969216

5 https://www.nytimes.com/2024/04/09/books/review/the-weight-of-nature -clayton-page-aldern.html

6 https://www.yourweather.co.uk/news/science/climate-change-humans -evolution.html

7 https://www.worldatlas.com/articles/is-climate-change-making-us-more -vulnerable-to-infectious-diseases.html

8 https://www.ctvnews.ca/climate-and-environment/could-climate-affect -our-eyes-canadian-study-finds-higher-temperatures-linked-with-vision -impairment-1.6465207

9 https://theweek.com/articles/482188/climate-change-making-crazy

10 https://www.nytimes.com/2021/08/30/climate/biden-climate-change-health -equity.html

11 https://abcnews.go.com/US/rise-heart-disease-explained-extreme-weather -conditions-study/story?id=88259158

12 https://aafa.org/asthma-allergy-research/our-research/climate-health/

13 https://www.wired.com/story/fungi-climate-change-medicine-health/

14 https://www.wired.com/story/climate-change-substance-abuse-tobacco -alcohol-india/

15 https://www.forbes.com/sites/willskipworth/2023/09/26/hotter-temperatures

-from-climate-change-could-increase-drug-and-alcohol-hospitalizations
-researchers-suggest/?sh=7d876d3b502f

16 https://www.cbsnews.com/miami/news/climate-change-may-trigger-increase
-in-headaches-migraines/

17 https://www.cnn.com/2017/03/20/health/climate-change-type-2-diabetes
-study/index.html

18 https://thehill.com/changing-america/well-being/prevention
-cures/3739994-climate-change-linked-with-worsening-neurologic-diseases
-review/

19 https://www.reuters.com/article/us-bangladesh-climatechange-displacement
/i-did-it-only-for-the-money-climate-displacement-pushes-girls-into
-prostitution-idUSKCN1MR1BP

20 https://www.cbsnews.com/news/climate-change-taliban-strengthen/

21 https://www.mrctv.org/blog/new-york-magazine-editor-predicts-spike
-murder-rates-and-rape-domestic-assault-thanks-climate

22 https://nymag.com/intelligencer/2017/07/climate-change-earth-too-hot-for
-humans.html?gtm=bottom

23 https://www.motherjones.com/environment/2014/02/climate-change-murder
-rape/

24 https://www.sciencedirect.com/science/article/abs/pii
/S0095069613001289#:~:text=Under%20the%20IPCC%D7%B3s%20A1B
%20climate%20scenario%2C%20the%20United,of%20vehicle%20theft
%2C%20compared%20to

25 https://it.usembassy.gov/how-climate-change-affects-the-food-crisis/

26 https://www.wsj.com/articles/climate-change-to-be-treated-as-public-health
-issue-11630315800?mod=djemVentureCapitalPro&tpl=vc

27 https://www.whitehouse.gov/wp-content/uploads/2021/10/National-Strategy
-on-Gender-Equity-and-Equality.pdf

28 https://www.washingtonpost.com/climate-environment/2022/10/13/heat-hate
-speech-aggression-climate/

29 https://www.foxnews.com/media/climate-change-effects-begin-womb-warns
-new-york-times-op-ed-pushes-govt-action

30 https://www.nature.com/articles/s41558-021-01058-x.epdf?itid=lk_inline
_enhanced-template

31 https://www.washingtonpost.com/climate-environment/interactive/2023/hot
-cold-extreme-temperature-deaths/

32 https://www.youtube.com/watch?v=TMrtLsQbaok

33 https://www.bloomberg.com/news/newsletters/2023-07-20/hotter-summers
-are-hurting-our-mental-health?sref=7LFAVbXk

34 https://time.com/4719009/climate-change-mental-health/

35 https://twitter.com/tomselliott/status/1733875285374693505

36 https://www.thelancet.com/journals/lanplh/article/PIIS2542-5196(21)00278-3
/fulltext

37 https://www.pewresearch.org/short-reads/2023/08/09/what-the-data-says
-about-americans-views-of-climate-change/

38 https://time.com/person-of-the-year-2019-greta-thunberg/

39 https://twitter.com/CNN/status/1175760675592970250

40   https://www.newyorker.com/culture/cultural-comment/what-if-we-stopped
      -pretending

41   https://abcnews.go.com/US/climate-change-americans-reconsidering
      -children-poll/story?id=94577495

42   https://www.npr.org/2016/08/18/479349760/should-we-be-having-kids-in-the
      -age-of-climate-change

43   https://www.nysun.com/article/defying-the-ecological-prophets-of-doom

44   https://www.google.com/books/edition/The_Population_Bomb
      /8WxeQAAACAAJ?hl=en

45   https://www.youtube.com/watch?v=jtRsnyWp468

46   https://www.smithsonianmag.com/science-nature/why-didnt-first-earth-days
      -predictions-come-true-its-complicated-180958820/

47   https://www.france24.com/en/20181202-un-climate-change-talks-open
      -poland-cop24-urgent-action-paris-agreement

48   https://books.google.com/books?id=cMlBE3umGzMC&pg=PA390&dq=%22%E2
      %80%9Ccivilization+will+end+within+15+or+30+years+unless+immediate+action
      +is+taken+against+problems+facing+mankind.%E2%80%9D%22&hl=en&sa=X
      &ved=0ahUKEwjStaXC3IbfAhVmplkKHfUqANUQ6AEIKjAA#v=onepage
      &q=%22%E2%80%9Ccivilization%20will%20end%20within%2015%20or%2030
      %20years%20unless%20immediate%20action%20is%20taken%20against
      %20problems%20facing%20mankind.%E2%80%9D%22&f=false

49   https://nypost.com/2021/11/12/50-years-of-predictions-that-the-climate
      -apocalypse-is-nigh/

50   https://www.pop.org/obamas-population-fundamentalist/

51   https://www.nytimes.com/1982/05/11/world/un-ecology-parley-opens-amid
      -gloom.html

52   https://wattsupwiththat.com/wp-content/uploads/2019/06/U.N.-Predicts
      -Disaster-if-Global-Warming-Not-Checked.pdf

53   https://www.nzherald.co.nz/world/news/article.cfm?c_id=2&objectid
      =10007899

54   https://blogs.nature.com/news/2007/10/nine_slaps_on_the_wrist_for_al.html

55   https://www.newsbusters.org/blogs/business/julia-seymour/2017/01/23/gore
      -rewrites-inconvenient-claim-about-nyc-flooding-sequel

56   https://www.france24.com/en/20181202-un-climate-change-talks-open
      -poland-cop24-urgent-action-paris-agreement?fbclid=IwAR1
      _UorfTqBmLlRnke5Jhurp1ir6heTxGhQPIIVfqTn4ieMD03uxa8JtdW8&ref
      =fb_i&utm_utm_medium=facebook

57   https://www.nrdc.org/stories/climate-scientists-world-we-have-only-20-years
      -theres-no-turning-back

58   https://www.npr.org/2021/11/04/1052267118/climate-change-carbon-dioxide
      -emissions-global-carbon-budget

59   https://www.smithsonianmag.com/smart-news/world-was-just-issued-12-year
      -ultimatum-climate-change-180970489/

60   https://www.washingtonpost.com/climate-environment/2023/03/20/climate
      -change-ipcc-report-15/

61   https://www.usatoday.com/story/tech/science/2018/11/24/alzheimers-vaccine
      -aims-cut-dementia-half-may-see-human-trials/2097609002/

62   https://www.cancer.org/research/acs-research-news.html
63   https://data.worldbank.org/topic/poverty
64   https://ourworldindata.org/grapher/death-rate-in-state-based-conflicts-by
     -type
65   https://ourworldindata.org/grapher/emissions-of-air
     -pollutants?time=1970.2016
66   https://ourworldindata.org/grapher/death-rate-by-source-from-air-pollution
67   https://www.npr.org/sections/goatsandsoda/2015/06/01/411265021/there-are
     -200-million-fewer-hungry-people-than-25-years-ago
68   https://www.whitehouse.gov/briefing-room/speeches-remarks/2022/09/23
     /remarks-by-president-biden-at-a-democratic-national-committee-event/a
69   https://x.com/ewarren/status/1133185531972673537
70   https://www.warren.senate.gov/newsroom/news-coverage/2016/10/10/politico
     -warren-highlights-drought-and-039s-toll-on-cranberry-farmers-2
71   https://twitter.com/RyanMaue/status/1131676480281427968
72   https://www.dailysignal.com/2019/05/24/its-just-the-weather-meteorologist
     -fact-checks-ocasio-cortez-on-climate-change/
73   https://www.weather.gov/ilm/Feb1973Snow
74   https://www.cbsnews.com/news/is-katrina-first-of-many/
75   https://www.nasa.gov/feature/goddard/no-major-us-hurricane-landfalls-in
     -nine-years-luck/
76   https://www.scientificamerican.com/article/global-warming-causes-fewer
     -tropical-cyclones/
77   https://www.theguardian.com/us-news/video/2021/sep/07/this-is-code-red
     -biden-sounds-alarm-on-climate-crisis-as-he-tours-new-york-damage-video
78   https://www.wsj.com/articles/hurricane-ida-henri-climate-change-united
     -nations-un-galsgow-conference-natural-disaster-infrastructure-carbon
     -emissions-11630704844
79   https://www.nature.com/articles/s41467-021-24268-5
80   https://www.nws.noaa.gov/om/hazstats.shtml
81   https://apnews.com/article/hurricanes-science-florida-storms-tampa
     -c872d318c12e44b7836171470cd6140d
82   https://www.nytimes.com/2022/09/27/climate/climate-imf-world-bank
     .html?smid=tw-share
83   https://twitter.com/tomselliott/status/1575062381763461124
84   https://www.statista.com/statistics/621238/number-of-hurricanes-that-made
     -landfall-in-the-us/
85   https://www.nhc.noaa.gov/pastdec.shtml
86   https://en.wikipedia.org/wiki/List_of_United_States_hurricanes
87   https://www.npr.org/2017/11/30/566950355/the-tempest-at-galveston-we-knew
     -there-was-a-storm-coming-but-we-had-no-idea
88   https://www.weather.gov/mfl/miami_hurricane
89   http://www.hurricanescience.org/history/storms/1930s/LaborDay/
90   https://projects.fivethirtyeight.com/mortality-rates-united-states/
91   https://www.washingtonpost.com/politics/the-green-new-deal-a-green-new
     -deal-whatever-it-is-2020-democrats-support-it/2019/01/30/a75166d4-2340
     -11e9-ad53-824486280311_story.html

92 https://www.scribd.com/document/399182602/Green-New-Deal-FAQ#from
_embed

93 https://www.climatedepot.com/2021/09/04/study-in-journal-nature-covid
-passports-tracking-apps-home-smart-meters-are-key-to-implement-personal
-carbon-allowances-restrictions-on-individuals-that-were-unthinkable-only
-one-year-befo/

94 https://twitter.com/EricHolthaus/status/1252952128131342336

95 https://www.eia.gov/tools/faqs/faq.php?id=33&t=6

96 https://www.nytimes.com/2020/09/16/us/politics/biden-trump-coronavirus
-vaccine.html

97   https://grabien.com/getmedia.php?id=1002333&key
=18ce8d3a2d997a54ff445badccb28a9e

98 https://thehill.com/policy/healthcare/521672-cuomo-public-should-be-very
-skeptical-about-covid-19-vaccine/

99 https://www.nytimes.com/2020/03/09/health/trump-vaccines.html

100 https://publications.aap.org/pediatrics/article-abstract/135/2/280/33437
/Geographic-Clusters-in-Underimmunization-and?redirectedFrom=fulltext

101 https://www.realclearscience.com/journal_club/2014/10/20/are_liberals_or
_conservatives_more_anti-vaccine_108905.html

102 https://www.nbcnews.com/health/health-news/portland-ore-last-big-city-add
-fluoride-water-flna994892

103 https://www.washingtonpost.com/dc-md-va/2020/07/17/black-anti-vaccine
-coronavirus-tuskegee-syphilis/

104 https://geneticliteracyproject.org/2013/12/23/patents-personal-genetics-and
-progress-the-top-10-genetics-stories-of-2013/

105 http://www.geneticliteracyproject.org/wp-content/uploads/2013/08/GLP
-Science-and-GMOs.pdf

106 https://www.pewresearch.org/science/2015/07/01/chapter-6-public-opinion
-about-food/

107 https://www.nytimes.com/2016/03/29/us/earthquake-risk-in-oklahoma-and
-kansas-comparable-to-california.html

108 https://money.cnn.com/2016/03/29/investing/earthquakes-fracking-usgs-oil
-gas/

109 https://www.theguardian.com/environment/2014/jun/19/russia-secretly
-working-with-environmentalists-to-oppose-fracking and https://www.forbes
.com/sites/jeffmcmahon/2015/03/12/russians-financed-the-u-s-anti-fracking
-movement-oil-tycoon/?sh=7e0ae44285ea

110 https://www.americanthinker.com/articles/2014/09/the_science_is_settled
_fracking_is_safe.html

111 https://archive.nytimes.com/www.nytimes.com/gwire/2011/05/10
/10greenwire-gao-death-of-yucca-mountain-caused-by-politica-36298
.html?pagewanted=all

112 https://www.washingtonpost.com/news/volokh-conspiracy/wp/2014/02/16/the
-7-political-groups-most-likely-to-believe-in-astrology/

113 https://www.pewresearch.org/religion/2009/12/09/many-americans-mix
-multiple-faiths/#3

114 https://big.assets.huffingtonpost.com/tabs_ufo_0906072013.pdf

CHAPTER 10: STEAL FROM THE POOR, GIVE TO THE PLUTOCRATS

1   https://time.com/longform/alexandria-ocasio-cortez-profile/
2   https://www.statista.com/statistics/188185/percent-change-from-preceding
    -period-in-real-gdp-in-the-us/
3   https://www.nytimes.com/1991/04/23/nyregion/new-york-killings-set-a-record
    -while-other-crimes-fell-in-1990.html
4   https://www.nytimes.com/2017/12/27/nyregion/new-york-city-crime-2017.html
5   https://www.bls.gov/iif/#:~:text=There%20were%205%2C190%20fatal
    %20work,increase%20from%204%2C764%20in%202020.
6   https://www.statista.com/statistics/183995/us-college-enrollment-and
    -projections-in-public-and-private-institutions/
7   https://www.federalreserve.gov/econres/feds/files/2018080pap.pdf
8   https://www.npr.org/2018/11/30/672103209/why-arent-millennials-spending
    -more-they-re-poorer-than-their-parents-fed-says
9   https://www.usnews.com/news/us/articles/2017-12-06/us-homeless-count
    -rises-pushed-by-crisis-on-the-west-coast
10 https://www.statista.com/statistics/184902/homeownership-rate-in-the-us
    -since-2003/
11 https://www.radiologybusiness.com/topics/quality/cancer-death-rate-down
    -27-percent-last-25-years
12 https://fee.org/articles/you-are-richer-than-john-d-rockefeller/
13 https://www.nytimes.com/2021/09/15/style/aoc-met-gala-dress.html
14 https://www.newsweek.com/80-americans-bothered-corporations-wealthy
    -dont-pay-fair-share-taxes-poll-1588063
15 https://www.nerdwallet.com/article/taxes/federal-income-tax-brackets
16 https://www.cnbc.com/2021/08/18/61percent-of-americans-paid-no-federal
    -income-taxes-in-2020-tax-policy-center-says.html
17 https://www.cnbc.com/2023/11/27/white-house-supply-chain-bidenomics-wins
    .html
18 https://pages.stern.nyu.edu/~adamodar/New_Home_Page/datafile/margin.html
19 https://www.aei.org/carpe-diem/the-public-thinks-the-average-company
    -makes-a-36-profit-margin-which-is-about-5x-too-high-part-ii/
20 https://www.macrotrends.net/stocks/charts/WMT/walmart/net-profit-margin
21 https://www.youtube.com/watch?v=25AKNA28nBY
22 https://www.facebook.com/watch/?v=663683751541741

EPILOGUE: YOU DON'T HAVE TO BE CRAZY TO WIN

1   https://www.axios.com/2021/12/08/poll-political-polarization-students?utm
    _campaign=organic&utm_medium=socialshare&utm_source=twitter

ACKNOWLEDGMENTS

Thanks to Eric Nelson for bringing me the idea of writing a book about the conspiratorial left. It is a target-rich topic with a long history. It was also a pleasure working with my editor, James Neidhardt, whose insights and suggestions improved the book in every way. Indeed, I am appreciative of everyone at HarperCollins who worked so hard to make me look good. You did the best you could—any mistakes are mine.

Jack Elbaum (with the help of Emily Jashinsky and the National Journalism Center) and Cecelia Vederman offered valuable help researching the insanity of the modern left. It is appreciated.

Mollie Hemingway and Sean Davis, friends and colleagues, are always patient and supportive when I go off on one of these adventures. Thanks, as well, to all my former colleagues at *The Federalist* for making my job such a pleasure.

Over the years, the editors at *National Review*, the *New York Post*, and the *Washington Examiner* have also given me space to refine and research some of the arguments found in *The Rise of BlueAnon*. I appreciate it.

Then, of course, there is my friends and family, to whom I am indebted for everything that matters most.

INDEX

ABOUT THE AUTHOR

DAVID HARSANYI is a senior writer at the *Washington Examiner* and a contributor to the *New York Post* and *National Review*. His work has appeared in the *Wall Street Journal*, the *Washington Post*, the *Daily Telegraph*, *USA Today*, and numerous other publications. Harsanyi has been featured on Fox News, CNN, MSNBC, NPR, *ABC World News Tonight*, *NBC Nightly News*, and dozens of radio talk shows across the country. He is the author of six books, including *Eurotrash: Why America Must Reject the Failed Ideas of a Dying Continent* and *First Freedom: A Ride Through America's Enduring History with the Gun*.